Supporting Dyslexic Adults in Higher Education and the Workplace

Praise for *Supporting Dyslexic Adults in Higher Education and the Workplace*

Dyslexia is a lifelong condition and, depending on severity, it can have a negative impact on educational achievement and career prospects. The message of this book, however, is that, if managed well, dyslexia need not be a barrier to success. By bringing together experts on dyslexia in higher education and in the work place, the book signals a 'coming of age' of research and practice on dyslexia in adulthood. The book is not just about screening, assessment and examination arrangements but rather its scope is wide, covering support for learning, key transitions, preparation for the workplace and psychosocial aspects. Within the legal framework of the Disability Discrimination Act it also explores sensitive issues surrounding the disclosure of dyslexia in the work place, and the extent to which dyslexia support is also appropriate for people of lower ability who have poor levels of literacy. In bringing together best practice on the management of adults with dyslexia, this book provides much food for thought and will be an important reference for all those who work in the field.

Maggie Snowling, Professor of Psychology, University of York

Supporting Dyslexic Adults in Higher Education and the Workplace

Edited by Nicola Brunswick
BSc (Hons), Dip, PhD, PGCertHE

Department of Psychology
School of Health and Social Sciences
Middlesex University
The Burroughs
Hendon
London
NW4 4BT
UK

WILEY-BLACKWELL
A John Wiley & Sons, Ltd., Publication

This edition first published 2012

Wiley-Blackwell is an imprint of John Wiley & Sons, formed by the merger of Wiley's global Scientific, Technical and Medical business with Blackwell Publishing.

Registered Office
John Wiley & Sons Ltd, The Atrium, Southern Gate, Chichester, West Sussex, PO19 8SQ, UK

Editorial Offices
350 Main Street, Malden, MA 02148-5020, USA
9600 Garsington Road, Oxford, OX4 2DQ, UK
The Atrium, Southern Gate, Chichester, West Sussex, PO19 8SQ, UK

For details of our global editorial offices, for customer services, and for information about how to apply for permission to reuse the copyright material in this book please see our website at www.wiley.com/wiley-blackwell.

Library of Congress Cataloging-in-Publication Data

Brunswick, Nicola, 1970–
Supporting dyslexic adults in higher education and the workplace / Nicola Brunswick.
p. cm.
Includes index.
ISBN 978-0-470-97479-7 (hardback) – ISBN 978-0-470-97478-0 (paper)
1. Dyslexics–Education (Higher)–Great Britain. 2. Dyslexics–Employment–Great Britain. 3. Dyslexia–Great Britain. I. Title.
LC4818.38.B76 2012
371.91'44–dc23

2011043295

A catalogue record for this book is available from the British Library.

Wiley also publishes its books in a variety of electronic formats. Some content that appears in print may not be available in electronic books.

Set in 9.5/12 pt Futura by Toppan Best-set Premedia Limited
Printed in Malaysia by Ho Printing (M) Sdn Bhd

1 2012

Contents

About the Contributors

Vikki Anderson (University of Birmingham, UK) is a dyslexia specialist who has worked in a number of schools, FE colleges and universities over the last 15 years.

Nicola Brunswick is a Senior Lecturer in psychology at Middlesex University, UK. She completed her PhD in the neuropsychology of dyslexia from the University of Warwick and her postdoctoral training at the Wellcome Department of Imaging Neuroscience (University College London), the MRC Cognitive Development Unit (London) and the Department of Epidemiology and Public Health (UCL Medical School). She is a trustee of the British Dyslexia Association.

E.A. Draffan trained as a speech and language therapist before specializing in Assistive Technologies. She has worked with disabled students in further and higher education, set up an Assistive Technology Centre, and contributed to the work of TechDis. She is now a research fellow at the University of Southampton, UK, and has worked on the LexDis project.

John Everatt is a Professor of Education in the College of Education at the University of Canterbury, New Zealand. His work focuses on children and adults with educational problems, particularly those with literacy learning difficulties and dyslexia.

Rob Fidler is a disability advisor at the University of Surrey, UK, where he completed his PhD in 2009 on The Reading Comprehension Skills of Adult Students with Dyslexia.

Vivien Fraser retired from her post as Dyslexia Academic Co-ordinator at Middlesex University, UK, in August 2010. She now works on a freelance basis as a dyslexia consultant and tutor.

Paul J. Gerber is Professor of Education at Virginia Commonwealth University's School of Education in Richmond, USA. He is the Ruth Harris Professor of Dyslexia Studies in the Department of Special Education and Disability Policy. His research focuses on adults with learning disabilities, employment and life span issues.

Ruth Gwernan-Jones is a research fellow at the Graduate School of Education, University of Exeter, UK. She recently completed her PhD looking at the experience of having difficulty learning to read and write, and how identifying oneself as dyslexic impacts this experience. She was a trustee of the British Dyslexia Association from 2006–2011.

Robert Hillier is a Senior Lecturer at Norwich University College of the Arts, UK. His practice and research as a designer is currently focused on Sylexiad, a series of typefaces he designed, tested and developed specifically for the adult dyslexic reader.

Bernadette Kirwan is an independent dyslexia consultant with Independent Dyslexia Consultants, London, UK. She trained in language and literature teaching, and in cognitive–behavioural coaching techniques. She specializes in working with adults, providing skill development, IT support and coaching to university students and dyslexic individuals in the workplace, and in providing advice to employers.

Morag Kiziewicz is a creative dyslexic individual whose first career as an environmental designer led to her second career as course director of spatial design. Her research into the development of spatial ability led her to the connection with dyslexia, which in turn led to 12 years, before retirement, developing and managing learning support provision at the University of Bath, UK.

Carol Leather is an independent dyslexia consultant with Independent Dyslexia Consultants, London, UK. She provides advice and coaching to dyslexic adults in the workplace and to their employers. She conducts workplace skills sessions and workplace assessments, and advises on provision of services, policy and reasonable adjustments. She also works with students in further and higher education.

John Mackenzie is a Discrimination Law and Employment Law Consultant, in Henley-on-Thames, UK, registered by the Ministry of Justice. He is a leading expert in dyslexia discrimination and has conducted landmark cases in this area of disability. He is a trustee of the British Dyslexia Association.

Margaret Malpas is Chair of Trustees of the British Dyslexia Association, UK. Her background is in personnel and training and she has developed a series of workshops for parents, teachers and employers. These cover issues relating to raising dyslexia awareness, dyslexia screening, and making reasonable adjustments to enable dyslexic people to succeed in education and work.

Alan Martin is Head of the Psychology Department at the University of Buckingham, UK. He is a chartered psychologist whose research interests include dyslexia in adults, both in terms of adults' experiences in the workplace and the assessment of adults, and other areas of education such as children's understanding of science and emotion detection.

David McLoughlin is an educational and occupational psychologist who provides diagnostic assessments to dyslexic people of all ages. He also provides career guidance for adolescents and adults. He is a visiting professor at the University of Buckingham, UK, and has acted as an adviser to the British Dyslexia Association.

Richard Mendez is the Work-related Learning Manager at the University of Leicester, UK. His remit includes teaching and assessment input on employability-hybrid modules within various academic departments across the university. He is also the Programme Director for the award-winning 'Access to Employability', an employability training programme for students with disabilities.

Sylvia Moody is a clinical psychologist who specializes in adult dyslexia assessment. She runs the Dyslexia Assessment Service in London, UK, and has written books for dyslexic teenagers, students and people in employment.

Sarah Nichols works as an assessor and specialist academic support tutor for students with specific learning difficulties, both privately and at the University of Worcester, UK. She has worked in special education since 1975.

Sue Onens is a dyslexia specialist and tutor who has worked in a number of schools, FE colleges and universities over the last 15 years, including the University of Birmingham, UK.

David Pollak retired in 2009. Prior to this he was Principal Lecturer in Learning Support at De Montfort University in Leicester, UK. His PhD explored the life histories of undergraduate students with dyslexia. He continues to do some work, post-retirement, as a supervisor and examiner.

Geraldine Price retired in 2011. Prior to this she was a Lecturer at Southampton University, UK. She set up Dyslexia Services for the University in 1993 and was course director for the MSc in SpLD, training teachers to AMBDA standard. She was a Director of PATOSS, a member of the BDA accreditation board, and of Sir Jim Rose's Expert Advisory Group which looked into dyslexia provision in schools. She took part in the SpLD/Dyslexia Trust work to develop competency scales for specialist teachers, and she is the author of the popular study skills book 'Effective Study Skills'.

Lynda A. Price is Associate Professor of Special Education at Temple University's College of Education in Philadelphia, USA. Her research interests centre on international issues about dyslexia, along with the employment, transition, and psychosocial issues of adults with learning disabilities.

Qona Rankin is Dyslexia Co-ordinator at the Royal College of Art, London, UK, and has been since 2002 when the post was created. She has degrees in Three-dimensional Design and in Design Education. Before retraining in Adult Dyslexia Support in 1997, she was a senior lecturer in Product Design and a freelance jewellery designer–maker.

Rosanne Rieley is a careers advisor who works as part of the Student Support and Development Team at the University of Leicester, UK.

Pauline Sumner is a Senior Lecturer, Dyslexia/SpLD Co-ordinator and Dyslexia/SpLD support tutor at Middlesex University in North London, UK.

Fiona White is a study adviser who works in the AccessAbility Centre at the University of Leicester, UK. Her duties include screening for dyslexia, providing one-to-one study support for dyslexic students, and negotiating and arranging reasonable adjustments for these students.

Acknowledgements

My greatest debt of thanks must of course go to all the authors who kindly contributed chapters for this book. The many examples of good practice they describe have been an inspiration to me, and I'm sure they will be to many others. I also thank them for their patience during the production of this book – they have been unfailingly generous with their time and goodwill.

My thanks also go to Karen Shield, my editor at Wiley-Blackwell, who has been helpful and supportive throughout the editorial process; to my colleague Dr Neil Martin, who has once again provided helpful feedback on my writing; to two anonymous reviewers whose positive comments on the original proposal for this book helped to set this process in motion; to Jon Galliers for his ongoing help, support and encouragement, and last but not least, to Daniel who I very much look forward to meeting.

Nicola Brunswick
London, June 2011

1

Dyslexia in UK Higher Education and Employment

An Introduction and Overview

Nicola Brunswick, Middlesex University, UK

The number of dyslexic students entering higher education has increased over the last few years as a result of government efforts to widen access and participation. These efforts include the introduction of the Special Educational Needs and Disability Act, which makes it unlawful for higher education institutions to:

> discriminate against a disabled person[1] [i.e. to treat him less favourably because of his disability] in the arrangements it makes for determining admissions to the institution; in the terms on which it offers to admit him to the institution; or by refusing or deliberately omitting to accept an application for his admission to the institution. (*Department for Education and Skills 2001, Section 28R (1)*)

Between the years 2000 and 2004, spanning the introduction of this Act, figures from the Higher Education Statistics Agency show that the number of dyslexic students entering university increased by almost 100% (Higher Education Statistics Agency 2006) although the actual numbers are still fairly low at around 3.2% of all UK students (Higher Education Statistics Agency 2010). It is, of course, possible that this number underestimates the true figure, as around 43% of dyslexic students are identified as being dyslexic only after they have started at university (National Working Party on Dyslexia in Higher Education 1999).

However, gaining a place at university is only one step of the dyslexic adult's journey. As Osborne (2003, p. 18) points out:

> Improving access is one thing, but ensuring progression both within and beyond higher education is another

and evidence regarding the progression of dyslexic university students is mixed. While some researchers have suggested that dyslexic students are more likely than non-dyslexic students to withdraw from their studies during the first year (Richardson and Wydell 2003; Stampoltzis and Polychronopoulou 2008), others have shown that dyslexic students are just as likely to pass their first- and second-year exams and to progress through their studies as are non-dyslexic students of the same sex and age (McKendree and Snowling 2011).

[1] See later in this chapter for a section on dyslexia and disability legislation.

Supporting Dyslexic Adults in Higher Education and the Workplace, First Edition. Edited by Nicola Brunswick.

For those dyslexic students who do complete their degree courses, their chances of graduating with either a first class degree or an upper second class degree are lower than those of their non-dyslexic peers. Figures of 41% versus 52% (National Working Party on Dyslexia in Higher Education 1999) and 44% versus 54% (Richardson and Wydell 2003) have been reported. These figures highlight the need for good, evidence-based dyslexia support to be provided to dyslexic students in higher education to give them the best possible chance of achieving completion rates and final degree results that are equivalent to those of non-dyslexic students.

Of course, the difficulties of dyslexic adults do not stop once they leave university, and the need for appropriate support continues into the workplace unless the individual chooses to enter a career that minimizes the need for reading and writing. For example, dyslexic adults who become teachers will face difficulties every day relating to their impaired literacy skills while those who become professional athletes are likely to face no such difficulties. This consideration may guide the career choices of many dyslexic readers. As Maughan and colleagues noted in their study of poor readers from adolescence to midlife:

> At the time they entered the labour market, childhood poor readers were . . . much more likely to have obtained jobs with limited literacy demands. (*Maughan, Messer, Collishaw* et al. *2009, p. 895*)

An interesting study of the occupational choices of 365 adults with and without dyslexia was undertaken by Taylor and Walter (2003). In line with Maughan *et al.* (2009), they found that adults with dyslexia were less likely than those without dyslexia to work in science/computing, management or business/finance (with their heavy reliance on the written word), and more likely to enter 'people-oriented professions' such as sales or nursing.

The potentially large numbers of dyslexic nurses (although the actual figure is not known – Wright 2000), and the fact that around 80% of clinicians in the UK are nurses (Jasper 2002) has led to a large body of research being undertaken with this occupational group. Much of this research has focused on the difficulties that dyslexia might cause in terms of patient safety. Studies with dyslexic nurses, for example, have highlighted concerns regarding the 'potential to confuse medical terminology or drug names' (Wright 2000, p. 39) and the 'presumed or potential risk to patient health and safety posed by dyslexia-induced performance error (e.g. problems with drug administration)' (Millward *et al.* 2005, p. 341).

Such concerns lead some nurses not to disclose their dyslexia to their employer or colleagues for fear of discrimination and ridicule (Morris and Turnbull 2006). However, evidence suggests that such fears are largely ill-founded, and that, where appropriate support is provided, dyslexia poses no risk in terms of effective nursing practice (Wright 2000; Shepherd 2002; Millward *et al.* 2005), and no barrier to career progression (Morris and Turnbull 2007).

Once again, however, the provision of appropriate support depends on individuals disclosing their dyslexia to their employer and colleagues, and this disclosure being met with understanding of the nature of dyslexia and the strengths and difficulties that it can bring.

What is Dyslexia?

Developmental dyslexia is a specific learning difficulty that affects between 5 and 15% of speakers of English (Pennington 1991; Snowling 2008). It is characterized by problems with reading and spelling (the word 'dyslexia' comes from the Greek words *dys* – 'impaired', and *lexis* – 'word'). However, it may be more accurately described as a collection of reading, spelling, naming, spoken language and memory difficulties. Combined, these difficulties render dyslexic readers relatively less able than non-dyslexic readers to do some of, or all, the following:

- read and spell words quickly and accurately
- read and write passages of text without missing out words, losing their place, and becoming distracted
- distinguish between similar-looking words such as *with* and *which*, *lots* and *lost* when reading and spelling
- comprehend written material without considerable effort
- hold verbal information, such as telephone numbers, people's names or directions, in short-term memory
- learn sequences of things such as the months of the year, poetry, or times tables
- recognize common sounds in groups of spoken words, such as '*sun*, *sea* and *sand*'
- pronounce long words, such as *parallelogram*, quickly and accurately
- display a similar level of ability in their spoken and written work.

In around 30 to 50% of cases, dyslexia occurs with at least one other developmental disorder (Kaplan *et al.* 1998; McArthur *et al.* 2000; Kadesjö and Gillberg 2001). These disorders include problems such as poor handwriting, difficulty remembering numbers, and problems with balance and coordination, specifically:

- impaired motor skills, balance and coordination (dyspraxia/developmental coordination disorder);
- poor hand–eye coordination, slow and messy handwriting, difficulty copying written text, and poor fine motor control of the hands (dysgraphia, although these symptoms might also reflect the fine motor difficulties of dyspraxia);
- poor concentration, inattention, impulsivity and hyperactivity (attention deficit/hyperactivity disorder);
- difficulty with counting, performing mental arithmetic, understanding and applying mathematical concepts (dyscalculia);
- difficulty with processing visual information – individuals may experience visual stress (or glare) from reading black text against a white background, symptoms of fatigue when doing close work, and they may see printed letters that appear to move or float above the page (scotopic sensitivity syndrome or Meares–Irlen syndrome).

However, individuals differ in the severity of their reading difficulties just as non-dyslexic readers differ in their reading abilities. The specific difficulties of dyslexia may depend on factors such as family background (whether other close relatives also have dyslexia), educational experience (the level of support and specialist teaching provided), and the individual's use of compensatory strategies.

Compensatory Strategies

Dyslexic readers can often apply skills, tactics or technical aids to help them cope with, or even hide, their reading difficulties (Lefly and Pennington 1991; Kirby *et al.* 2008; Logan 2009). Strategies might include avoiding situations in which reading or writing may be required; delegating to others tasks that involve reading and writing; using the spell-check and grammar-check facilities on a computer; using mind maps to organize ideas; having other people read through written work to check for errors; and recording lectures or meetings to avoid the need to take contemporaneous written notes.

However, even with the assistance of compensatory strategies, dyslexic readers often need to invest greater time and effort in order to complete a piece of work (that still may not reflect their actual ability). Furthermore, even the most seemingly-effective compensatory strategies are prone to break down under pressure, for example when the individual is required to read rapid subtitles on television, or to write quickly and accurately in front of other people (van der Leij, de Jong and Rijswijk-Prins 2001; Bartlett, Moody and Kindersley 2010).

Signs of Dyslexia in Adulthood

While dyslexia is often first identified in childhood, it is a lifelong difficulty. Some of the characteristic signs of the adult dyslexic reader are:

- poor spelling
- slow reading
- poor time management – often arriving late for appointments or missing them completely
- difficulty taking down messages, especially if these involve strings of numbers, such as telephone numbers
- difficulty with tasks that require sequencing, such as filing or looking up information in an alphabetized list or directory
- difficulty concentrating in a noisy environment.

Individuals may also show low self-esteem, lack of confidence, anxiety and frustration, particularly if their reading difficulties have not been recognized or supported properly.

A Legal View of Dyslexia

Some people have challenged the view of dyslexia as a disability, preferring instead to describe it as a learning *difference* (see, for example, Griffin and Pollak 2009; Hendrickx 2010). The UK Equality Act (2010), however, is quite unequivocal: dyslexia *is* a disability representing a:

> mental impairment which has a substantial and long-term adverse effect on a person's ability to carry out normal day-to-day activities. (*Office for Disability Issues, 2010, Chapter 1, Section 6*)

In this definition, 'mental impairment' specifically includes learning disabilities such as dyslexia and dyspraxia. The difficulties of dyslexia are more than a minor inconvenience – they either increase the time that might normally be required to perform an activity, or they prevent the performance of this activity altogether – and they last for at least 12 months. Finally, the activities affected include everyday aspects of life that depend on spoken and written language, memory and the ability to concentrate, learn or understand.

According to this legal definition, people with dyslexia cannot be discriminated against when they apply for or undertake educational courses or employment. This means that they cannot be denied a place on a course or an employment opportunity because of their dyslexia; neither can they be dismissed from a job or denied promotion because of their reading and writing difficulties. On the contrary, they are legally entitled to receive tailored support in the form of 'reasonable adjustments'; these adjustments will remove barriers that might otherwise prevent these individuals from having equal training and employment opportunities with their non-dyslexic peers.

'Reasonable adjustments' in higher education

The UK's Code of Practice for the Assurance of Academic Quality and Standards in Higher Education requires that:

> The delivery of programmes should take into account the needs of disabled people or, where appropriate, be adapted to accommodate their individual requirements . . . (*The Quality Assurance Agency for Higher Education, 1999, Section* 3, *Precept 10*)

The Code also states that:

> Assessment and examination policies, practices and procedures should provide disabled students with the same opportunity as their peers to demonstrate the achievement of learning outcomes . . . (*Section* 3, *Precept 13*)

The 'individual requirements' of dyslexic students can be met, and these students can be helped to demonstrate 'the achievement of learning outcomes', through the implementation of simple 'reasonable adjustments'. These might include: encouraging dyslexic students to sit near the front of the lecture theatre so that they may see and hear as clearly as possible; providing comprehensive handouts and lecture notes (preferably before the lecture) rather than requiring students to make their own notes during lectures; encouraging students to ask questions whenever anything is unclear; developing methods of assessment that require minimum amounts of writing; and asking dyslexic students if there is anything else that might be done to assist them with their studies. These adjustments, and evidence for their efficacy, are discussed in much more detail in Section One of this book.

'Reasonable adjustments' in the workplace

Many of the strategies suitable for helping dyslexic students in higher education can also be adopted in the workplace. For example, dyslexia-friendly employers might (depending on the nature of the job): encourage dyslexic employees to intersperse periods of computer work with other activities; provide dyslexic employees who suffer from visual glare with an anti-glare screen filter whenever they need to use a computer; provide a quiet working space for their dyslexic employees, where this is possible, to minimize distractions; and encourage dyslexic employees to ask questions whenever they are unsure of something.

These strategies, and evidence of the beneficial effects that they can have on dyslexic adults in the workplace, are discussed in more detail in Section Two.

An Overview of This Book

The aim of this book is to provide an overview of current research and practice in supporting the needs of dyslexic adults in education and employment. It combines evidence and data from academic research with practical advice drawn from years of working with, and supporting, dyslexic adults. The book is divided into two sections, focusing on supporting dyslexic students in higher education and supporting dyslexic adults in the workplace. These sections are outlined below.

Section One: Supporting dyslexic students in higher education

This first section explores issues relating to dyslexic students in higher education. It considers how the policy, provision and practice of educational institutions are responding to the specific needs of these students. The main focus is on recognizing and identifying dyslexia in adulthood and providing practical support for dyslexic individuals, once identified, to help them to develop the skills necessary for higher-level study. Tailored support might be provided through the use of computer-based elearning materials, multimedia teaching materials, helping students to develop effective metacognitive strategies (i.e. teaching them *how* to learn) and considering alternative forms of assessment that are not so focused on the traditional written exam. The section ends by considering ways in which dyslexic adults might best be prepared to make the move from education into the workplace. Many examples of good practice have been provided by the chapter authors in this section. All these examples have been developed as a result of years of experience of providing support to dyslexic students in colleges and universities and, as the authors report, there is evidence for their efficacy in enhancing the teaching and learning of dyslexic students in these institutions (see also McLoughlin, Leather and Stringer 2002).

In Chapter 2, Ruth Gwernan-Jones considers the socio-emotional aspects of dyslexia. She looks at different views that people – dyslexic individuals, their parents, friends and teachers – hold about dyslexia, and how these views can impact upon the educational experiences and outcomes of dyslexic students. Many of the dyslexic students mentioned in this chapter describe a school background in which they were identified as being lazy and where they were frequently humiliated in front of their peers for their difficulties with reading and spelling. Yet it is how individuals perceive themselves (perceptions that are often shaped by positive attitudes of teachers, parents and employers) that determines how they make sense of their dyslexia; these perceptions either hold dyslexic adults back or spur them on to achieve their goals.

Vikki Anderson and Sue Onens (Chapter 3) explore how well prepared students with Specific Learning Difficulties (SpLDs) are for making the transition from school or college through to the end of the first term of university. Initial interviews with these students revealed that most felt 'fairly well prepared', mostly by friends and family members, for study at university. In later interviews, however, most participants reported feeling shocked by the volume of work and the amount of independent learning that was expected of them at university and, with hindsight, several changed their earlier responses to indicate that they would have benefited from more preparation to help them through this period of transition.

In Chapter 4, Sarah Nichols discusses the merits and problems associated with measures that are commonly used to screen for dyslexia and other SpLDs in adults in higher education. She presents the results of an evaluation of a screening package that effectively and reliably identifies students who should be referred for a full dyslexia assessment. The sooner students are screened, and if necessary assessed, the sooner support can be provided to ease their progress into and through higher education.

Vivien Fraser's chapter (Chapter 5) picks up on some of these issues by exploring the complex nature of dyslexia support at university, and the tools and strategies available for dyslexia support tutors to use. Specific examples are provided in the form of case studies of individual students who brought different strengths and weaknesses with them into higher education, and who were therefore able to engage with the process of learning support to a greater or lesser degree.

In Chapter 6, Geraldine Price considers ways in which dyslexic students can be taught to take control of their own learning through metacognitive strategy instruction. Students can be shown how to identify through experience which skills and strategies to use in any learning environment and how to evaluate the relative success of these strategies. In this way, dyslexic students may develop effective learning skills alongside improved self-confidence and self-regulation, which enable them to become independent learners.

In Chapter 7, David Pollak continues the theme of supporting dyslexic learners in higher education. He identifies the particular difficulties faced by dyslexic students and discusses assistive technology that can be used to alleviate these difficulties. Strategies that university tutors can use when planning their lectures, seminars, handouts and assignments are suggested, as are strategies that students can use to help them with reading, writing, note-taking, and writing examination answers.

Dyslexia support at the Royal College of Art is described by Qona Rankin in Chapter 8. This support includes the production of Mp3 recordings of tutorials; video recordings of practical demonstrations; the use of colour and space to help students to differentiate between different technical processes; the use of pictorial handouts; and small-group work in which all students have the opportunity to practise techniques they have just seen demonstrated. Qona also describes how the dyslexic art students themselves are identifying problems that they are experiencing in the classroom and the workplace, and using their unique abilities to solve these problems in creative ways.

The creative use of technology, including electronic learning and virtual learning environments, is described in Chapter 9 by E.A. Draffan. She explains how the presentation of materials online can be customized by the user to change background colour, font size and character spacing, and this material can be accompanied by podcasts, audio presentations, videos and links to further material. The importance of text-to-speech is also discussed, as are text magnification, the use of headings and subheadings, and clear contents tables or menus to enable individuals to navigate easily around large interactive files.

Chapter 10, by Rob Fidler and John Everatt, describes a study of the reading comprehension skills of dyslexic university students. Five interventions designed to improve comprehension were put in place and ability was assessed before and after the intervention. The most successful intervention strategies were those that involved the use of mind-mapping techniques and the writing of summary notes. These metacognitive strategies, which required the students to engage with the text and to think about its content, enabled the dyslexic students to spend longer reading and thinking about the material, and this improved their comprehension.

The final two chapters of Section One explore ways in which dyslexic adults at university can be supported and prepared for the world of work. In Chapter 11, Pauline Sumner outlines some of the different strategies used by specialist dyslexia support tutors during tutorials to boost students' confidence and self-esteem. She also discusses issues pertinent to students who are about to embark on a work placement. These include disclosure about one's dyslexia, workplace strategies, and good work placement practice; all of these can be discussed and rehearsed in the supportive environment of the one-to-one tutorial.

Finally, Fiona White, Richard Mendez and Rosanne Rieley from the University of Leicester consider how well dyslexic undergraduates make the transition into the workplace. Focus groups held with dyslexic students at different stages of their university education revealed that most – particularly those in their final year – were anxious about obtaining employment. Key to this anxiety was uncertainty regarding potential employers' perceptions of their dyslexia and about how their dyslexia might prevent them from meeting the demands of the workplace. Following on from this study, the University set up an 'Access to Employability' programme designed to support students with dyslexia and other disabilities to make the transition from higher education into work. This programme is described in this chapter.

Section Two: Supporting dyslexic adults in the workplace

The second section of this book considers ways in which the difficulties of dyslexia might affect the employment performance of dyslexic adults and how these might be overcome. Chapters in this section provide tips and strategies regarding how best to disclose dyslexia to employers and colleagues; how to increase self-confidence in the workplace; how to obtain reasonable adjustments; and a look at legal aspects of dyslexia support, including a summary of disability legislation as it applies to people with special educational needs. This section ends by highlighting the particular skills and strengths that dyslexic adults can bring to the workplace. Chapters in this section have been written by researchers and practitioners who have drawn on a wealth of experience in supporting and advising dyslexic adults in the workplace, and numerous examples of evidence-based practice are provided. Many chapters include case studies designed to capture the immediate experiences, good and bad, of dyslexic adults at work.

This section opens with a chapter by Alan Martin and David McLoughlin, who discuss the issue of disclosure in the workplace: when and how to disclose a learning difficulty to employers and colleagues, and why some people choose not to disclose at all. Results of a study tracking dyslexic alumni of the University of Buckingham revealed that fewer than 17% had disclosed details of their learning difficulties to their employers. The most common reasons given for non-disclosure were that individuals felt that their dyslexia was not relevant to their work and that they feared they would be discriminated against in the workplace. The chapter ends with advice for dyslexic people who do choose to disclose, focusing on when to say something, whom to tell and what to say.

Chapter 14, written by Paul Gerber and Lynda Price, continues this theme of self-disclosure by considering the contexts and circumstances that might persuade an individual to disclose his or her dyslexia to their employers and colleagues, and the reactions of others following disclosure. Paul and Lynda's own research into disclosure is discussed in terms of risk management, i.e. the 'acceptable loss' and 'potential gain' that self-disclosure might bring for an individual.

In Chapter 15, Sylvia Moody presents a series of case studies to illustrate different situations in the workplace in which (i) an employee is aware of his or her difficulties but is not aware that these are the result of dyslexia; (ii) an employee is aware that he or she has dyslexia but fears that disclosing this to the employer will lead to discrimination; and (iii) an employee has disclosed his or her dyslexia to an employer but this disclosure has been met with a lack of sympathy, sometimes leading to hostility and bullying. Suggestions for bringing about a successful outcome in each of these cases are presented.

In order for dyslexic people to achieve success in the workplace they need self-understanding; to be working in a job in which they can use their strengths; to be able to use technological and creative solutions; and the support and understanding of their employer and colleagues. These issues are discussed in Chapter 16 by Carol Leather and Bernadette Kirwan. They consider ways of increasing awareness and understanding of dyslexia, of helping individuals to explore different ways of working to maximize their efficiency, and of developing skills of self-advocacy to increase dyslexic adults' sense of control over their working lives and, ultimately, of their self-confidence.

Chapter 17, by Margaret Malpas, examines the skills and knowledge that specialist tutors need to coach and support dyslexic adults at work to help them to perform their jobs effectively. These skills include counselling skills; motivation skills; tact and diplomacy; knowledge of government funding available to pay for the introduction of reasonable adjustments; and knowledge of grievance and disciplinary procedures, as well as an understanding of equality legislation.

A detailed look at dyslexia and disability discrimination is provided by John Mackenzie in Chapter 18. He summarizes UK legislation as it applies to people with special educational needs throughout their education and in the workplace. John also describes the process whereby individuals bring claims against schools, universities and employers where they feel that they have been discriminated against because of their dyslexia. Examples of discrimination may include dyslexic employees being victimized or harassed, having appropriate support or reasonable adjustments withheld, being denied promotion or even being dismissed from their jobs.

In Chapter 19, Robert Hillier describes the process through which he designed and developed the Sylexiad typeface, specifically intended to help dyslexic adults to distinguish more easily between letters and words when reading printed text. As part of the development process, Sylexiad was tested against other 'dyslexia-friendly' fonts for its readability and legibility. Results showed that most dyslexic readers preferred the long ascenders and descenders, light letter weights and generous inter-word spacing of the Sylexiad font to the other fonts tested. Sylexiad has since been adopted by various institutions across the UK, and examples of its use are provided in this chapter.

Finally, in Chapter 20, Morag Kiziewicz presents evidence of some of the strengths that dyslexic adults can bring to the workplace. These strengths include creativity, persistence, adaptability and an ability to 'think outside the box'. As long as dyslexic individuals are respected and valued for these strengths, they should have every opportunity to take their place in the workforce and be an asset to society.

The central aim of this book is to provide information and advice on supporting adults with dyslexia. Of course, much of what can be done applies across the age range and so there are areas of overlap across the two sections of this book. The UK Equality Act 2010, for example, is mentioned in both sections as it influences the way that dyslexic individuals are treated across the lifespan. Similarly, many examples of good practice apply in the university just as much as in the workplace.

A strength of this book is the wealth of practical experience possessed by its contributors. It includes chapters written by specialist dyslexia tutors and learning support tutors in colleges and universities, a speech and language therapist, independent dyslexia consultants and coaches, a clinical psychologist, a lawyer, a careers advisor, a disability advisor, and academic psychologists, educationalists and designers. The years of specialist experience encapsulated in the chapters of this book should help to increase awareness and understanding of the challenges faced by dyslexic adults, whether these are students, clients, employees or colleagues, and of the role that we can all play in supporting and enabling them to meet these challenges in higher education and the workplace.

References

Bartlett, D., Moody, S. and Kindersley, K. (2010) *Dyslexia in the Workplace: An introductory guide*, 2nd edn, John Wiley & Sons, Ltd, Chichester.

Department for Education and Skills (2001) *Special Educational Needs and Disability Act*, Author, London.

Griffin, E. and Pollak, D. (2009) Student experiences of neurodiversity in higher education: insights from the BRAINHE project. *Dyslexia*, 15, 23–41.

Hendrickx, S. (2010) *The Adolescent and Adult Neuro- Diversity Handbook*, Jessica Kingsley, London.

Higher Education Statistics Agency (2010) *Students in Higher Education Institutions 2008/2009*, Author, Cheltenham.

Higher Education Statistics Agency (2006) *Students in Higher Education Institutions 2004/2005*, Author, Cheltenham.

Jasper, M. (2002) Editorial. *Journal of Nursing Management*, 10, 4, 189–190.

Kadesjö, B. and Gillberg, C. (2001) The comorbidity of ADHD in the general population of Swedish school-age children. *Journal of Child Psychology and Psychiatry*, 42, 487–492.

Kaplan, B.J., Wilson, B.N., Dewey, D., and Crawford, S.G. (1998), DCD may not be a discrete disorder. *Human Movement Science*, 17, 471–490.

Kirby, J.R., Silvestri, R., Allingham, B.H. *et al.* (2008) Learning strategies and study approaches of postsecondary students with dyslexia. *Journal of Learning Disabilities*, 41, 85–96.

Lefly, D.L. and Pennington, B. F. (1991) Spelling errors and reading fluency in compensated adult dyslexics. *Annals of Dyslexia*, 41, 143–162.

Logan, J. (2009) Dyslexic entrepreneurs: the incidence; their coping strategies and their business skills. *Dyslexia*, 15, 328–346.

Maughan, B., Messer, J., Collishaw, S. *et al.* (2009) Persistence of literacy problems: spelling in adolescence and at mid-life. *Journal of Child Psychology and Psychiatry*, 50, 893–901.

McArthur, G.M., Hogben, J.H., Edwards, V. T. *et al.* (2000) On the 'specifics' of specific reading disability and specific language impairment. *Journal of Child Psychology and Psychiatry*, 41, 869–74.

McKendree, J. and Snowling, M.J. (2011) Examination results of medical students with dyslexia. *Medical Education*, 45, 176–182.

McLoughlin, D., Leather, C., and Stringer, P. (2002) *The Adult Dyslexic: Interventions and outcomes*, Whurr, London.

Millward, L.J., Bryan, K., Everatt, J. and Collins, R. (2005) Clinicians and dyslexia – a computer-based assessment of one of the key cognitive skills involved in drug administration. *International Journal of Nursing Studies*, 42, 341–353.

Morris, D. and Turnbull, P. (2006) Clinical experiences of students with dyslexia. *Journal of Advanced Nursing*, 54, 238–247.

Morris, D. and Turnbull, P. (2007) A survey-based exploration of the impact of dyslexia on career progression of UK registered nurses. *Journal of Nursing Management*, 15, 97–106.

National Working Party on Dyslexia in Higher Education (1999) *Dyslexia in Higher Education: Policy, provision and practice*, University of Hull, Hull, UK.

Office for Disability Issues (2010) *Equality Act 2010*, Office for Disability Issues, London.

Osborne, M. (2003) Increasing or widening participation in higher education? – A European overview. *European Journal of Education*, 38, 5–24.

Pennington B.F. (1991) *Diagnosing Learning Disorders*, Guilford, New York.

Richardson, J.T.E. and Wydell, T.N. (2003) The representation and attainment of students with dyslexia in higher education. *Journal of Reading and Writing*, 16, 475–503.

Shepherd, K. (2002) People with dyslexia are quite capable of nursing. *Nursing Standard*, 16, 36, 30.

Snowling, M.J. (2008) Specific disorders and broader phenotypes: the case of dyslexia. *Quarterly Journal of Experimental Psychology*, 61, 142–156.

Stampoltzis, A. and Polychronopoulou, S. (2008) Dyslexia in Greek higher education: a study of incidence, policy and provision. *Journal of Research in Special Educational Needs*, 8, 37–46.

Taylor, K. E. & Walter, J. (2003) Occupational choices of adults with and without symptoms of dyslexia. *Dyslexia*, 9, 177–185.

The Quality Assurance Agency for Higher Education (1999) *Code of Practice for the Assurance of Academic Quality and Standards in Higher Education, Section 3 Students with Disabilities*, Author, Gloucester.

van der Leij, A., de Jong, P.F. and Rijswijk-Prins, H. (2001) Characteristics of dyslexia in a Dutch family. *Dyslexia*, 7, 105–124.

Wright, D. (2000) Educational support for nursing and midwifery: Students with dyslexia. *Nursing Standard*, 14, 41, 35–41.

Section 1

Supporting Dyslexic Adults in Higher Education

2

Socio–Emotional Aspects of Dyslexia

We're all in this Together

Ruth Gwernan-Jones University of Exeter, UK

In this chapter I would like to give a flavour of the experience of being dyslexic, and how important other people's attitudes toward dyslexic-type difficulties are to how well a dyslexic person is able to succeed, first at school/further education/higher education, and then at work. I discuss experiences in education at some length because it is during these years that dyslexic individuals often come to believe that they are not capable. Their work lives become a time when self-perceptions can change as the scope for non-writing-based activities widens and possibilities can expand for success (Dale and Taylor 2001). I would like to do more than share the perspectives of some dyslexic people, however; I would also like to share my own experiences, which have brought me to the realization that it is possible to impact dyslexic people negatively by viewing dyslexic-type difficulties as impairments. This is something that I have done for years whilst understanding myself to be an advocate for dyslexic people. I would like to offer other 'understandings' of dyslexia, the adoption of which enable conceptualisations that sustain positive self-perceptions and back constructive action for dyslexic adults.

My undergraduate degree is in psychology and my favourite module was called 'Brain and behaviour'. It looked at modular theories of the brain, for example the kinds of relationships proposed by Paul Broca (1861) and Carl Wernicke (1874) where damage to specific areas of the brain resulted in impairment in speaking and understanding speech, and I found it absolutely fascinating. Fifteen years later, when my six-year-old son was identified as dyslexic, I began to read literature on dyslexia and was once again fascinated by theories about brain dysfunction and links to behaviour, this time in relation to developmental difficulties in learning to read and write. While completing a Diploma in Specific Learning Difficulties, I enjoyed reading literature on cognitive psychology and neuropsychology and, when I decided to pursue a PhD, my first proposal involved comparing functional Magnetic Resonance Imaging (*f*MRI) scans of fluent and non-fluent readers. My supervisor talked me out of this idea, persuading me that contributing to knowledge about the human aspects of dyslexia would be more beneficial, and I have recently completed a life history study of dyslexic adults instead (Gwernan-Jones 2011).

This change in attitude was initiated by my supervisor. However, my further development of change in attitude was the result of two things: a change in understanding about the nature of language and knowledge, and a response to the things I have read about or been told by dyslexic adults about their experiences. The first has influenced the way I have made sense of the latter; so I will begin by discussing constitutive aspects of language and finish the chapter by discussing the experiences of dyslexic adults.

Supporting Dyslexic Adults in Higher Education and the Workplace, First Edition. Edited by Nicola Brunswick.

Constitutive Aspects of Language

For my PhD thesis I wanted to explore the experience of dyslexia. My background is in science and psychology, where to develop knowledge one measures systematically. However, I wanted to develop knowledge about human experience, and this is not so easy to measure. During my MSc in Educational Research I was introduced to the idea of social constructionism, the belief that knowledge is constructed through relationships between human beings and their interaction with the world (Crotty 1998). Rather than 'tree-ness' being an inherent aspect of a tree, social constructionism would describe a person's understanding of a tree as the result of what people have said to him or her about trees, and what his or her experiences with trees have been. A social constructionist understanding of 'tree-ness' makes it possible to see how, for example, a lumberjack and an environmentalist can hold very different, complex and possibly opposing attitudes and understandings about trees. It provides a way to take account of the meaning-making process that is involved in any aspect of human experience.

From this perspective, language and knowledge do not neutrally reflect the world, people and relationships but rather they play an integral part in creating them. Knowledge is an outcome of the way the world is categorized, it develops historically, is culturally-specific, is created and maintained by social processes and establishes what is normal and what is unthinkable, and so it has social consequences (Phillips and Jørgenson 2002).

In relation to dyslexia, my understanding and knowledge of it framed the way I thought about researching it. Before thinking about dyslexia from a social constructionist perspective, I prioritized its more measureable aspects, for example, attainment and/or ability scores, and cognitive measures such as phonological skills. It is not that I was unaware of social and emotional aspects of dyslexia – seeing the socio-emotional impact of dyslexia on my family was what spurred me to want to do research in order to address the negative effects I had witnessed. However, I had difficulty in knowing how I might address such issues. Perceptions and emotions are not easily instrumentalized, and measurable aspects were the only ones about which I believed knowledge could be established. This had the result of limiting the development of my knowledge and attitudes to a non-human focus. In effect I was valuing quantifiable aspects of dyslexia above experiential ones. Both these tendencies – narrowing issues of dyslexia to their measureable aspects and prioritizing these – can impact dyslexic people negatively, as will be discussed below. When I began to approach dyslexia from a social constructionist way of understanding knowledge, I was better able to take social and emotional impacts of dyslexia seriously because this concept frames these aspects as key, giving a structure for considering the human meaning-making process as important. What do people say about dyslexia? How does a dyslexic person feel about what is said? What kinds of frameworks are available for dyslexic people to understand themselves?

In addition to discussing constructionism, I have described the way adopting it enabled me to address questions of dyslexia in a new way to give an example of the way that language can be constitutive. I will now discuss the manner in which different ways of understanding dyslexia impact the way dyslexic individuals may perceive their own value and what they are capable of, and how they may act in response to these beliefs.

Different Ways of Understanding Dyslexia

My first acquaintance with dyslexia was in relation to my son's identification. As a mother, dyslexia represented to me the possibility of a different approach to teaching reading and writing that meant my son would be able to learn. The cognitive aspects I read about explained how he could be intelligent and still have the difficulties he was having. I perceived dyslexia positively because it provided a structure from which to support my son educationally as well as a constructive way to understand his difficulties, that is, because it clarified that he was, indeed, intelligent and capable of learning. I realize now that this attitude is relatively common amongst parents (e.g. see Augur 1981; Riddick 2010). This way of understanding dyslexia was motivating to me and I responded with action; I paid for a specialist tutor for my son and I volunteered at his school to support him and other children with work recommended by his tutor and teachers. He was predicted to achieve 'Working towards Level 1' in his Key Stage 1 Standard Attainment Tests (SATs),[1] but by the end of that year he reached 'Level 1', an improvement I attributed to his receiving more appropriate support. Once I became a specialist tutor I maintained this positive perspective about dyslexia, dismissing alternative views as uninformed.

However, as I began my PhD, I had to address the range of views about dyslexia. I began to appreciate the scope for differences in perceptions about what is meant by it, and correspondingly different actions in response to it. For example, Kerr (2001) reports a small, qualitative study about the perceptions held by providers of (what was then known as) Adult Basic Education about students who were identified as dyslexic:

> 'Dyslexia', respondents all agreed, if it is to be meaningful at all, is a neurological deficit, a miswiring of some kind somewhere in the brain. A miswiring is, par excellence and by definition, an innate and irremediable attribution of causation. Even if such miswiring were to exist, such an attribution is unavoidably maladaptive. (*Kerr 2001, p. 84*)

Kerr (2001, p. 83) also describes the teachers as responding to the students with learned helplessness, noting that:

> A majority of respondents appeared to believe that for a 'dyslexic' the learning of literacy is so formidable and arduous a task that real victory is improbable. This relative hopelessness was, in many instances, sympathetically, but nonetheless clearly, transmitted to the student in question.

Here, 'neurological' (i.e. brain) deficit is interpreted to mean 'there's nothing to be done – the difficulties cannot be remediated', and Kerr describes correspondingly negative changes to the teaching approach such that 'wherever tuition was altered this was invariably a "dumbing-down"' (p. 83). This latter perception of dyslexia as an insurmountable brain deficit is related to less helpful belief systems and action in both non-dyslexic and dyslexic people, as will be shown further below.

The Experiences of Dyslexic People

I have described two opposing perspectives on dyslexia as neurological deficit: the first my own as a parent and then specialist teacher, the second that of practitioners teaching Adult Basic Education. But what of the perspectives of dyslexic people themselves? Research that examines the experience and emotions involved with being dyslexic is relatively rare. Most of the research carried out about dyslexia is from a professional perspective, for example that of educational psychologists, teachers, or cognitive psychologists. Predominance of professional perspective rather than first-hand experience in relation to wider disabilities is also common.

Academic Michael Oliver, a wheelchair user, describes his introduction to the academic literature about disability in the following way:

[1] These were National Curriculum assessments for the subjects English, maths and science, taken by children in school year 2 (they are no longer statutory). The levels of attainment were: Working towards Level 1, Level 1, Level 2c, Level 2b, Level 2a and Level 3. Children were expected to achieve Level 2.

> When I began to read some of the things that able-bodied academics, researchers and professionals had written about disability, I was staggered at how little it related to my own experience of disability or indeed, of most other disabled people I had come to know. Over the next few years it gradually began to dawn on me that if disabled people left it to others to write about disability, we would inevitably end up with inaccurate and distorted accounts of our experiences and inappropriate service provision and professional practices based upon these inaccuracies and distortion. (*Oliver 1996, p. 9*)

All those – employers, lecturers, academics, family members – who interact with dyslexic people would benefit from understanding their perspective, as indeed it is possible to offer inappropriate service provision and professional practices through lack of understanding. Below I discuss experiences of school to give background knowledge about how and why the socio-emotional issues that many dyslexic adults face develop. The way in which teachers' attitudes to dyslexic people impact them positively or negatively in these extracts can be extrapolated to situations of higher education and/or employment for dyslexic adults.

When dyslexic people are interviewed, a common theme is their awareness, often as young children and long before they are identified as dyslexic, that they are different from their peers (Burden 2005; Hellendoorn and Ruijssenaars 2000; Ingesson 2007; McNulty 2003; Pollak 2005). McNulty (2003), in his narrative analysis of the life stories of 12 dyslexic adults, characterizes them as coming to understand that 'something's wrong with me' (p. 371). This understanding is the hinge on which their life stories about being dyslexic revolve; that is, it is the 'exposition' that sets the story in motion. Struggling to come to grips with this issue forms the body of the stories these individuals tell. In other words, the experience of being dyslexic is about realizing that one is different from one's peers, and then working towards making sense of that difference.

There are very few ways to understand difficulty learning to read and write that allow one to make positive sense of it. In interview studies with dyslexic children and adults, some said they decided they must be unintelligent and/or lazy (Dale and Taylor 2001; Ingesson 2007; McNulty 2003). Others said they felt as though they didn't belong (Burden 2005; Dale and Taylor 2001). Moving back to a constructionist perspective about the development of knowledge, the way people make sense of such difficulties will be related to the way important people in their lives – employers, teachers/lecturers, parents, peers – respond to these difficulties. A common description found in interviews with dyslexic people is being humiliated in school for their difficulties (Dale and Taylor 2001; Gerber, Ginsberg and Reiff 1992; Hellendoorn and Ruijssenaars 2000; Hughes and Dawson 1995; McNulty 2003; Riddick 2010; Singer 2005); some to the extent that they still feel traumatized by the experience as adults (Edwards 1994; Gerber, Reiff and Ginsberg 1996; Hughes and Dawson 1995; McNulty 2003). Such experiences convey the idea that difficulties with reading and writing are a problem for which the pupil bears sole responsibility, and about which he or she should be ashamed. This is exemplified by two participants I interviewed for my thesis, Country Boy[2] and Alice:

Country Boy

Country Boy says of his days at school: 'I can remember the headmistress of the junior school saying to me that she didn't know what [the headmaster of the senior school] was going to do with me because I was completely thick and I went to the senior school with that as a legacy.'

[2] All participants chose their own pseudonyms to maintain anonymity.

Country Boy 'proved' his headmistress wrong: he was successful in business in spite of his difficulties with reading and writing, first rising quickly through the ranks to be a top buyer, then running his own business. As he observes:

> 'I got away with being dyslexic by having a secretary . . . who I could dictate letters to. And she would . . . do the spelling and the punctuation . . . and I've got a fair vocabulary so I would write reasonable letters and things.'

He goes on to describe how employment changed his perceptions of himself:

> 'What changed [my lack of confidence], it didn't happen all at once, it was a gradual process . . . the RAF made me more confident because I was . . . given the job of being watch supervisor of the whole communications setup at Mount Batten.. another thing that boosted my confidence was being consulted by [the boss] . . . I was working amongst the big boys . . . and I wasn't being stupid.'

He now holds a Bachelor's degree and a Master's degree.

Alice

Alice, another participant in this study, offers examples of both negative and positive impact of teacher expectations as she recalls:

'by the time I got to the second class I started to realize everybody was reading and I wasn't . . . I was unbelievably ingenious at getting out of doing anything . . . I can remember panicking, absolutely panicking every time I had to do written work but luckily never really had to do much, because the school didn't make you . . . I was very good at working out that they took your temperature by putting a little strip across your forehead and if you put your forehead on a radiator first of all the little windows lit up very quickly . . . I just got home, every day, if I could . . .

[then when we moved I] went from doing no work for school to where I really had to work . . . they were strict as anything and I hated it and I wanted to go home but they didn't believe me when I stuck my head on the radiator at this school . . . I really struggled. My spelling was awful . . . I could have quite easily just decided I wasn't going to work. And every time you did a spelling test, if you got it wrong, you did those ones again, and if you got it wrong, you did them again, and you were kept in at break time and you did it again. And in some ways, people probably think it's mean, but it made me realize by the end of the week when I did get them all right that I could. It might take me longer than everybody else, but that doesn't mean you shouldn't try. And, that was the best thing that that school did for me. And I think if I hadn't gone to that school, I wouldn't be [a dentist now].'

These two cases provide examples of how self-perceptions, developed on the basis of the way teachers' attitudes are perceived, can impact the way that individuals with dyslexia can make sense of their difficulties with reading and writing. In Alice's case, her perception of teacher expectations impacted her future actions. As she says, at her first school, 'I could have quite easily just decided I wasn't going to work.' Instead, she was required by teachers at her new school to learn that she could overcome her difficulties through persistence. She attributes her ability to become a dentist to this realization. This demonstrates the importance that high but realistic expectations of others can have on people with dyslexia.

Having discussed how teachers' negative attitudes and low expectations can impact the way a person makes sense of their reading and writing difficulties, but how these can change for the better through more positive interactions, I now turn to dyslexia as an explanatory concept. My own experience of the label 'dyslexia' was that it is a positive way of making sense of these kinds of difficulties. However, I was not the one being identified with a disability; going through such an experience oneself can be painful and confusing even if it offers positive explanation, and this is not always the case. It depends on what a person understands dyslexia to mean, which, in turn, depends on the way those around them understand and explain it. Both Ingesson (2007) and McNulty (2003) note that identification carried out insensitively can add to a sense of trauma.

Armstrong and Humphrey (2009), in their study of 20 dyslexic students in further education, developed a resistance-accommodation model that sought 'to explain the psycho-social processes of "living with the label" and how such processes might impact upon later outcomes' (p. 95). In this model, the authors associated accommodation (integration of a positive notion of dyslexia into the sense of self) to positive adjustment in that these students were aware of personal strengths but also areas of weakness, and were willing to take action to offset those weaknesses. In contrast, those who resisted identifying with dyslexia avoided confronting their areas of weakness. Those who avoided identifying themselves as dyslexic understood it to mean 'stupid'. It is important for those who support dyslexic adults in higher education or the workplace to be aware of the relevance and potential challenge that identification may pose. It is also important to appreciate that providing both emotional support and positive information about what dyslexia means are equally important to the aspects of a cognitive profile that lead to identification.

Pollak (2005), in analysing interviews with 33 dyslexic students in higher education, identified four discourses[3] of dyslexia. All 33 interviewees spoke about dyslexia from a *Patient* discourse using medical terminology such as 'diagnosis' and brain deficit (e.g. phonological deficit, difficulties with auditory short-term memory, and slow processing speed), though only nine individuals spoke about dyslexia *primarily* from this perspective. Pollak links the discourse through which students talk about dyslexia to their ability to understand themselves positively, and to act to compensate for their difficulties. As he says: 'the informants who adopt the "patient" discourse are farthest from being able to do this, believing themselves to be deeply flawed' (p. 136). These nine individuals were also those with the lowest levels of self-esteem and self-efficacy. The *Patient* discourse links back to Kerr's (2001) findings about the impact of understanding dyslexia to be a neurological/brain deficit.

In contrast, those who spoke about dyslexia primarily from the perspective of other discourses were able to make more positive sense of their differences, and they acted in a way that accorded with each framework of understanding. Those who talked about dyslexia from a *Student* discourse (so-called because it is a notion of dyslexia based on a discrepancy between school attainment and intelligence), still understood dyslexia from a deficit perspective but they perceived themselves to be intelligent and so capable of learning study skills to compensate for their difficulties.

These individuals were therefore motivated to work to succeed academically. They also compartmentalized dyslexia as an aspect of their educational lives only, and this supported positive self-perceptions outside of academia.

[3] A discourse is 'a particular way of talking about and understanding the world (or an aspect of the world)' (Phillips and Jørgensen 2002, p. 1).

Hemispherists (so-called because this discourse stems from ideas about dyslexia in relation to left-brain *versus* right-brain function) had highly developed understanding of the way they learned, what they were good at and what they found difficult. They conceptualized these as personal patterns of strengths and weaknesses and they made practical decisions about how to maximize success in all walks of life using such knowledge (e.g. choosing a university course that assesses through coursework rather than exams and/or employment that requires minimal processing of the written word). Use of the *Hemispherist* discourse supports the development of more positive self-perceptions because of its celebration of personal strengths. Furthermore, the practical application of knowledge of weakness and strength engenders constructive action, both by drawing attention to the need to avoid situations of disadvantage, as well as by seeking situations where personal strengths will be valued.

Finally, *Campaigners* (so called because this idea of dyslexia conceptualizes it in relation to civil rights) talked about dyslexia in terms of social, cultural and educational barriers and their own rights to education and employment. For example, a *Campaigner* would view dyslexia as a result of the way our culture demands high levels of literacy in relation to almost any qualification and/or job with cultural status; this is a cultural barrier that disadvantages dyslexic people. An example of a social barrier would be the historical association between being educated and being intelligent. Dyslexic people are often held in contempt for things like spelling mistakes, regardless of their level of intelligence. An example of an educational barrier is the way pupils and students are judged about how much they understand primarily by how well they are able to write about what they know; of course, for them this is a highly inaccurate measure. The *Campaigner* discourse supports the most straightforward means to positive self-perceptions because from this perspective dyslexic difficulties are a result of the structures and mores of society rather than a deficit in the person. However, in terms of action, this discourse is limiting because it downplays the power individuals have to act (by overcoming their areas of difficulty, as in the *Student* discourse, or by choosing contexts to maximize strengths, as in the *Hemispherist* discourse); instead it focuses on campaigning for institutional and societal change, over which the individual has little power.

The Social Model of Disability in Relation to Dyslexia

The UK Disability Movement began in the 1970s, initiating a representation of disability as the result of societal barriers rather than impairment and it has been successful in supporting more positive perceptions of disability, particularly for disabled people. The idea originally put forward by The Union of the Physically Impaired Against Segregation (UPIAS) that 'it is society which disables physically impaired people' (UPIAS 1976, p. 14), was later developed by several disabled academics (e.g. Barnes 1991; Finkelstein 1980; Oliver 1990) into what is now called 'the social model of disability'. The social model of disability views disability as the barriers that society creates for people with impairment, and this has been the 'battle cry' of the Disability Movement, encouraging a trend toward active, vocal disabled people. Many of these people perceive their disability to be part of a positive personal and social identity and up to half of them, given the choice, would prefer to keep their disability rather than have it 'cured' (Gwernan-Jones 2009).

Before the Disability Movement began, and to a lesser degree still today, disability tended to be conceived as a person's physical or mental shortcoming, making that person passive and needy in relation to powerful professionals (e.g. doctors or teachers) who make choices about their care. This conceptualisation justifies the segregation and/or marginalisation of disabled people on the basis that they are less valuable due to a biological cause (Morris 1991). Dyslexia, like other disabilities, can be understood from this perspective.

Historically, dyslexia has been viewed with social scepticism. This is illustrated, for example, by the suggestion that 'dyslexia is the middle class name for stupid'. Such dismissive or negative cultural attitudes challenge and undermine attempts to develop positive self-perceptions in relation to the disability, and this issue is of great importance to dyslexic people. Social attitude as a barrier features strongly as subject matter in interviews with dyslexic people, though participants are rarely able to verbalize that the source of the disability lies in society and not in themselves. As was demonstrated above, dyslexic people frequently describe in interviews negative attitudes that other people have shown about their difficulties, and the disabling impact of these statements is often more obviously detrimental than how well the person is able to read and write.

The structure of Western education, and the requirement for qualifications related to employment, particularly disables dyslexic people. Our educational system both communicates what is to be learned and measures pupils' learning primarily through the written word. Dyslexic children are required by law to remain in this context, which highlights their weaknesses and often ignores their strengths, for 12 formative years. Most qualifications necessary for employment are gained through written exams regardless of the extent to which writing skills are needed to carry out work in a particular job. And all this despite the fact that the use of computers now makes most weaknesses related to reading and writing surmountable.

An alternative view of dyslexia, as a variation of 'normal' brain function, provides a different slant. Rather than trying to 'fix' what is normal, we could be focusing on the structures in society that make this normal variation disabling. As Pablo, one of the participants interviewed for my thesis, says:

> There isn't enough stuff in visual formats. Just in such a frustratingly obvious way sometimes, the way stuff is still being bandied about on paper when people are discussing dyslexia. There's so much text. I'd strip it down and do a short animation . . . I understand [dyslexia] not just as difficulty with words but the way we see and perceive and are experiencing slightly differently . . . and the way you perceive yourself and the way others perceive you as the kid in the remedial class, whereas he probably wouldn't be perceived that way if we were all stood around having a pint. But in school, a fish out of water. Bird out of the sky . . . but beating anyone in a running race because I can do that, I can create film. I can do so many things.

Conclusion

In this chapter I have shared my own process of viewing dyslexia from a positivist perspective with a particular interest in brain deficit, to the development of more constructionist views leading to an understanding that brain difference is only one potential barrier in the multifaceted process that is learning to read and write. I have discussed a number of studies that demonstrate that paying attention to socio-emotional aspects of dyslexia is important in supporting dyslexic people, and that the way dyslexia is understood, by dyslexic and non-dyslexic people alike, is important to how well dyslexic adults are able to make sense of their experiences, and to respond proactively.

The dominance of a medical/cognitive focus, positivist approaches and intervention based almost exclusively on remediating reading mean that not only are socio-emotional aspects of dyslexia relatively ignored, but the attention focused on deficit can actually impede healthy socio-emotional development in dyslexic people. In this chapter I have highlighted non-deficit aspects of dyslexia, acknowledging the complex, reciprocal and social nature of learning to read and write, and brought attention to society's role in structuring and perpetuating difficulties. Acknowledging that individual difference is only one part of a much larger picture can help dyslexic people and those who support them to put difficulties into a less reductive, less personal and more positive perspective.

References

Armstrong, D. and Humphrey, N. (2009) Reactions to a diagnosis of dyslexia among students entering further education: Development of the 'resistance-accommodation' model. *British Journal of Special Education*, 36, 95–102.

Augur, J. (1981) *This Book Doesn't Make (Sens, Scens) Sense*, Whurr, London.

Barnes, C. (1991) *Disabled People in Britain and Discrimination*, Hurst & Co., London.

Broca, P. (1861) Remarques sur le siège de la faculté du langage articulé, suivies d'une observation d'aphémie. *Bulletin de la Société Anatomique de Paris*, 6, 330–357.

Burden, R. (2005) *Dyslexia & Self-Concept: Seeking a dyslexic identity*, Whurr, London.

Crotty, M. (1998) *The Foundations of Social Research: Meaning and perspective in the research process*, Sage, London.

Dale, M. and Taylor, B. (2001) How adult learners make sense of their dyslexia. *Disability & Society*, 16, 997–1008.

Edwards, J. (1994) *The Scars of Dyslexia*, Cassell, London.

Finkelstein, V. (1980) *Attitudes and Disabled People*, World Rehabilitation Fund, New York.

Gerber, P.J., Ginsberg, R. and Reiff, H.B. (1992) Identifying alterable patterns in employment success for highly successful adults with learning disabilities. *Journal of Learning Disabilities*, 25, 475–487.

Gerber, P.J., Reiff, H.B. and Ginsberg, R. (1996) Reframing the learning disabilities experience. *Journal of Learning Disabilities*, 29, 98.

Gwernan-Jones, R.C. (2011) *Making sense of dyslexia: A life history study with dyslexic adults mapping meaning-making and its relationship to the development of more positive self-perceptions and coping skills*. Unpublished doctoral dissertation. University of Exeter.

Gwernan-Jones, R.C. (2009) *Identity and disability: a review of the current state and developing trends*. Futurelab. www.beyondcurrenthorizons.org.uk, Bristol.

Hellendoorn, J. and Ruijssenaars, W. (2000) Personal experiences and adjustment of Dutch adults with dyslexia. *Remedial and Special Education*, 21, 227–239.

Hughes, W. and Dawson, R. (1995) Memories of school: Adult dyslexics recall their school days. *Support for Learning*, 10, 181–184.

Ingesson, S.G. (2007) Growing up with dyslexia. *School Psychology International*, 28, 574–591.

Kerr, H. (2001) Learned helplessness and dyslexia: A carts and horses issue? *Reading, Literacy and Language*, 35, 82–85.

McNulty, M.A. (2003) Dyslexia and the life course. *Journal of Learning Disabilities*, 36, 363–381.

Morris, J. (1991) *Pride against Prejudice: Transforming attitudes to disability*, The Women's Press Ltd, London.

Oliver, M. (1990) *The Politics of Disablement*, Macmillan, Basingstoke.

Oliver, M. (1996) *Understanding Disability: From theory to practice*, Macmillan, London.

Phillips, L. and Jørgenson, M.W. (2002) *Discourse Analysis as Theory and Method*, Sage, London.

Pollak, D. (2005) *Dyslexia, the Self and Higher Education: Learning life histories of students identified as dyslexic*, Trentham Books, Stoke on Trent.

Riddick, B. (2010) *Living with Dyslexia: The social and emotional consequences of specific learning difficulties/disabilities*, 2nd edn, Routledge, London.

Singer, E. (2005) The strategies adopted by Dutch children with dyslexia to maintain their self-esteem when teased at school. *Journal of Learning Disabilities*, 38, 411–423.

UPIAS (1976) *Fundamental Principles of Disability*, Union of the Physically Impaired Against Segregation.

Wernicke, C. (1874) *Der Aphasische Symptomenkomplex*, Cohen and Weigert, Breslau, Poland.

3

How Well Are Students with Specific Learning Difficulties Prepared for Higher Education? A case study of a pre-1992 university

Vikki Anderson and Sue Onens

Introduction

The transition from school or college to higher education can be challenging for many students. A number of studies explore students' experiences of transition to higher education, referring in particular to student expectations, achievement and retention (see for example Lowe and Cook 2003; Wingate 2007; Yorke and Longden 2008). Some research suggests that the transition process can be particularly fraught for 'disabled students' who 'already have "added bits" to manage in the transition from school to university' (Goode 2007, p. 44) but few studies explicitly consider the views and experiences of students with specific learning difficulties during their transition to higher education. Two reports commissioned by *Aimhigher* [1] sought the views of 'disabled learners', including some students with specific learning difficulties. Madriaga (2005) focused on the transition of 21 students (15 of whom were dyslexic) from further to higher education, while Elliott and Wilson (2008) investigated the perceptions of students with 'hidden impairments' in relation to their experiences of transition to higher education. Eighteen students (ten with dyslexia), attending five different higher education institutions, participated in this study.

The majority of students in Elliott and Wilson's (2008) study felt ill equipped for higher education and only a few thought they had had sufficient pre-entry experience to prepare them for its potential challenges. The absence of a family tradition of higher education meant that 3/4 of the students were dependent on information from schools, colleges and the Connexions Service.[2] Some students had received useful input from advisors such as further education course tutors and a private study skills tutor, whilst others felt their teachers and personal advisors had limited knowledge of the issues related to studying in higher education as an individual with a hidden impairment.

In both Madriaga's (2005) and Elliott and Wilson's (2008) studies, participants did not expect the differences in teaching and learning between school or further education and higher education to be so great, and they were surprised to find that teaching methods were organized around the expectation that they would be self-directed learners. Students felt they

[1] www.aimhigher.ac.uk/sites/practitioner/home/index.cfm.
[2] www.connexions-direct.com.

Supporting Dyslexic Adults in Higher Education and the Workplace, First Edition. Edited by Nicola Brunswick.

were required to become independent learners too quickly and they needed additional support to make the change from the more structured approaches of school and further education.

Madriaga's (2005) and Elliott and Wilson's (2008) research focused largely on students entering higher education from further education. Our study adds a new dimension to this area as it considers the views of students with specific learning difficulties entering higher education from more traditional routes. The aim was to examine the extent to which students felt prepared for studying at university and to elicit their views on ways of improving the transition process.

Our Study

By listening to the voice of students with specific learning difficulties, we sought to identify some of the 'connections between structural conditions and the lived reality of people' (Barton 1996, p. 1, cited in Fuller *et al.* 2004, p. 304), with the aim of responding to their views and facilitating change. The definition of transition is by no means straightforward. According to the National Disability Team and Skill (2004), the term is used to describe 'the myriad of changes that occur as a person moves from child to adult' (p.14). Individuals moving through the UK's education and training system can go through a number of major transitions, including:

- the move from nursery to primary school
- the change from primary to secondary school
- the move from compulsory education to post-16 education or training
- progression into higher education
- the move into employment (Hudson 2009).

Although it is recognized that there is a cycle of transition in higher education, with transitions occurring from pre-entry to the first year, from one academic year to the next, and possibly from undergraduate to postgraduate study, for the purpose of our research transition was taken to mean the period between accepting a place at university and completing the first term.

The research was carried out at a pre-1992 Russell Group university at which approximately 700 students had identified themselves as having specific learning difficulties. It aimed to garner the views of newly enrolled first-year undergraduates with specific learning difficulties, regarding transition from school or college, and to compare these with their subsequent experiences of studying at university. This was achieved through the repetition of questions in interviews conducted shortly after enrolment (late September/early October 2008) and after one term at the university (January 2009). In the first phase of the study, 51 students (31 male, 20 female) from a wide range of subject areas agreed to be interviewed at the end of an introductory appointment with a learning support advisor. Thirty-nine students had dyslexia, five had dyspraxia and the remainder experienced overlapping conditions – five with dyslexia and dyspraxia, one with dyslexia and attention deficit hyperactivity disorder (AD/HD) and one with dyslexia and hearing loss. Eighteen of these students (eleven male, seven female), sixteen with dyslexia and two with dyspraxia, volunteered to be interviewed again at the beginning of the second term.

The following research questions were addressed:

1 How were students with specific learning difficulties prepared for studying at university?
2 Who did they think had been the most influential in preparing them, and why?
3 In what ways did they perceive transition issues to be different for students with specific learning difficulties?
4 What, with hindsight, could be done differently in order to better prepare students with specific learning difficulties for higher education?

Findings and Discussion

The majority of participants (44 out of 51) had studied for A-levels[3] at school or sixth-form college. Only one student had a BTEC[4] National Diploma. Seven were mature students, six of whom had attended further education colleges and completed Access to Higher Education programmes. Fewer than half of the students had taken preparatory modules or courses at school or college (for example, Study Skills or Critical Thinking) and only the mature students said they would have attended an organized event such as a summer school, had the opportunity been available. Thirty-five students said they had not done any pre-entry work for university. The others reported that they had explored departmental web sites and read some of the books on the reading list. However, not all reading lists arrived in time and a number of students said they were not sent reading lists at all. In contrast, two students from the same Science department were pleased to have received a comprehensive study guide giving them an indication of what to expect when they joined the course. Eight of the nine students who had taken a gap year felt that it had been highly advantageous, particularly with regard to being self-reliant and feeling confident about easing into independent-living skills. For example, one student commented:

> Taking a gap year has settled me down, giving me independent living skills such as cooking and meeting people. I can now concentrate on my academic studies.
>
> *BSc Economics student*

However, one student expressed concern about having spent time away from studying:

> Having a gap year has meant I've spent a whole year not doing any academic work. I'm worried I won't be able to get back into it.
>
> *BA Media, Culture and Society student*

The majority of students interviewed were aware of the Disabled Students' Allowances (44 out of 51 had received information about DSAs before coming to university) but most said they did not regard themselves as being 'disabled'.

Of the 51 students with specific learning difficulties interviewed in the first phase of the research, 34 said they 'felt fairly well prepared' for study at university; 14 felt they 'needed more preparation'; two thought they were 'not prepared at all' and only one felt 'very well prepared'. Twenty-five students thought they had been best prepared by family members (parents or siblings at university, or who had previously been to university), and/or friends who had informed them about the academic and social requirements of higher education. Guidance from family and friends is an important factor in the transition experience of a number of students (UCAS 2002). However, it cannot be assumed that all students will have this support and, as Crozier *et al.* (2008) and Elliott and Wilson (2008) point out, it can be difficult when students seek advice from family members who have no prior experience of higher education.

Fifteen students thought that teachers or college tutors had prepared them by teaching relevant skills and informing them about university life. However, some of those interviewed a

[3] Advanced level exams taken in the UK, generally at the age of 18.
[4] Business and Technology Education Council.

second time felt their teachers had understated the extent of the difference between studying at school and at university. The following comments illustrate this feeling:

> My teachers stressed the need for independent study but the reality came later.
> *BA Media, Culture and Society student*

> I had no idea about the volume of work – it's a huge step up from A-level.
> *BA International Relations student*

> At school it was handed to us on a plate. Teachers were on tap but you can't just go and ask tutors here. Teachers could have given us more self-directed learning.
> *BSc Economics and Geography student*

The majority of participants in the second phase of the study said they were shocked by the degree of independent learning expected; the pace of delivery in lectures; the volume of work and the range of organizational strategies needed. Nine of these students changed their minds about the extent to which they felt prepared. Eight changed from 'fairly well prepared' to 'needed more preparation' and one, a BSc Psychology student, changed from 'needed more preparation' to 'not prepared at all', remarking:

> I was spoon-fed at school, so it's going from one extreme to the other. Here you get given the basics and the rest is down to you.

These reports of difficulty in adapting to learning and teaching approaches in higher education correspond with the findings of other research. For example, in Piggott and Houghton's (2007, p. 581) study, a dyslexic student commented:

> When I got to university, it wasn't so structured, you were teaching yourself, I mean my organisation is not the best, let's put it like that...I mean at school, you had everything structured for you 9 to 5.

There were mixed views as to whether the transition to studying at university was different for students with specific learning difficulties. Twenty-six of the 51 students in the first phase of the study felt it was more challenging for them, mainly due to difficulties with multi-tasking, speed of processing and organization. The following comments were typical:

I have a slower processing speed than others and I can't think and write at the same time.

BSc Geology student

I need to spend more time on academic work. Some people can 'bang out' essays easily. For me, they can take for ever.

BSc Geography student

I'm slow. Other people are better at organization and probably don't find note-taking as difficult.

BA War Studies student

It's harder for me to cope – I experience overload more easily.

BSc Biochemistry student

One student felt there were degrees of difference, with dyslexic students who had studied for A-levels being in a better position than those who had not:

It's worse for me because I come from a BTEC background. I had to do BTEC because of my dyslexia.

BA Sport, Physical Education and Community Studies student

Having experienced a term at university, two students changed their minds, saying they now felt studying at university was more difficult for students with specific learning difficulties, mainly because they had to work much harder and invest a lot more time in their work. As these students said:

I find it harder to absorb information – others just get it. I need at least two weeks to write essays; my friends need two days. It's much harder for me to keep on top of deadlines.

BA Geography student

And:

It takes me much longer to read things than other people. My flatmates do a lot more socialising than me.

BA International Relations student

However, on reflection, one student decided that the difficulties he experienced in adapting to higher education were no different from those of any other student:

> It's a matter of getting used to it, how everything works. I find referencing difficult but so do other people.
>
> *BA Politics student*

Research has shown that many students, with or without specific learning difficulties, are concerned about being under-prepared for the demands of independent learning (see for example Hocking, Cooke and Bowl 2007; Richardson 2003; Lowe and Cook 2003; UCAS 2002). However, Elliott and Wilson (2008), Goode (2007), and Piggott and Houghton (2007) argue that these concerns can be magnified for disabled students, as they may experience them in addition to other challenges linked specifically to their impairments, such as having to work harder than their peers to achieve the same results.

Our results appear to accord with other research findings, particularly regarding the amount of time needed to complete tasks, and issues with listening and writing simultaneously. In Fuller *et al.*'s (2004) study of a post-1992 university, 2/3 of the students with dyslexia reported difficulties with learning in lectures, including problems with taking notes while listening, and lecturers talking too quickly or removing visual material before the student could absorb the information. Mortimore and Crozier (2006) surveyed the perceived difficulties and support needs of a sample of 62 dyslexic students from a wide range of degree programmes across 17 universities (4 pre-1992 and 13 post-1992) and compared their responses with those of a matched group of students not identified as having dyslexia. They found that the dyslexic students reported considerably more difficulties with a range of learning and study skills, particularly note taking, organizing essays and expressing ideas in writing.

At a pre-1992 university, Carroll and Iles (2006) compared 16 students with dyslexia with 16 others (matched for sex and age) with no history of learning difficulties. The dyslexic students were found to have slower reading speeds than the controls, together with higher levels of state anxiety – 'an emotional reaction to a specific self-threatening situation' (Carroll and Iles 2006, p. 653) – and elevated levels of academic and social anxiety. However, only five students in our study referred to anxiety, remarking:

> Most things are harder for people with dyslexia. Because of my dyslexia I think I experience more stress and anxiety.
>
> *BA Philosophy student*

> My dyspraxia makes me feel more apprehensive and worried that I won't succeed.
>
> *BA Media, Culture and Society student*

> I've had some bad experiences of education in the past. I get stressed and anxious, particularly about revision.
>
> *BA Political Science student*

> I'm anxious about my dyslexia. I'm so forgetful.
>
> *BA Media, Culture and Society student*

> I feel more anxious because I've got to deal with my dyslexia as well as everything else.
>
> *BA French and Maths student*

Although it is evident that some dyslexic students experience more difficulties than their non-dyslexic counterparts, almost half the students interviewed in the first phase of our study did not think that the transition to higher education was different for students with specific learning difficulties. For example:

> I don't think it's all that different. I've done well throughout school. I have my own strategies and will probably cope as well as anyone else.
>
> *BSc Economics student*

> It's the same for everyone – change causes everyone to worry, it's just that people with dyslexia have different worries.
>
> *BA Philosophy student*

Healey *et al.* (2008) caution against treating 'disabled students' as a 'separate category', arguing that: 'they fall along a continuum of learner differences and share with other higher education students similar challenges and difficulties; sometimes the barriers are more severe for them, but sometimes they are not' (p. 1). Students' expectations and support requirements are likely to vary depending on their personal characteristics and their individual circumstances and experiences. In both phases of our research, some of the participants said that overall they thought it was difficult to prepare for studying at university, remarking:

> I don't know what I'm preparing for!
>
> *BA International Relations student*

It's difficult to anticipate what you need – I thought the study skills help at school would be useful, but it's so different studying at university. It's the pace of work and the volume of reading that's difficult for me.

BA History student

There's not a lot you can do really. You just have to deal with situations as they occur.

BA Social Policy student

There's very little that anyone can do to prepare you for university. You have to experience it before you know what you need.

BSc Biochemistry student

Focusing on the promotion of inclusive learning, Heathcote and Brindley (2006, p. 40) argue that it is important to explore the advantages and disadvantages of both 'universal and targeted' approaches, together with the implications for learners with specific learning difficulties in targeting provision and classifying them as different. We asked the participants in our study to suggest how a range of stakeholders might ease the transition to higher education of students with specific learning difficulties. Suggestions for improvement were made by the students who were interviewed twice and therefore able to view the process with hindsight. For schools and colleges, students suggested:

- less 'spoon feeding', with more emphasis on independent learning and research skills
- workshops focusing on changes related to academic work, such as the volume of reading; fast pace of teaching; note-taking; styles of writing; time management and issues around self-directed learning
- subject-specific sample lectures and seminars, preferably delivered by guest speakers from higher education.

In relation to the last point, *Aimhigher* has done a large amount of outreach work in schools and colleges but this may not have extended to all students with specific learning difficulties and there may still be gaps in provision.

The students also made a number of suggestions for university departments. These included:

- sample lectures at open days
- more information about the logistics and requirements of the course, for instance the number of essays per term, how seminars work, examples of assignments and printed lecture notes
- reading lists sent well in advance, identifying *key* texts
- vodcasts (video podcasts) of lectures so that students can practise note-taking
- a directed piece of work to be completed over the summer and discussed at the beginning of the course
- subject-specific support with reading strategies, note-making, essay and report-writing and referencing in the first few weeks of university.

These suggestions give weight to Wingate's (2007) view that academic tutors should support *all* students in the process of learning to learn in higher education and that a subject-specific approach is needed to help students assimilate into the practices of their disciplines. Shevlin, Kenny and Mcneela (2004) highlight the need to ensure that the inclusion of disabled students in higher education 'is treated as a cultural change that will transform the practices of the institution and of personnel at all levels who work in it' (p. 29). This involves continuous, effective communication and collaboration between the institution's academic departments and learning support service, eliminating the gap or 'glass wall' (Mortimore and Crozier 2006, p. 248) that can exist between them.

Within our study, students suggested that the university's learning support service make the following available:

- an induction checklist for students with specific learning difficulties
- vodcasts of students with specific learning difficulties relating their experiences of transition to university
- a web-based resource, including information on note-taking; different types of referencing; essay planning and writing; time management and organization
- an information-giving event during induction week to include second- and final-year students with specific learning difficulties speaking about their experiences
- a 'buddy' support system.

The learning support service has since implemented the majority of the students' suggestions and is in the process of evaluating its response. It is anticipated that the vodcasts in particular will go some way towards supporting the transition of students without a family tradition of studying in higher education.

Conclusion

Focusing mainly on 'traditional' students entering a pre-1992 Russell Group university, this small-scale study makes an important contribution to research into the transition experience of students with specific learning difficulties. The main findings show that many students thought they had been best prepared by family members, and some reported that, although teachers had made a positive contribution to the transition process, with hindsight, the difference between studying at school or college and university had been underemphasized. The majority of students in the first phase thought they were 'fairly well prepared' for study at university but over half of those interviewed a second time felt they had overestimated their preparedness.

There were mixed views on whether the transition process was different for students with specific learning difficulties. Some concluded that it was difficult to prepare for 'the unknown' in more than general terms, suggesting that they needed to experience study at university over a period in order to establish exactly what was required. It is apparent that the level of preparedness varies from student to student, together with the inclination to participate in pre-university activities. In our study, only around 1/4 of students had undertaken any pre-entry work and it was only the mature students who said they would have been willing to attend an organized event such as a summer school.

Our research has clear implications for the ways in which transition to studying at university is conceptualized and supported. It cannot be assumed that all students are the same, and clearly one size does not fit all. Many of the students in our study said they did not regard themselves as 'disabled' and would prefer not to be singled out as such. The importance of students being proactive in managing their expectations and endeavouring to prepare for studying at university cannot be overestimated. However, they need access to appropriate guidance and support as and when they require it, which is likely to involve subject-specific, contextualized provision throughout most of the first term. The emphasis should be on a whole-institution approach to preparing *all* students for the different stages of the transition cycle, with some 'targeted' support available for those who choose to use it.

In line with other studies, our findings indicate that ongoing work is needed to ensure that partnerships between the various education providers are effective and take account of the student voice. Preparation for transition to higher education is important for all students, particularly those with specific learning difficulties, and should be a shared responsibility between the students, their schools and colleges, relevant support services and university departments.

References

Barton, L. (1996) Sociology and disability: some emerging issues, in *Disability and Society: Emerging issues and insights* (ed. L. Barton), Longman, London.

Carroll, J.M. and Iles, J.E. (2006) An assessment of anxiety levels in dyslexic students in higher education. *British Journal of Educational Psychology*, 76, 651–662.

Crozier, G., Reay, D., Clayton, J. *et al.* (2008) Different strokes for different folks: diverse students in diverse institutions?–?experiences of education. *Research Papers in Education*, 23, 167–177.

Elliott, T. and Wilson, C. (2008) The perceptions of students with hidden disabilities of their experience during transition to higher education, Aimhigher East of England, available at: http://www.impact-associates.co.uk/hidden_disabilities.html.

Fuller, M., Healey, M., Bradley, A. and Hall, T. (2004) Barriers to learning: a systematic study of the experience of disabled students in one university. *Studies in Higher Education*, 29, 303–318.

Goode, J. (2007) 'Managing' disability: early experiences of university students with disabilities. *Disability & Society*, 22, 35–48.

Healey, M., Roberts, H., Fuller, M. *et al.* (2008) *Reasonable adjustments and disabled students' experiences of learning, teaching and assessment*, available at: http://www.tlrp.org/dspace/retrieve/2993/Fuller+M+-+C__Documents+and+Settings_emm…E5_3I7PXLPQ_spring2008%5B2%5D.pdf.

Heathcote, V. and Brindley, F. (2006) *16–18 year old students with Specific Learning Difficulties: Transition into HE*. Aimhigher South Yorkshire, available at: http://www.actiononaccess.org/resources/files/Y&H_SpLD%20Main%20Report.pdf.

Hocking, C., Cooke, S. and Bowl, M. (2007) Academic engagement within a widening participation context – a 3D analysis. *Teaching in Higher Education*, 12, 721–733.

Hudson, C. (2009) *A review of literature relevant to transitions and widening participation in HE Art and Design*. Available at: www.arts.ac.uk/media/oldreddotassets/docs/CH_transitions_LitReview.pdf.

Lowe, H. and Cook, A. (2003) Mind the gap: are students prepared for higher education? *Journal of Further and Higher Education*, 27, 53–76.

Madriaga, M. (2005) *Research report on the transition of disabled learners from Further Education to Higher Education: Final report*. Aimhigher, South Yorkshire.

Mortimore, T. and Crozier, W.R. (2006) Dyslexia and difficulties with study skills in higher education. *Studies in Higher Education*, 31, 235–251.

National Disability Team and Skill (2004) *Aspiration raising and transition of disabled students from Further Education to Higher Education: Final report*. National Bureau for Students with Disabilities, London.

Piggott, L. and Houghton, A. (2007) Transition experiences of disabled young people. *International Journal of Lifelong Education*, 26, 573–587.

Richardson, D. (2003). *The transition to degree level study*, The Higher Education Academy, York.
Shevlin, M., Kenny, M. and Mcneela, E. (2004) Participation in higher education for students with disabilities: an Irish perspective. *Disability & Society*, 19, 15–30.
Universities and Colleges Admissions Service (UCAS) (2002) *Paving the Way*, UCAS, Cheltenham.
Wingate, U. (2007) A framework for transition: Supporting 'learning to learn' in higher education. *Higher Education Quarterly*, 61, 391–405.
Yorke, M. and Longden, B. (2008) *The First-year Experience of Higher Education in the UK*, The Higher Education Academy, York.

Additional Resources

Preparing for university study if you have dyslexia. Available at: http://www.as.bham.ac.uk/studentlife/disability/learningsupport/transition/index.shtml.
A guide for disabled learners interested in higher education. Available at: http://www.actiononaccess.org/resources/files/resources__dis-AH-guide.pdf.
Bridging the Gap: A guide to Disabled Students' Allowances in higher education 2010/2011. This more recent guide is available for download from: http://www.direct.gov.uk/prod_consum_dg/groups/dg_digitalassets/@dg/@en/documents/digitalasset/dg_194349.pdf.
Thinking about higher education? Tips from students with dyslexia, mental health difficulties and Asperger's syndrome. Available at: http://www.impact-associates.co.uk/hidden_disabilities.html.
DfES (2004) *Working with Dyslexic Students in Higher Education*, Department for Education and Skills, London.

4

Screening for Specific Learning Difficulties in Higher Education

Sarah Nichols University of Worcester, UK

Introduction

The first article on dyslexia published in the UK appeared in *The Lancet* in 1895 (Hinshelwood 1895). The Dyslexia Institute (now Dyslexia Action[1]) was founded in 1972, the British Dyslexia Association (BDA[2]) in 1984, and both have worked tirelessly since then to raise awareness, in schools and among the general public, of the condition. Miles published the first Bangor Dyslexia Test in 1983, and Fawcett and Nicolson's Dyslexia Adult Screening Test appeared in 1998.

Gubbay wrote about 'the clumsy child syndrome' as early as 1975 and, although we now call this Developmental Coordination Disorder (DCD) or dyspraxia, his definition remains virtually unchanged. The Dyspraxia Foundation[3] was founded in 1987 as the Dyspraxia Trust.

In the early 1980s, Olive Meares and Helen Irlen both published their findings on the frequent value of tinted lenses for people with reading problems (Meares 1980, Irlen 1983), and their work led to a plethora of studies into what came to be known as Meares–Irlen Syndrome (M–IS).

Yet still very many adults with specific learning difficulties (SpLDs) and/or M–IS are not identified until they enter higher education (40% of dyslexic students according to Singleton, 2004a). While this may be understandable in the case of mature students who left school in the 1980s or early 1990s, in the case of 18-year-old entrants it seems increasingly remarkable that they have escaped recognition throughout their school careers.

Support in Higher Education

However, higher education institutions (HEIs) in the UK have no time for recriminations. Our duty is to catch all those who have slipped through previous nets, and to do so quickly. Those who are at risk need the benefit of full diagnostic assessment by a professional: either a qualified educational psychologist or a tutor holding a Practising Certificate in Assessment

1 www.dyslexiaaction.org.uk.
2 www.bdadyslexia.org.uk.
3 www.dyspraxiafoundation.org.uk.

Supporting Dyslexic Adults in Higher Education and the Workplace, First Edition. Edited by Nicola Brunswick.

awarded by the BDA or by the Professional Association of Teachers of Students with Specific Leaning Difficulties (Patoss).[4] Those found to have specific learning difficulties can then access funding – the Disabled Students' Allowance (DSA)[5] administered by regional Student Finance boards for England, Wales, Northern Ireland and Scotland, and by the Open University. The DSA will pay for one-to-one support and for appropriate technological aids and software. It is well established that the sooner such support is in place, the more likely students are to succeed. This whole process can be arranged well in advance through the student's HEI as soon as an offer has been accepted, or in some cases earlier.

Screening in Higher Education

Our task then, in every HEI, is to establish a net of our own that catches as many students as possible with unidentified SpLD, and to send them on to full diagnostic assessment, without mistakenly catching those who are unaffected. This net is called a screening test. The term 'screening' can be used in two different ways: screening a whole population (of students), or simply checking those who refer themselves because they have concerns about their own work, to see if they show sufficient positive indications to warrant assessment. Some HEIs adopt one policy and some the other.

Whichever kind of screening is adopted, the process stands or falls on the size of the mesh of the net. If the screening test lets slip those who genuinely have SpLD, it has failed them. They will not proceed to full-scale assessment, they will not access the DSA, nor achieve their potential; they may well drop out of university, demoralized and disillusioned, before completing their course. On the other hand, every time the screening test 'catches' students who do not in fact have SpLD, their time will be wasted, they will suffer unnecessary stress and anxiety, and the HEI will spend increasingly scarce funds (which might have been better spent elsewhere) on an assessment that ultimately proves negative. The efficacy of the net in catching the 'positive' SpLD students is called the sensitivity of the screening test, and its efficacy in excluding the 'negative' ones is called its specificity. It is in terms of sensitivity and specificity that we must judge screening tests.

In the field of dyslexia there is now a wide variety of such tests on the market. Some are simple checklists such as Vinegrad's revised adult dyslexia checklist (Vinegrad 1994), which can be completed by the individual. Some consist of a barrage of subtests such as the York Adult Assessment battery (Hatcher, Snowling and Griffiths 2002; see also [6]), the Bangor Dyslexia Test (Miles 1997), Wolff and Lundberg's (2003) group screening test, and the Dyslexia Adult Screening Test (DAST) (Fawcett and Nicolson 1998), and each of these must be delivered by a tutor who has received training on the test. The scores of individual students determine whether they reach a cut-off point that indicates the need for full assessment.

Also available are screening tests that can be taken by any student, via the internet, for a fee. The BDA, for example, currently offers 'spot your potential',[7] which includes advice on learning styles, while amidyslexic?com[8] provides support advice as part of its feedback.

Alternatively, the HEI can buy a site licence to install a computer-based screening programme and make it available on a number of terminals across campus so that students can access the tests at will. These tests include Quickscan and Studyscan,[9] and the Lucid Adult Dyslexia Screening test (LADS) (Singleton 2004b; see also[10]). Computerized versions usually

4 www.patoss-dyslexia.org.
5 www.direct.gov.uk/en/DisabledPeople/EducationAndTraining/HigherEducation.
6 www.york.ac.uk/media/psychology/crl/documents/YAA.pdf.
7 www.spot-your-potential.com.
8 www.amidyslexic.com.
9 www.studyscan.com.
10 www.lucid-research.com.

give a printout of results and advice but, as they are not delivered by another person, the opportunity for feedback and reassurance is necessarily limited.

All screening instruments for dyslexia aim to test some combination of the student's phonological processing, visual processing, working memory, spelling, reading, comprehension and, sometimes, underlying non-verbal ability. In other words, they aim to test most of the same things as a full assessment but in less depth. Which 'things' to test is the central question – which are the best predictors of dyslexia? The content of every screening instrument, however delivered, is the result of a decision about this.

Experience at the University of Worcester

At the University of Worcester (UW), we had for some years relied on tutor-delivered tests to self-referring students. We used a combination of seven subtests from the Dyslexia Adult Screening Test (DAST) and eight from the Bangor Dyslexia Test (BDT). While the DAST is well standardized, the BDT is not normed for those above 17 years but was continuing to prove itself useful. It was originally intended as a brief assessment to identify dyslexia in children (van Daal and Miles 2001), but has latterly been used extensively as a screening test. The BDT was devised in the early 1980s, before much attention had been focused on phonological processing deficit, and its subtests chiefly emphasize difficulties of working memory, sequencing and orientation, and provide, for example, an objective measure of *left/right confusion*. The test also asks two questions: one about *familial incidence* and one about *b/d* letter confusions. After experimentation during a pilot study, we decided to use the *digit span* test from DAST but not from BDT.

DAST draws from work on the phonological deficit (Frith 1999; Snowling 1995), and on the cerebellar hypothesis (see, for example, Fawcett 2001; Nicolson and Fawcett 1999). It has proved very successful in higher education, as Reid and Kirk (2001) reported: 'the data it provides is more than one would expect from a screening test' (p. 33). It was devised as a screening test from the outset, and provides an 'at risk' measure for dyslexia.

Harrison and Nichols (2005) found that, overall, DAST had a sensitivity of 74% and a specificity of 84%. They found that the subtests that were most reliable at discriminating between dyslexic and non-dyslexic readers were: *nonsense passage reading, two minute spelling, phonemic segmentation, one minute reading* and *one minute writing*. However, they maintained that the *postural stability, nonverbal reasoning* and *semantic fluency* subtests were not effective discriminators. Gunn (2000) also found that *semantic fluency* and *nonverbal reasoning* did not distinguish dyslexic adults from those with general learning difficulties. In a study using similar measures to DAST, Hatcher, Snowling and Griffiths (2002) found that the best predictors were *nonword reading, spelling, digit span* and *writing speed*.

Landerl, Frith and Wimmer (1996) found phonemic difficulties to be a central problem in dyslexia. We therefore decided that the balance of evidence was in favour of including the *phonemic segmentation* subtest. It was our own experience that this is a particularly good discriminator for well-compensated dyslexic students. We also decided to include *rapid naming*, as this seemed to us to be a valuable measure of the students' ability not only to access but to articulate their internal lexicon, and thus might be an indicator of dyspraxia as well as of difficulties in phonological processing.

The more of the DAST subtests employed, the higher their combined predictive value, according to Fawcett and Nicolson (1998). We decided to use all the subtests whose efficacy was demonstrated either by Harrison and Nichols (2005), or by Hatcher, Snowling and Griffiths (2002), plus *rapid naming*. So the subtests we used were: *one minute reading, phonemic segmentation, two minute spelling, digit span, nonsense passage reading, rapid (object) naming* and *one minute writing*.

We had some reservations about the use of the *postural stability* subtest on students in a confined space (in this test the individual is pushed gently in the lower back to see how much he or she wobbles). Moreover, a recent meta-analysis found that impaired balance did not have a specific enough association with dyslexia to be used in identification (Rochelle and Talcott 2006). We therefore excluded this subtest from our battery.

DAST uses a four-point scoring system of 0, 1, 2 or 3. Zero equates to the student performing within the normal range on that task, and 1, 2 and 3 represent points successively below that normal range. These scores are achieved by comparing the raw score with age-related score keys for population norms. The seven subtests together give a partial quantitative 'At Risk Quotient' (ARQ) by dividing the student's total score (3, 2 or 1) on each subtest by seven (the number of subtests). Our cut-off for full assessment was 'six or more'. This meant that our ARQ, the cut-off warranting referral for assessment, was 0.857 (6/7), rather than the original DAST recommended ARQ of 1. This necessarily gave our chosen group of subtests a higher sensitivity than would be expected when using the full DAST.

We also employed eight subtests from the Bangor Dyslexia Test: *subtraction, left/right confusion, polysyllables* (verbal repetition of multi-syllabic words), (multiplication) *tables*, (reciting) *months forward*, (reciting) *months reversed, b/d confusion*, and *familial incidence*. BDT uses a three-point scoring system, 0, 0.5 or 1, where 0 equates to success at the test, 0.5 equates to satisfying some of the criteria and 1 equates to failing to satisfy the criteria. Our cut-offs for full assessment on the BDT were 2.5 positive indicators on our selected eight subtest battery.

We knew from experience that altogether this was a good package for predicting dyslexia and dyspraxia (even though none of the tests was specifically designed to identify signs of the latter). We wanted to establish whether a computerized screener such as LADS might be as good a net as this method, and particularly how it might compare for sensitivity and specificity. Moreover, computerized screening tests can be taken by large cohorts of students at the same time, perhaps saving much time and money. Indeed, HEIs can even screen the whole of one year's entry at once rather than relying merely on self-referral. Many students with SpLD have developed such good ways of coping with their difficulties that they are not really fully aware of them. This usually means that they underestimate their own underlying ability, and have perhaps internalized school reports that may have included comments such as 'needs to concentrate more' or 'careless and lazy'. These are the students that we suspected we might be missing because they were not referring themselves.

LADS employs an algorithm that weights performance on its nonverbal *reasoning* test against performance on its subtests of *word recognition, word construction* and *memory*. In other words, the student who scores highly on *reasoning* will have to do worse on the other subtests to be identified as at high risk of dyslexia than the student who does less well on *reasoning*.

There is considerable dispute as to whether this kind of discrepancy model is wholly valid. Stanovich and Stanovich (1997), for example, criticized the inclusion of any measurement of underlying ability in the definition of dyslexia, arguing that there is no correlation between reading disability and underlying intelligence. Miles and Miles (1999) have also argued cogently that children at any level of intelligence can have a specific learning disability and, according to this thesis, the same must hold true for adults. However, in the absence of other confounding factors, a statistically significant discrepancy between literacy skills and underlying ability is often at the very least indicative of SpLD, and LADS does not rely wholly on such anomalies.

LADS gives a risk result for each element separately and a brief summary identifying the student as at *high, moderate, borderline* or *low* risk of dyslexia. Like BDT and DAST, it is not intended or designed to indicate the presence of any other SpLD, nor of M–I syndrome. We referred for assessment all those identified by LADS as being at *borderline* risk of dyslexia or above, as recommended in the LADS manual (Singleton, Horne and Thomas 2004).

Meares–Irlen Syndrome

We also wanted to shorten our screening test if possible so that we could include screening for Meares–Irlen syndrome, also sometimes known as 'visual stress' or 'scotopic sensitivity'. Readers with M–IS read faster, or more comfortably, when using a coloured acetate overlay or coloured lenses, than when reading black text on a white background. M–IS is not currently defined as an SpLD, but it is known to occur more frequently among people with dyslexia than in the general population (Kriss and Evans 2005; Singleton 2008), and it certainly hampers full or easy access to any HE curriculum. The Irlen website[11] provides a helpful self-administered quiz, and a more objective screening test can be administered by any teacher using Cerium[12] coloured overlays and the Wilkins Rate of Reading Test® (Wilkins *et al.* 1996). Another way to screen for this syndrome is via the Lucid Visual Stress Screener (ViSS).[13] An appropriately qualified optometrist can then make a full visual assessment both of M-IS and of difficulties with, for example, tracking, binocular instability, or convergence, which may also seriously hinder fluent reading.

Research at the University of Worcester

In 2007 to 2008 a team at the University of Worcester ran a small research project to explore all this (Nichols *et al.* 2009). We recruited 100 students to undertake both LADS and a tutor-delivered screening, and of these the results from 74 students were ultimately included in our study. None of the participants had previously been identified as having SpLD.

The comparison between the tutor-delivered screening and LADS indicated that the former gave a stronger overall performance. LADS has a higher specificity but a lower sensitivity than our tutor-delivered screening; this means that it will miss a higher proportion of students with disabilities. In this case it missed 12 of the sample as against three missed by the tutor screening. However, the corollary was that the tutor battery resulted in eight assessments that proved negative as against only four from LADS, and this clearly had implications in terms of both cost and student stress levels.

Eventually, statistical analysis of our database yielded surprising conclusions.

First, Meares–Irlen Syndrome itself proved an excellent stand-alone predictor of SpLD. If we had employed this at the screening stage instead of at assessment, we would have immediately identified 51% of those with a disability. This means that anyone who shows positive results (an increase of 5% or more in reading speed on the Wilkins Rate of Reading Test® using a Cerium overlay) should be fully assessed for SpLD straightaway and should also go to see a specialist optometrist.

Second, the best combination of screening instruments turned out to be LADS *plus* positive results on a combination of just four of the subtests delivered by the tutor. These four were *polysyllables* and *familial incidence* (from BDT) and *digit span* and *one minute writing* (from DAST). Data from these four tests and from LADS, when subjected to statistical analysis (for details see Nichols *et al.* 2009), resulted in both high sensitivity (94%) and high specificity (92%) given suitable cut-offs. This combination is more sensitive than LADS alone (which has a sensitivity of 66%), more specific than our previous tutor-delivered package (which has a sensitivity of 79%), and outclasses any other combination.

[11] www.irlen.org.uk.

[12] www.ceriumoptical.com/vistech.aspx.

[13] www.lucid-research.com/vissvideo.htm.

Our research ultimately resulted in the UW Dyslexia and Disability Service (DDS) buying a site licence for LADS and installing the programme at various terminals on campus. Our students are now encouraged, via the university web site, to take the LADS test if they have any anxieties about spelling, punctuation, grammar, or the timing or structure of their work; they are also encouraged to refer themselves immediately to the DDS for further screening and advice if the result is borderline or above. We emphasize that they should come in anyway if they are still anxious. As outlined above, LADS is not wholly reliable as a stand-alone screening programme.

Subsequent Developments

As already mentioned, none of the dyslexia screening tests on offer is designed to spot dyspraxia/Developmental Coordination Disorder (DCD), nor indeed any other SpLD such as Attention Deficit (Hyperactive) Disorder. The fact that our screening system picks up some students with dyspraxia may well be due to the fact that the articulation of multisyllable words is often hard for dyspraxic people, so the *polysyllables* element of the BDT may be doubly valuable for that reason. Similarly, *writing speed* may be slowed either by dyslexic problems of remembering what to write and how to spell it, or by dyspraxic problems of managing the pen, or both. *Digit span*, which aims to measure working memory, is usually a component of both dyslexia and dyspraxia, and indeed of AD(H)D.

Recently it has been suggested that significant discrepancy between working memory and underlying intelligence is a defining characteristic of dyslexia (Lawrence, 2009). However Lawrence's study employed the Wechsler Adult Intelligence Scale (WAIS) measure of working memory and it must be noted that, to assess this, WAIS includes letter–number sequencing and a timed mental arithmetic test, as well as digit span.

LADS also employs a *working memory* task. This is delivered slightly differently from the DAST *digit span* task as the student must respond by keyboard rather than by voice. Indeed, all the LADS subtests are undertaken by keyboard, and are strictly timed, and both poor keyboard skills and poor time management may be indicative of dyspraxia too.

Since our investigation took place, work by Kirby and Rosenblum at the Dyscovery Centre in Newport has resulted in a valuable standardized checklist for dyspraxic characteristics in adults.[14] This checklist can either be self-administered or undertaken through discussion with a tutor. It has proved a valuable addition to our armoury and we now routinely include it in the screening process, with tutor input. Dyspraxia can be fully identified only by a medical practitioner (as other clinical conditions such as cerebral palsy and multiple sclerosis need to be definitively ruled out), but the identification of any dyspraxic characteristics in the student's profile are helpful to students themselves, to their assessors, to their needs assessors and, ultimately, to their support tutors.

Screening for AD(H)D is undertaken at UW only if the student reports serious difficulties with such things as maintaining concentration or sitting still, and it is usually explored only at assessment level. A simple checklist is used based on the symptoms listed in the *Diagnostic and Statistical Manual of Mental Disorders* (American Psychiatric Association 1994). This can be found online,[15] but again a reliable diagnosis of AD(H)D can be made only by a medical practitioner, and students need to be referred to a consultant via their GP to explore the possibility fully. There is now an Association for Adult Attention Deficit Disorder, which gives good advice about this.[16]

[14] http://www.newport.ac.uk/research/researchcentres/Centres/Dyscovery%20Centre/Research/Screening%20Tools%20-%20Adults/Pages/default.aspx.

[15] www.hcp.med.harvard.edu/ncs/ftpdir/adhd/18%20Question%20ADHD-ASRS-v1-1.pdf.

[16] http://aadd.org.uk/faqs.html.

As for M–IS, we have increasingly found that considerations of vanity play an understandably important part. It is crucial to emphasize to the student that sensitivity to black-on-white that is relieved by a coloured overlay does not necessarily mean that they will have to wear coloured spectacles for ever, or indeed at all. Specialist optometrists can often improve tracking or convergence with the use of clear prescription lenses worn for only a few months. Some optometrists specialize in this kind of work and have formed the Society for Coloured Lens Prescribers.[17] It seems that sensitivity to colour possibly acts as a marker for a wide variety of visual processing difficulties, only one of which is clear-cut M-IS *per se* (Evans 2001).

Value to the Assessor

Screening records can be invaluable to assessors. On a purely practical front, apart from any considerations of their diagnostic value, reading and writing speeds have to be tested at some stage if any recommendation is to be made about exam concessions.

Notes made by the screener about a student's history and reasons for coming forward provide valuable openings that reassure them that each is not simply a cog in a machine, but a person whose real deep-seated anxieties have been acknowledged and recorded.

If visual stress has been identified, the assessor can allow the student to use his or her preferred overlay for all reading tasks during the assessment to minimize confusing visual effects and allow a clearer profile to emerge.

The LADS test of underlying non-verbal intelligence is black and white. This is sometimes helpful in that, if the student does better or worse here than on a coloured non-verbal intelligence test, such as the *Matrices* subtest of the Wide Range Intelligence Test (Glutting, Adams and Sheslow 2000), this difference also may indicate visual processing problems that need further investigation.

Discrepancy between the *digit span* result from DAST and the *working memory* result from LADS is sometimes revealing, or indeed confusing, but always worth further exploration.

Conclusions

To sum up, we continue to find that there is no substitute for a human. No computer screener can yet measure the student's ability to pronounce polysyllabic words such as 'anemone' or 'specific', nor test writing speed (though both tasks may be technically possible in the future). No computer can yet reliably deliver a Cerium overlay check or a reading speed test. Talking through a dyspraxia checklist with a tutor may reveal characteristics in students' profiles that they themselves had never suspected might hamper them academically.

So the mesh of our net has widened considerably. We now refer for assessment all those who reach our cut-off on the *LADS* plus *polysyllables, familial incidence, one minute writing* and *digit span* combination; plus all those who score above 60 on the Kirby/Rosenblum checklist; plus those who achieve more than a 5% increase in reading speed on the Wilkins test when using a coloured overlay. This has resulted in a much improved 'hit-rate'. Of the 112 students assessed at UW in the last eight months only two were assessed as negative for SpLD (University of Worcester 2011).

This tutor-screening takes under an hour, leaving time for conversation and exploration of the student's anxieties, and some more elements of DAST if these seem appropriate. Our screeners also routinely include *one minute reading* as this is helpful both to diagnostic and needs assessors.

[17] www.s4clp.org.

Table 4.1 The UW screening package.

	Working memory	*Phonological processing*	*Visual processing*	*Sequencing/ orientation*	*Hand–eye coordination*	*Underlying intelligence*	*Reading*	*Spelling*	*Writing*	*Genetics*
BDT Polysyllables		■								
BDT Familial incidence										■
DAST 1-minute writing			■	■	■				■	
DAST Digit span	■									
LADS	■	■	■		■	■	■	■		
Cerium + Wilkins			■				■			
Kirby-Rosenblum checklist	■			■	■				■	

The shaded boxes indicate the specific SpLD indicators measured by each test in the package

Our final screening package is perhaps best understood from Table 4.1, which makes clear that all the different aspects of concern about dyslexia, dyspraxia and M–IS in any student profile are being addressed by this combination.

As far as student welfare is concerned, it is vitally important that no one should ever be left worrying about the results of a computerized test without easy access to support. We make it absolutely clear on-screen that even a *'high-risk'* score on LADS is no cause for panic, and that help is at hand. Students who find that they have a 'borderline' score or above on LADS are naturally encouraged to refer themselves to the DDS for advice about the next stage.

It is also important to advertise as widely as possible what the process of assessment, application for the DSA, Needs Assessment, etc. may be like. Students are naturally anxious about 'tests', cost, privacy, 'labelling', and future job prospects. Any publicity that raises the profile of those with SpLD is valuable here, as are flow charts explaining the process itself, and reassurances about both confidentiality and cost.

Damage by Delay

Readers will have realized by now that the whole process of screening and assessment is very long-drawn-out. Students may not think of undertaking any screening test at all until their second semester, when they get an unexpectedly poor mark, or realize how terribly hard they are working just to keep up. The tutor screening must be booked. The assessor and the optometrist must, if necessary, be booked and assessment undertaken. Reports must be written. If results are positive a Needs Assessment must be booked and carried out. By the time students actually receive any appropriate tutorial support or technological aids, weeks will have passed, and by that time they may have become seriously discouraged and depressed. It is very hard to compensate later for time, energy and self-confidence wasted in this way. The first semester of university life is confusing enough; students must adapt quickly to a new existence away from home, managing their own money, their housekeeping and their social lives, let alone the new demands of academe, without suffering unidentified SpLD.

All this means that any students bound for HE who have any suspicion at all that they may have SpLD, or whose family or teachers suspect it, should undertake a screening test (either online or administered by a teacher) plus a screening test for M–IS, and refer themselves for full assessment if necessary, well before they arrive at university. If the DSA is provided, support can be in place as soon as they arrive, untold anxiety and stress can be avoided, and they will have the chance they deserve to fulfil their potential from day one.

References

American Psychiatric Association (1994) *Diagnostic and Statistical Manual of Mental Disorders*, 4th edn, American Psychiatric Association, Washington, DC.

Evans, B. (2001) *Dyslexia and Vision*, Whurr, London.

Fawcett, A. (2001) Dyslexia and the cerebellum. *Patoss Bulletin*, November, 2–5.

Fawcett, A. and Nicolson, R. (1998) *The Dyslexia Adult Screening Test*, The Psychological Corporation, London.

Frith, U. (1999) Paradoxes in the definition of dyslexia. *Dyslexia*, 5, 192–214.

Glutting, J., Adams, W. and Sheslow, D. (2000) *Wide Range Intelligence Test*, Wide Range, Inc., Wilmington, DE.

Gubbay, S.S. (1975) *The Clumsy Child: A study of developmental apraxic and agnosic ataxia*, Saunders, Philadelphia.

Gunn, L. (2000) The Dyslexia Adult Screening Test (DAST) a review. *The Application of Occupational Psychology to Employment and Disability*, 2, 37–44.

Harrison, A. and Nichols, E. (2005) A validation of the Dyslexia Adult Screening Test (DAST) in a post-secondary population. *Journal of Research in Reading*, 28, 423–434.

Hatcher, J., Snowling, M. and Griffiths, Y. (2002) Cognitive assessment of dyslexic students in higher education. *British Journal of Educational Psychology*, 72, 119–133.

Hinshelwood, J. (1895) Word-blindness and visual memory. *The Lancet*, 2, 1564–1570.

Irlen, M. (1983) *Successful treatment of learning difficulties*. Paper presented at The Annual Convention of the American Psychological Association, Anaheim, California, USA.

Kriss, I. and Evans, B. (2005) The relationship between dyslexia and Meares–Irlen Syndrome. *Journal of Research in Reading*, 28, 350–364.

Landerl, K., Frith, U. and Wimmer, H. (1996) Intrusion of orthographic knowledge on phoneme awareness: strong in normal readers, weak in dyslexic readers. *Applied Psycholinguistics* 17, 1–14.

Lawrence, D. (2009) Analysis of the test results of 447 adult students assessed for dyslexia. *Patoss Bulletin*, November, 14–17.

Meares, H. (1980) Figure/ground, brightness contrast, and learning disabilities. *Visible Language*, 14, 13–29.

Miles, T.R. (1997) *The Bangor Dyslexia Test*, 2nd edn, Learning Development Aids, Cambridge.

Miles, T.R. and Miles, E. (1999) *Dyslexia: 100 Years On*, 2nd edn, Open University Press, Milton Keynes.

Nichols, S., McLeod. J., Holder, R. and McLeod, H. (2009) Screening for dyslexia, dyspraxia and Meares–Irlen syndrome in higher education. *Dyslexia*, 15, 42–60.

Nicolson, R. and Fawcett, A. (1999) Developmental dyslexia: the role of the cerebellum. *Dyslexia*, 5, 155–177.

Reid, G. and Kirk, J. (2001) *Dyslexia in Adults: Education and employment*, John Wiley & Sons Ltd, Chichester.

Rochelle K.S.H. and Talcott, J.B. (2006) Impaired balance in developmental dyslexia? A meta-analysis of the contending evidence. *Journal of Child Psychology and Psychiatry*, 47, 1159–1166.

Singleton, C. (2004a) *Dyslexia in FE and HE: recent developments*. NADO Spring Conference on Dyslexia, London, March 11, accessed May 20, 2007 from www.nadp-uk.org/events/docs/chris_singleton.ppt..

Singleton, C. (2004b) *Lucid Adult Screening Test*, Lucid Research Ltd, Beverley.

Singleton, C. (2008) Visual stress and dyslexia. In C. Singleton (ed.) *The Dyslexia Handbook 2008/9*, British Dyslexia Association, Reading.

Singleton, C., Horne, J.K., and Thomas, K.V. (2004) *LADS Administrator's Manual*, Lucid Research Ltd, Beverley.

Snowling, M. (1995) Phonological processing and developmental dyslexia. *Journal of Research in Reading*, 18, 132–138.

Stanovich, K.E. and Stanovich, P.J. (1997) Further thoughts on aptitude/achievement discrepancy. *Educational Psychology in Practice*, 13, 3–8.

University of Worcester (2011) *Disability and Dyslexia Service statistics*, unpublished.

van Daal, V. and Miles, T.R. (2001) *A Comparison of the Dyslexia Screening Test with the Bangor Dyslexia Test*. Presented at the British Dyslexia Association's 5th International Conference, April 18–21, University of York.

Vinegrad, M. (1994) A revised adult dyslexia checklist. *Educare*, 48, 21–23.

Wilkins, A.J., Jeanes, R.J., Pumfrey, P.D., and Laskier, M. (1996) Rate of Reading Test: its reliability, and its validity in the assessment of the effects of coloured overlays. *Ophthalmic and Physiological Optics*, 16, 491–497.

Wolff, U. and Lundberg, I. (2003) A technique for group screening of dyslexia among adults. *Annals of Dyslexia*, 53, 324–339.

5

The Complex Nature of Dyslexia Support in the Context of Widening Participation

Vivien Fraser, retired from Middlesex University, UK

What Do Dyslexia Support Tutors Do?

The simple answer is that they help students to develop study strategies that compensate for their particular difficulties caused by dyslexia. The tutor will introduce individual students to a range of approaches to reading, writing and other aspects of study that seem to fit the student's cognitive profile, while continuing to encourage them to reflect on how they learn best, and to build on their strengths. This is how support tutors are taught to see their role. However, if a student's low underlying level of ability and/or lack of preparation for HE study are factored in, the answer to the question of what support tutors actually do becomes far more complicated. In this chapter I will explore the ways in which support for an increasing number of students whose study difficulties appear to be multi-determined present some interesting challenges for the tutor. But first, another question:

How Much Support Should a Student Be Given?

Recently, some concern has been expressed by the Disabled Students' Allowance funding bodies over the quantity of support tutorials provided for increasing numbers of students, sometimes for the duration of their course. It was argued that compensatory study skills could be covered in about 10 hours and that 60 hours or more was excessive. This concern was allayed, however, by the Association of Dyslexia Specialists in Higher Education (ADSHE). It was shown that there are a number of reasons why students cannot learn the strategies they require in the recommended ten sessions: reasons to do with co-morbidity (e.g. overlaps with dyspraxia or Attention Deficit Hyperactivity Disorder), the severity of their dyslexia, changing demands of the course, the need to over-learn and revisit, and so forth.

One reason that has been somewhat neglected, however, is the student's previous educational experience. Yet this can be a major factor underlying the need for continued support. There can sometimes be quite a mismatch between the academic demands of the course and the amount of preparation for HE study the student has received. Dyslexia tutors are not subject specialists, and they are aware that they should not be addressing subject-specific areas nor, for that matter, areas relating to widening participation and the possible lack of HE preparation. There is no wish to disadvantage those students who are not dyslexic, but who are equally needy, who do not receive much support.

Supporting Dyslexic Adults in Higher Education and the Workplace, First Edition. Edited by Nicola Brunswick.

Tutors are meant to be addressing dyslexia-related problems but attempting to extricate the effects of a student's previous education from those of dyslexia is difficult, if not impossible. To begin to address the complex and interlinked needs arising from both dyslexia and inadequate education, many hours of support will be needed.

Why Dyslexia May not be the Only Issue of Concern

For a student to be assessed as dyslexic it is necessary to show that he or she has had the 'opportunity to learn' and to be able to exclude other possible barriers to learning, such as a low level of underlying ability (DfES 2005). Although a diagnosis of dyslexia is no longer based on the identification of a discrepancy between underlying ability and literacy levels (Stanovich 1991), it is 'expected that in most cases university students will demonstrate such a discrepancy in the assessment' (Jamieson and Morgan 2008, p. 9).

However, in the case of a number of students assessed with dyslexia, overall levels of achievement as documented in their reports may not rise above the tenth percentile even though a discrepancy between various scores may be present. Some assessors will not diagnose dyslexia when all the scores are very low, but others will.

Similarly, it is difficult in many cases to see how much of an educational opportunity students have had. Dyslexia support tutors often find that they are supporting students who have had a limited exposure to print, and who appear to have gained but a rudimentary education in literacy and/or numeracy skills. It is almost impossible to gauge to what extent this shortfall is due to an underlying learning difficulty as opposed to poor schooling, low expectations and the lack of inculcation of any kind of academic culture. Even if an underlying cognitive deficit can be seen, such as poor phonological processing, it is hard to determine if this is a cause or an effect. Either way, if a poor basic education underlies the student's difficulties, dyslexia support tutors cannot simply rely on the toolkit of strategies they have been trained to deploy.

How Does Support Normally Work?

Tutors are trained to base their support on the cognitive profile of the individual student whilst 'paying attention to the way individuals internalize information' (Stacey 2010, p. 18). They will work on strategies that circumvent phonological and working memory difficulties underlying slow or inaccurate reading, note-taking difficulties, and difficulties with expressing ideas clearly, accurately and in a structured fashion. They may work on, for example, organizational techniques, time management, breaking down questions, proofreading and revision strategies. By drawing on the student's strengths, tutors will use multi-sensory techniques such as chunking, highlighting, mind mapping, the development of frameworks or schemas, the use of the voice and visualizing. They may help students to develop alternative ways of representing ideas and organizing concepts to overcome difficulties with sequential structures. Even for a recently assessed dyslexic student who *has* been prepared for HE study, a series of support tutorials that addresses strategies such as these may be all that is needed; for the student who has had minimal preparation for HE, far more may be required.

What Else Might be Needed?

Take reading skills, for example. Many students find extracting meaning from an academic text somewhat onerous. The dyslexic student may be hampered by decoding and short-term memory difficulties that, in turn, may have resulted in an avoidance of written texts and a consequently smaller sight vocabulary. In these circumstances, tutors may encourage the use of text-readers, and the development of active reading skills such as:

- asking questions and pre-guessing content
- surveying and skimming the material
- identifying key elements within the overall text, paragraph and sentence
- seeing the difference between content and function words, ideas and examples, main and subsidiary themes.

Students may be helped to quicken their reading speed, to maintain a forward momentum, to allow for uncertainty, but also to know when rereading is needed. However, for the unprepared student with little familiarity with academic texts and conventions, or for those whose knowledge of the subject matter is limited, no amount of active reading skill can compensate effectively for this lack. Being advised to highlight key words or to map the concepts is pointless if the text is fundamentally meaningless. If you don't really know what a concept is or what certain words actually *mean*, how on earth can you know if they are 'key'? In these circumstances, the tutor might suggest turning to an easier text on the same subject, or consulting Wikipedia for a quick overview but, if the concepts are meaningful only as part of a wider subject-specific discourse, no quick overview will suffice. It becomes necessary to return to basics, to the fundamental questions that underlie this particular discourse. Such an activity takes a significant amount of time and drifts uncomfortably close to subject-specific support.

In addressing this issue, one experienced tutor recounts how he often found himself having to explain basic concepts, ones that he felt should really be understood prior to undergraduate level. However, aware that he was not meant to be teaching the subject as such, he used the opportunity to explain a simple concept by introducing a learning method that might be new to the student – for example, ways of breaking down difficult texts, or using imagery. The teaching of basic concepts is, in other words, justified on the grounds that it is a way of teaching a learning strategy, an approach that is highly effective but also highly time consuming.

Another alternative is for the tutor to attempt to 'translate' the text into everyday language, which may be successful up to a point but presupposes that academic language is merely a gloss, even an obfuscation, of a simpler message. This is sometimes true, but often not.

Or the tutor may attempt, through judicious questioning, to relate the student's existing knowledge and experience to the text's message. This can be an effective way of opening up the text for the student but it is not working on strategies; it is attempting to make up for lost education. There is catching-up to be done not just in the subject area but in the very language in which, and with which, the student is supposed to be working. This too presents a significant challenge. A good deal of vocabulary development has to take place. However, it is often the nuances of the academic register that can cause difficulties: its underlying structure, extended metaphors, the passive voice, embedded clauses, or even the function of a word such as 'whereas' or 'despite' at the start of a sentence. If a student is new to this kind of discourse, it may take many hours of support to begin to decipher its mechanics and meaning.

So much for academic comprehension. But what about the medium through which students are actually evaluated, graded and obtain qualifications and jobs, namely, academic writing? Here, the tutor may model diagrammatic ways of getting thoughts down on paper or encourage the taping of ideas; the tutor may help to develop templates or schemas for essay writing, help break the task down and then later thread text together so that it forms a coherent response to a question. The idea is to demystify what essay-writing is all about. For the dyslexic student buzzing with ideas, strategies for creating structure will often suffice. But for students who have few ideas about their subject, no amount of mind mapping or schema creation will create content. What can a tutor do in these circumstances? Socratic questioning[1] perhaps, close reading of the lecture notes, paraphrasing techniques, and of course – perhaps above all, because students are supposed to *read* for a degree, are they not? – a return to reading and deciphering texts, i.e., *studying* them. These all offer ways in to academic writing but not ones that can be travelled along quickly. Even if a *viva voce* replaces the need for written expression – an accommodation that might benefit a dyslexic student – it still presupposes knowledge of the subject area, and thus the need to *engage* with texts; this is often knowing somewhat more than merely what a text 'says' but also what it *means*, *presupposes*, *implies*, and so on. It returns us to the problems outlined above.

The Spectrum of Difficulties: Some Examples

Clearly then, the work a tutor engages in with a student will depend on the level of need and the individual student's particular cognitive profile and personality. Equally, the spectrum of difficulties a support tutor may encounter often relates as much to the student's previous education as to the severity of his or her dyslexia. A few examples of students' work will exemplify this.

The following original piece of writing was produced by a mildly dyslexic student (identified here as student A) who had been well prepared for HE:

> Inflammation is the response of living tissues to cellular injury. Its purpose is to eliminate the causative agent, limit tissue injury and instigate repair. Acute inflammation involves interaction between cells and soluble molecules of the innate immune system.

This brief example of original writing typifies the kind of work student A produced throughout her course. Despite her slower-than-average reading skills, some difficulties in extracting meaning from text, and slightly wonky spellings, her work was always first rate. Her academic success rested not only on her high general ability and previous education but on sheer hard work, along with organizational and memory strategies. The student needed help in organizing the workload in order for all aspects of the course to be given due attention; this also meant that student A's anxieties, which had hampered her success in the past, would be allayed. Also, memory techniques were explored in order to circumvent working memory problems, and to ensure that she learned the large amount of difficult vocabulary that the course required.

Revision was built into the student's self-constructed timetable from the *second* week of term. A variety of techniques was employed: these included reading notes onto an Mp3 player to listen to when exercising, visual and verbal mnemonics, and mind maps that summarized each significant section of each course. By starting early, student A could revisit the material frequently, which improved her self-confidence and reduced her anxieties even further. The tutorials also offered her a chance to take stock of her progress, to discuss any worries and to continue to help develop her academic literacy skills. Student A engaged with great enthusiasm and skill with the assistive software she was given.

Student B was on a less demanding course but nonetheless found it very challenging. The extract below shows some of the 'classic' dyslexic mistakes that were common in her writing, and which are often to be found in the writing of other dyslexic students:

[1] This is systematic, in-depth questioning of the student by the tutor in order to explore the topic of interest.

> I will first start by giving a definition of Critical incident, than go on to identify my role as a student nurse. There will be clear explanation of my incident with an appropriate model used to reflect upon a reason will also be given on the choice of the model. In order analyse on the incident I will have to reflect on the incident to start I will give a short definition of reflection which is define by Jasper M (2003) cited Reid 1993 as a . . .

Here there are problems with homophones, morphemes, the omission of words, proofreading, sentences running into each other, and academic literacy. Yet student B's meaning is clear in both this paragraph and the rest of the work, and she was able to provide a coherent and structured argument with some support. With her tutor she learned to chunk essays into subheaded word-counted colour-coded sections, and to identify the main clause within a sentence. In order to identify her mistakes she was encouraged both to read her work aloud and to use a text reader. She learned to use common academic phrases such as 'to analyse something' correctly, and to reference appropriately. Once again, this student willingly employed all the software she had been given.

However, this was not the case with Student C, who did not use her software mainly due to lack of time and therefore lack of practice in its use. Not only were there a great many demands on her time from work and family, but she found the expectations of her course utterly overwhelming. She was also very unprepared for this level of work. Here is a typical example of her writing during her second year, an extract from a research critique essay:

> The problem with the title is that it failed to incorporate other professionals what took part in the research. According to Blaxter *et al.* 2006 stated that a research topic should be "as short as possible not exceeding more than 15 words". The word (P C C) research report topic serves as a key word in the title. The overall words like primary method of health topic reflects the research study. The research article also contain critical words like philosophical and underpinnings

With writing such as this, where does the support tutor begin? Clearly there are certain basic issues that can be addressed, such as how to reference and introduce a quote, noun/verb agreement, and vocabulary. Although there is no problem with the structure of the sentences as with Student B, say, here they make very little sense. The word that perhaps best sums up this kind of writing – the like of which is not at all uncommon on some courses – is 'alienated'. The student is being asked to critique a research paper that she can barely comprehend. She is expected to work with an academic register that to her appears impenetrable and unconnected with any kind of meaningful reality. Not only has she had limited exposure, at best, to such discourse but, as with many other students, her literacy skills are in great need of development. That is: the ability to write clearly, to comprehend a journal article, to summarize key points, to understand the function of a sentence and paragraph, and to develop vocabulary and coherent expression. However, such students find themselves truly in the deep end, trying to engage in the critique of what is to them an obscure piece of writing, to analyse critically the methodological procedures of experienced researchers, and possibly to challenge the 'philosophical underpinnings' of an approach based upon something grandly announcing itself as 'Heideggerian phenomenology'.[2] No wonder they are alienated.

[2] Heideggerian phenomenology, like all phenomenology, explores how various structures of consciousness operate. Heidegger examines, in particular, thought itself and ontology, what it means to 'be', and how, for example, empathy is possible.

There are many instances like that of Student C, when the support tutor sees the need to focus on what are essentially literacy skills, not only because they are vitally important for the student professionally. This focus is easily lost, however, with the need to develop 'graduate' skills of critical analysis. Many tutors are torn between meeting the responsibilities that all universities have of ensuring 'that students can write effectively and accurately even if they are admitted onto courses without that ability being fully developed' (Winch and Wells 1995 p. 86), and helping students find strategies to cope with their immediate assignments.

The Effects of Previous Education

As the nature of these assignments changes, many dyslexic students will need to develop new strategies and revisit old ones to address changing levels of tasks. But, once again, the development of students' independence in the use of these strategies will depend as much on a sound educational base as on the severity of their dyslexia. Perhaps most important of all, it is students with such a sound base who are most aware of what they can and cannot do. They will have developed meta-cognition (an awareness of how they learn) through trial and error, and know what works best for them. They will often make enthusiastic use of their assistive software. They will know what strengths to draw upon, and will also know what level of effort is expected in academic work. A dyslexic student who has struggled against all the odds to achieve at a higher academic level truly knows the meaning of studying hard. Such an awareness may be less well developed in students from schools with low expectations and mediocre results.

Knowing what learning consists of is a prerequisite for appropriate use of study methods. Indeed, students are sometimes shocked at the amount of reading and writing that is expected of them. Some have domestic or work responsibilities that preclude a large amount of studying. Some may have chosen a subject to study with little knowledge of what is expected of them, for example the statistics needed for psychology. But, perhaps most significant of all, many will have chosen to study what is essentially a vocational or creative subject – art, business studies, nursing – with little foreknowledge of the academic standards to be met to see it through successfully.

How Subject Based Must Support Become?

There is much evidence to suggest that generic study skills are ineffective, as students generally need help to work within their own academic discipline (Wingate 2006). For the well-prepared dyslexic student, however, it is often the non subject-specific strategies that are required; strategies that help students to stay organized and on track, on their course of study and within their essays. They may require strategies that help them to extract meaning from texts, to make useful notes, to spell and memorize facts. Tutorials offer such students a space for reflection on the effectiveness of their previous approaches, and for planning how to approach the next task.

For the less well prepared students, tutors can help them to recognize task requirements – a problem many non-dyslexic students may also have – and help them to see how demands will differ from task to task. They will help to build up their 'repertoire of methods' (Gibbs 1994). They can help to give them an overview of the area in which they are working – sometimes sadly absent from lecturers – so as to make the material meaningful and relate it to other, perhaps more concrete, concerns. This is something that many dyslexic students find essential, as they cannot learn what is not understood. Tutors will scaffold and model what needs to be done within the context of a particular discipline, show how to generate initial ideas that will guide research and how to appreciate the dialectical nature of research and planning. They can provide a supportive environment where mistakes are tolerated, and they will encourage self-assessment and self-supervision. Any helpful feedback can also be a focus of a support session.

For the very unprepared student, however, tutors also need to try to fill in many educational gaps if they are to begin to help the student to study. They will need to read through and explain lecture notes to the student, and to address some of the basic concepts with which the student is meant to be dealing. They will also need to read with the student to help them make sense of the texts. In other words, they will need to move way beyond the mere provision of strategies and start to address the kinds of educational needs that should have been addressed years ago at school. The alternative is to help the student tidy up the edges of a completely alienated and semi-coherent piece of work that has involved much cut and paste and little cognitive activity.

But does Support Work in the Context of Widening Participation?

Intensive dyslexia support works, yes. On some courses that attract 'widening participation' students, it is the ones with dyslexia (and therefore with individual support) who are outperforming their peers for whom there is limited support. Many non-dyslexic students from non-traditional educational backgrounds, and with differing levels of ability, do not receive the kind of support they need. It is the supported students too who never resort to plagiarism, as this is unlikely to get past a support tutor.

Perhaps then, rather than question the amount of support some dyslexic students receive, we should build on this effective support work. There is a great need for more support generally – i.e. for all the students who are paying for courses for which they are unprepared – and perhaps an even greater focus on basic education than is already provided. The educational system has let these students down once already; it is just not right to let it happen again. Ironically, there is a lack of academic tutorials in the very places where they are most needed. There is simply not the time in many universities to provide students with the kinds of academic tutorials – or even seminars – where they can explore responses to their writing and explore their understanding of their subject. It is not surprising, therefore, that they turn to their support tutor to provide that kind of feedback and exploration.

Other Forms of Help

Finally, there are many simple adjustments that institutions can make to meet the needs of all non-traditional students more effectively. These include:

- providing easy-to-follow module guidelines with clear instructions and deadlines
- providing meaningful overviews
- providing examples of good and bad essays, with perhaps the opportunity for students to grade these essays themselves
- offering peer review
- allowing students to organize and prioritize their work
- giving essay titles out early
- spacing work evenly through the year
- providing handouts before the lectures
- offering alternative forms of assessment

More contentiously, there could be a reconsideration of what constitutes 'graduateness' in the light of vocational or creative courses, so that students who have generally chosen to avoid academia but who wish to develop in their chosen profession should not need to overcome possibly irrelevant academic hurdles. Does the 'professionalization' of an area have to include the introduction of heavy and pointless concepts, models and theories that are then discarded at the conclusion of the course?

There are many instances – like that of Student C, above – when the support tutor would see the need to focus on what are essentially literacy skills, not least because they are vitally important for the student. This focus is easily lost, however, with the need to develop 'graduate' skills. Central to this is the need to be 'critical'. To many tutors, if a student is just beginning to grapple with the fundamental discourse of a particular discipline, this will not be the time to start raising 'epistemological doubt' or the 'essential relativity of knowledge' in order to develop academic literacies (Lee and Street 1998).

The notion of graduateness is not, of course, a question for the dyslexia support tutor; nor indeed is the issue of how well prepared students should be for HE study. But the ramifications of these issues – low literacy levels, lack of subject knowledge, limited exposure to academic texts, mismatches between the student's skills and the demands of the course – are often ones most keenly felt in the dyslexia support tutorial. It may be called 'dyslexia support' but it is dealing, unavoidably, with wider educational issues and is undoubtedly a sine qua non of the widening participation agenda.

References

DfES (2005) Final Report: SpLD Working Group 2005/DfES Guidelines, available from: http://www.patoss-dyslexia.org/DSA2.html.

Gibbs, G. (1994) *Improving Student Learning: Theory and practice*, Oxford Centre for Staff Development, Oxford.

Jamieson, C. and Morgan, E. (2008) *Managing Dyslexia at University*, Routledge, London.

Lee, M. and Street, B. (1998) Student writing in higher education: an academic literacies approach. *Studies in Higher Education*, 11, 182–199.

Stacey, G. (2010) Personalised strategies for effective study. *Dyslexia Review* Spring, 21, 16–18.

Stanovich, K.E. (1991) Discrepancy definitions of reading disability: Has intelligence led us astray? *Reading Research Quarterly*, 26, 7–29.

Winch, C. and Wells, P. (1995) The quality of student writing in higher education: a cause for concern. *British Journal of Educational Studies*, 43, 75–87.

Wingate, U. (2006) Doing away with 'study skills'. *Teaching in Higher Education*, 11, 457–469.

6

Why Can't I Learn? Metacognitive Strategy Instruction

Geraldine Price, University of Southampton, UK

Introduction

'My computer's on the blink. I've spent the last few days trying to fix it. I think that it's OK now but it doesn't seem to be working as fast as it was before.'

How many of us have had a problem like this and tried our best to solve it but it has taken a long time and a lot of effort, and in the end we are not totally satisfied with what we have done? Some people seem to do things effortlessly; others work conscientiously yet do not achieve the results they anticipated. Dyslexic students have often commented that, although they have spent a long time doing academic work, the results are disappointing. Perhaps the answer lies in the fact that we are not tackling the problem as an expert would. Learning is a complex process, and one that is vital for almost everything else we do in life. Thus, it is essential that we provide a teaching environment that encourages dyslexic students to learn how to learn.

Many dyslexic students in school and at university say that they spend more time than their friends do when carrying out written tasks. Some university students express frustration and annoyance about completing assignments. For example, Fiona, a second-year archaeology student, who says:

> I get really confused about what I'm expected to do. I was reading the wrong papers so wasted quite a bit of time doing this! Trying to get the right words and sorting out the paragraphs for the structure is what I spend most of my time doing. But when I get the essay back the tutors always say that I've not kept to the point. I wonder why I bother because it takes me so long to get my ideas down on paper.

For such students, the answer has been to provide study skills tuition that focused on time management schedules, speed-reading techniques and learning to keep to a prescribed structure for writing essays, which involves a beginning, a middle and an end. Doubtless, these surface factors are important for dealing with the day-to-day drudgery of school/university work. However, the answer lies at a deeper level involving knowledge of how experts work, and how to adapt to new tasks and challenges. It relates to how the learner is able to respond to new situations, drawing upon a knowledge of what works best in a given

Supporting Dyslexic Adults in Higher Education and the Workplace, First Edition. Edited by Nicola Brunswick.

circumstance and making *educated* decisions about which techniques to use to carry out the task. In other words, the learner is operating like an expert. Thus, the learner takes an *active role* in the process. In the words of Harrison (2000 p. 315):

> The self-managing learner is one who is self-aware, capable of exercising choice in relation to needs, of taking an active self-directing role in furthering his or her own learning and development.

This has an impact upon how dyslexic learners are taught. Whilst 'personalised learning' is advocated in the UK Department for Education and Skills Research Report No. 843 (Sebba *et al.* 2007, p. 15), it relies upon the teacher to tailor the teaching to meet the needs of the individual:

> Personalised learning offers a real opportunity for learners to participate fully in their own education and contribute to decisions about the supply and public value of education in general . . . Personalised learning demands teaching and learning strategies that develop the competence and confidence of every learner by actively engaging and stretching them.

The challenge for teachers is to ensure that students maximize their potential. So often teachers will try out something with their students and, if it does not provide the anticipated success, they turn to another method. This 'let's try this to see if it works' does our dyslexic students a disservice. It is vital to adopt a teaching approach that is the most reliable for dyslexic learners. One such approach is cognitive strategy instruction, which helps the learner to understand what skills are needed. It develops an ability to choose the most appropriate strategies to apply in any given learning environment.

The teaching of skills and processes is best done in the context of the curriculum. Using curriculum materials to develop skills ensures that learning has an immediate application. Thus, it becomes real for the student, who can put knowledge and learning into practice. This approach to learning cannot be started too soon. It provides the dyslexic learner with a ring of confidence to try out techniques, to get the job done, and then to reflect and evaluate what worked and what did not in those circumstances so that, when approaching a new situation, a best-fit choice is made based upon reflection and experience. This develops efficiency and effectiveness, which results in good grades for the time and effort put into the work.

Helping students to take control of their learning and to solve problems is life-enhancing. This process is known as metacognition and, as Price and Skinner (2007, p. 19) point out:

> If the student has an understanding of the learning process and can monitor progress throughout, there will be greater efficiency and quality of learning. Metacognitive strategies provide a barometer of success for the student and attempt to change the student from 'passive and anxious' (Brown 1992) to . . . an active learner.

Support for dyslexic students is best placed within a multidimensional teaching and learning environment that is made up of many layers and strands. It is a dynamic environment that incorporates flexibility of response. Thus, the teacher becomes the change agent in the contextualized environment. The learning support specialist makes connections between a learner's responses and the context in which they occur.

This proposed teaching framework hinges upon the teacher's ability to capitalize on individual strengths and weaknesses within the boundaries of a developmental continuum of learning. It encourages the development of learning skills, learner autonomy and the building up of self-esteem (Skidmore 2002).

There are four key elements in the teaching environment: developmental progression of skills, cognitive strategy instruction, apprenticeship modelling and metacognitive awareness (see Figure 6.1).

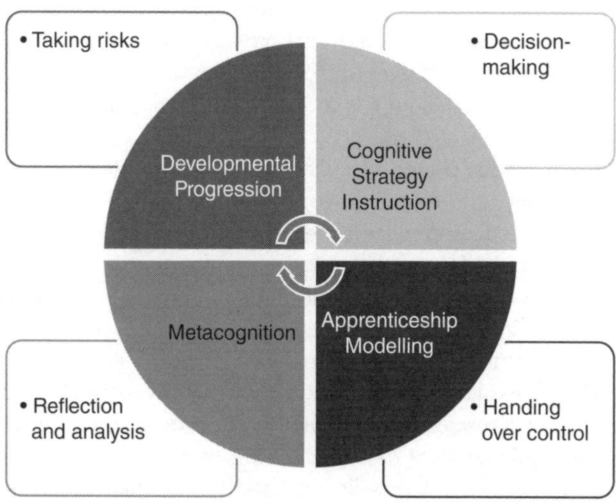

Figure 6.1 Elements of the teaching framework.

The four main components are the teaching approaches adopted in a cyclical manner and which provide an holistic environment. These instil the main skills that learners need to develop to become independent learners.

Developmental progression

The learning support specialist has to be aware of the hierarchy of stages of learning. This knowledge will provide a backdrop in which to assess the strengths and weaknesses, and the phase, that individual students have reached. It will afford a global picture of where each student is and what needs to be put in place, enabling the teacher to choose the best starting point, thus personalizing the progression.

Cognitive Strategy Instruction (CSI)

This approach will activate and enhance the process of metacognition. If we regard education as 'the passport to vocational competence and success' (Haywood 2004, p. 2) then we should use the teaching context to develop strategies that will become an integral part of the student's approach to new situations. CSI offers a thinking-skills framework that can be adapted to lifelong learning. The teacher demonstrates techniques that the individual will use strategically relating to the demands of a given activity. This element of the teaching framework delivers a 'mediated learning experience' (Feuerstein *et al.* 1980). At this stage the teacher takes control of the learning process, using the student's curriculum tasks and resources to bring the cognitive skills to the surface.

Apprenticeship/Modelling

An apprenticeship model can be compared with the master builders of medieval times who modelled skills to their apprentices. The apprentices were able to practise specific aspects of masonry and had many opportunities to overlearn the skills. This approach to learning was advocated by Vygotsky (1962). Key to Bandura's social cognitive theory, which explains how human nature and actions are guided by society (Bandura 2001), are the skills of self-regulation and self-efficiency. Zimmerman (2001) demonstrated how these could be achieved by modelling. Self-regulation ensures that learners monitor their own progress by constantly questioning what they are doing and evaluating what they have done. This leads to greater efficiency and ensures that such efficiency is in the hands of the apprentice/learner as part of an active approach to development of skills.

The use of modelling provides a type of collaboration as an effective teaching approach that encompasses partnership. It is set within a positive and secure learning environment, which is a critical factor for teaching vulnerable, dyslexic students.

Collaborative dialogues provide a platform for a developmental, interactive approach to metalinguistic awareness for dyslexic learners of all ages (Glynn, Wearmouth and Berryman 2006; Montgomery and Kahn 2003). Dyslexic students, because of a history of difficulties, are often unaware of language structures. Consequently, it is vital to ensure that teaching support makes linguistic knowledge explicit so that there is a conscious recognition of knowledge of language and linguistic structures such as sentence and paragraph construction, genre, syntax and semantics. In this way, the student becomes aware of his or her own use of language.

Problem-solving and decision-making skills are used to help the students to interact more confidently with abstract language. The teacher models a self-questioning technique to help the student become aware of the hidden language clues by way of collaborative dialogues. Steps to mastery are within a controlled environment to give familiarization, self-monitoring (the internal dialogues), and a deeper knowledge of how to evaluate new and novel tasks. In this way, the student gains confidence through metacognitive realization to work independently. This technique is further explored later in the chapter.

Metacognition

A teaching and learning environment in which students are challenged and construct knowledge is more supportive for dyslexic learners than one that relies mainly upon the transmission of knowledge. The latter does not develop metacognitive skills that can greatly increase learning potential, particularly for dyslexic learners. Knowing how to do things, what works and what does not work is vital to ensure efficiency and effectiveness. It enables the student to maximize potential and to cut down on fruitless attempts at tasks and written work. Self-reflection and self-analysis are crucial if the student is to take greater control of his or her own learning.

Operating the Teaching Framework

The starting point of the teaching framework is the adaptation of the dyslexic way of working in relation to the demands of the academic environment. The essence of the 'interactivity' of the model evolves from the combination of the bottom-up and top-down concepts. The starting point, therefore, has to be the dyslexic student's mindset and conceptions of procedures and methods of working. It is a student-led not a teacher-led approach. In this sense it is a bottom-up model that is student-driven. However, the teaching methods employed use explicit modelling to develop metacognition, metalanguage and metaskill performance in an environment that promotes success by scaffolding the learning and breaking skill acquisition into manageable steps. In this way, the teacher talks about the decision-making processes and their manipulation to demonstrate macro-organization (the ability to hold 'the big picture' for planning and organization) and the problem-solving skills that are involved in critical reading, text generation and editing.

Let us see how this operates in one aspect of learning: writing an essay. Writing is the poor relation in terms of research into teaching approaches yet it is the aspect of school and university work that causes the most concern for students. Producing a paragraph or a whole essay is a big challenge for dyslexic writers. It involves many choices that are vital to communicating ideas to others: choosing the right language, using the correct syntax and grammar, and sequencing ideas, not to mention grouping information into coherent paragraphs. It requires a great deal of multitasking. This puts pressure upon a person's working memory. The greater the working memory efficiency, the smoother and quicker the multitasking operations are. It is, therefore, little wonder that our dyslexic learners need support in the organization and management of this complex process.

Writing Like an Expert

To be an expert, a toolbox of techniques is needed. Expert writers rely upon a large toolbox to enable them to communicate ideas effortlessly and efficiently. When dealing with a new problem (such as a written task), the expert opens up the toolbox and decides which tools are relevant and appropriate to get the job done. Choosing a technique is a personal decision and is matched to the task demands and the written outcome, such that:

Task demands + choice of technique = personal strategy.

This flexible and dynamic method of working puts the learner in the driving seat. It means that he or she can adapt techniques to meet demands and thus be able to cope with new situations.

Dyslexic students need to be provided with learning environments that give them opportunities not only to learn new techniques but to learn how to make appropriate choices to solve the problem. There are various stages to learning techniques and filling up the student's toolbox. For example, the teacher:

1 explains a new technique – what it is, how it works, when it can be used and why it is useful
2 models the *hidden thinking skills* that experts use to make decisions about the choices
3 provides the student with lots of opportunities to make decisions about choice of technique
4 ensures that the student can justify the choice/decision, thus developing self-monitoring.

This type of study skills support is best done using curriculum tasks. They are real-life problems that the dyslexic learner is experiencing. The skills learned can be applied immediately to solve a pressing problem, such as homework.

Overlaying cognitive strategy instruction on the above procedures relies heavily on bringing the *thinking skills* to the surface. Many teachers find this difficult to start with because, as experts, they do many of the processes subconsciously. However, if dyslexic learners are to understand how experts operate, they need to have the questions and justifications for the decisions made explicit. This goes beyond modelling procedures mechanistically in a 'do this, do that' manner. It involves learning to ask the right questions to unravel the language. This is known as *metacognitive interrogation* of the problem. The inner questions are used to work out the language and at the same time to link the abstract language to an action.

The 'Language Detective'

Picture this scenario: a student has been given a written task. The first hurdle is working out what exactly the teachers want. For dyslexic students, the language of the task is alien and they need a simple technique that helps them to unpick the language and put it into action. I developed the BUG Method© in 1985 to help dyslexic students to manage their own learning (Price and Maier 2007). BUG stands for:

- **B**ox the action word
- **U**nderline the key (important) words
- **G**lance back.

By asking oneself simple questions, the language of an examination question or a written task can be demystified. So this method provides a platform for the teacher to introduce:

- metacognitive interrogation
- linkages between abstract language and written action
- self-monitoring techniques that develop a reflective and analytical approach.

The key to the success of this technique is that the answer to one question leads on to the next operation. For example, the expert would ask 'What do I have to *do*?' The response might be 'explain'. To help the student work out the key words to underline, the next question would be 'explain *what*?' Of course, those who are grappling with language are never confident that what they have underlined is correct. When learning this new technique, students often underline every word just in case. This is because they are not tuned in to language and do not have the inner voice to help them make decisions about which words to select and which to eliminate. Often these students will overlook simple, short words and lock on to longer words in the belief that size does matter! By putting the 'Glance back' into operation, they can be given questions that will help them to be more discriminating, for example, asking 'Have I missed anything?' 'Would it make a difference to what I have to do if this word stayed in/was left out?' Another bonus to this technique is that it has kinaesthetic features that help prevent the student freezing and being unable to work out difficult and complex language. Having to put a box around some words and to underline others, in addition to the inner prompts, psychologically takes the fear out of 'working out' language. An example of this process in action is provided by Graham.

Graham

Graham was a typical student who never seemed to answer the question. He was given the following task:

'Make notes for an essay on why it is difficult to reach agreement about elephant conservation.'

Before tuition, Graham underlined the words shown here in bold to reflect his understanding of what he had to do:

'Make notes for an **essay** on why it is difficult to reach agreement **about elephant conservation**.'

Of course, he had made assumptions that would have led to a lot of work but still would have resulted in a poor grade in this instance. The teacher explained why the BUG Method© would save him time and ensure that he did what was asked. His tutor spoke aloud all the questions she would ask to get down to the real task, at the same time boxing and underlining words.

- Question: What do you have '*to do*'?
- Student: Make notes
- Question: Is this different from 'writing an essay'?
- Teaching point: Clarify where to start teaching
- Question: Glance back at the words you have not underlined. Are any of them important/significant? Would any of them make a difference to the information you need?
- Teaching point: Bring thinking/decision-making skills to the surface

These questions were modelled for a dual purpose: first to show Graham how to clarify by interrogating the language of the task, and also as a starting point for teaching. If he does not know the difference between writing an essay and making notes, work would have to be done on this.

The tutor provided Graham with many short exercises to unpick the language of the question without having to carry out the written work, each time making him talk aloud his inner questions and justifying his actions. Many dyslexic learners like the fact that they can explain what they are doing without having to do the written essay! After a time, he was allowed to internalize the questions when they had become an automatic part of his routine. He was, at last, working subconsciously by applying the hidden thinking skills that experts draw upon automatically. When Graham decided that he was an expert, he was able to join a group of other students and demonstrate the technique. He was a more exacting tutor than his own teacher, and would pull up his peers if they were skipping the 'Glance back' part of the procedure, drawing from his own experiences and bitter disappointments.

Of course, dyslexic learners need to be exposed to the most frequently used 'action words' they will encounter in an academic year. Not only do they need to be able to pick out these words quickly (drawing on visual memory) but they also need to link them to a written action. Dyslexia tutors play a vital role in building up these word banks and providing crucial overlearning to secure word and meaning in memory. Pelmanism games[1] are a fun way to forge links in memory for quicker retrieval. They work best with the student's own definitions and language. Many definitions of 'to do' words can be found in textbooks but, if a student is struggling with language retrieval, using his or her own words will be a stronger trigger in the memory. There are three packs: action words, the action required, and the type of writing involved.

It's never too early to start. Working with Key Stage 2 children initiates this way of working. As the children move up the educational ladder, the action words may increase in difficulty but the linkages have been started and it is just a matter of topping up each year.

The combination of cognitive strategy instruction and dynamic support is a heady one because it provides all the ingredients that have proved effective for success for dyslexic learners and, invariably, the simple things work best. This article has explored how to hand over the skills to the learner in a progressive way. Once those providing support are aware of the need to bring the thinking skills to the surface, and how to model these, it is a method that can be used collaboratively with teaching assistants and with parents.

References

Bandura, A. (2001) Social cognitive theory: An agentic perspective. *Annual Review of Psychology*, 52, 1–26.

Brown, A. (1992) Reciprocal teaching: An approach to improving reading comprehension by training metacognitive strategies, in *Literacy without Frontiers* (eds F. Satow and B. Gatherer), United Kingdom Reading Association, Widnes.

Feuerstein, R., Rand, Y., Hoffman, M.B. and Miller, R. (1980) *Instrumental Enrichment*, University Park Press, Baltimore.

[1] These are matching card games often used by dyslexia tutors to improve memory.

Glynn, T., Wearmouth, G. and Berryman, M. (2006) *Supporting Students with Literacy Difficulties*, Open University Press, Maidenhead.

Harrison, R. (2000) Learner managed learning: managing to learn or learning to manage? *International Journal of Lifelong Learning*, 19, 312–321.

Haywood, C. (2004) Thinking in, around and about the curriculum: the role of cognitive education. *International Journal of Disability, Development and Education*, 51, 231–252.

Montgomery, J.K. and Kahn, N.L. (2003) You are going to be an author: adolescent narratives as intervention. *Communication Disorders Quarterly*, 24, 143–152.

Price, G.A. and Maier, P. (2007) *Effective Study Skills: Unlock your potential*, Pearson Education, Harlow.

Price, G.A. and Skinner, J.P. (2007) *Support for Learning Differences in HE: The essential practitioners' manual*, Trentham Books, Stoke-on-Trent.

Sebba, J., Brown, N., Steward, S. *et al.* (2007) *An investigation of Personalised Learning Approaches used by schools*, DfES Research Report RR843, University of Sussex.

Skidmore, D. (2002) A theoretical model of pedagogical discourse. *Disability, Culture and Education*, 1, 119–131.

Vygotsky, L.S. (1962) *Thought and Language*, MIT Press, Cambridge, MA.

Zimmerman, B.J. (2001) Theories of self-regulated learning and academic achievement: An overview and analysis, in *Self-regulated Learning and Academic Achievement: Theoretical perspectives*, 2nd edn (eds B.J. Zimmerman and D.H. Schunk), Erlbaum, Mahwah, NJ, pp. 1–37.

7

Supporting Higher Education Students Who Are Dyslexic

David Pollak, retired from De Montfort University, UK

Until the 1980s, people who were dyslexic were usually advised that higher education was not for them. Things are very different now as numbers of known dyslexic students at university have increased enormously and every university has staff to ensure quality of access. Many have guidelines on marking the work of students who experience learning differences, and legislation has ensured that a range of adjustments or accommodations is available everywhere. There is no need for academic staff to feel ignorant about dyslexia as most universities have online information available and face-to-face training on offer. There are also numerous websites and national projects to draw on.

The Current Higher Education Context in the UK

Over the past ten years, numbers of known dyslexic students in UK universities have increased tenfold. Awareness of dyslexia among staff means that the possibility of dyslexia is being suggested to more and more students. Government policy is to encourage increasing numbers of people to go to university, including those who lack formal qualifications from their schooldays. It is possible for such people to do special short courses to prepare them for higher education (see, for example, Access to Higher Education[1]).

All students have opportunities to disclose dyslexia on the national admissions form and the university's own enrolment form. It is important that they do this so that support arrangements can be 'triggered' as early as possible. Those who have never been formally identified as dyslexic can be screened by support staff at the university, and these staff teams play a key role in enabling students who are UK citizens to claim the Disabled Students' Allowance (DSA).[2] This is a grant set aside by the government to support disabled students in higher education by funding assistive technology, individual learning support and items such as coloured paper and photocopying. Claiming the DSA requires a post-16 psychological assessment and a formal assessment of needs. Comprehensive information about this, and much else, can be found in Jamieson and Morgan (2008), and Pavey, Meehan and Waugh (2010).

In terms of models of disability, the current gateway to services is via a medical model that locates impairment as a purely in-person factor, i.e. the 'problem' lies within the individual.

[1] www.accesstohe.ac.uk.

[2] The DSA is non-means tested, it is awarded to the student, not the university, and students do not have to pay it back.

Supporting Dyslexic Adults in Higher Education and the Workplace, First Edition. Edited by Nicola Brunswick.

Students have to accept categorisation as disabled and arrangements designed to help them fit in (social attitudes to disability have improved a great deal, but some students still find this difficult and hence do not visit the disability service).

Conversely, the social model of disability proposes that, if there is a problem, it is socially constructed and thus one for the institution as a whole to address. Students who are dyslexic may be disabled by inaccessible learning and teaching practices. Currently, this model does not prevail regarding dyslexia in higher education. Terminology can carry important overtones: 'learning difficulty' places the responsibility within the student, whereas 'learning difference' indicates that teaching must be adjusted. Ironically, the increase we have seen in the availability of training courses for dyslexia tutors and assessors has perpetuated the notion of dyslexia as a specialist matter that mainstream academic staff cannot hope fully to understand. This means that, in spite of the availability of information referred to above, many feel uncertain about how to support dyslexic students.

That said, the current system has one potentially positive feature: the process of identification as dyslexic can lead to a marked increase in self-knowledge (Cooper 2009). Good quality assessment reports contain plenty of information about individuals' strengths. However, as their main purpose is to support an application for the DSA, they also have to make unambiguous reference to deficits, leading one dyspraxic person to say recently: 'When I read the report, I wondered how I was able to cross the road, let alone get a degree.'

Dyslexia Assessment

We have something called screening, a process that can be carried out by a specialist tutor who is not a chartered psychologist. This always begins with a learning history because screening is a collaborative process with the student, and one can learn a lot from asking him or her about school experiences, memory issues, personal organization and many other things. Where the learning history and current differences both point to dyslexia, then a full assessment will often be recommended (although both the student and the institution may be satisfied with a good screening report).

Full assessment is carried out by a psychologist or by a specialist tutor who has completed a recognized training course in dyslexia assessment and support. Most psychologists use a model of dyslexia that focuses on a discrepancy between intelligence quotient (IQ) and academic attainment; they therefore begin with a detailed IQ test such as the Wechsler Adult Intelligence Scale (Wechsler 1981) followed by a range of attainment tests.

In the UK, the final stage of dyslexia assessment in higher education is known as Assessment of Needs (for students accessing the DSA). This is a collaborative process involving discussion of the study strategies the student is currently using. The nature of the student's course is a key element in determining his or her particular needs and how these might best be met. A summary of the results of these tests is then written up in a report.

A good assessment report has the following characteristics:

- self-esteem is not damaged by the process
- all technical terms are explained
- it describes strengths as well as weaknesses
- it takes account of the student's current strategies
- it refers to the particular demands of the student's course
- there are detailed recommendations and costings (e.g. regarding the use of technological aids)
- it states clearly the category of learning difference that applies to the student. This is needed by both the university, as evidence for adjustments, and the body that administers the DSA, as evidence of eligibility.

Of course, the report contains personal information about the individual, and so the student must be responsible for its distribution. It should not be automatically copied to anyone.

Particular Issues for Dyslexic Students at University

As they arrive at university, many dyslexic people have poor self-esteem as a result of years of struggle with the education system, as well as years of embarrassment because of their poor memory or poor personal organization. This sometimes feeds into social anxiety where a person becomes barely able to speak to others (Griffin 2007). Just as the world (society) is mainly designed by and for right-handed people, it is not designed with dyslexic people in mind. On the other hand, for younger people this is counterbalanced (in countries like the UK) by the number of openly dyslexic, successful people, many of whom are 'celebrities' (for examples, see www.xtraordinarypeople.com).

Dyslexic people are as varied as anyone else in terms of their strengths and weaknesses. However, in higher education it can be said that linear thought is a problem for the majority. Therefore, writing essays and dissertations, with a structure that moves from an introduction to a series of points or chapters and ends with a conclusion, can be very challenging. Many students describe their ideas as coming to them in a two-dimensional or three-dimensional way (Pollak 2005).Though it is not a panacea for dyslexic experiences, excellent assistive technology is available and the equipment itself is constantly improving (Draffan 2009). Voice recognition is enormously easier to use than it was ten years ago, and screen-reading programs are widely available. Technology does not of course make you a linear thinker, although concept mapping at least helps you to see all your ideas, and skilled individual support can develop strategies for writing in the expected manner.

Assistive Technology

These are the main categories of technological aid (hardware and software) that students use:[3]

- Planning: concept mapping
  Concept mapping is also known as 'mind mapping' and is a very good way for a holistic thinker to make notes, either in a lecture or to plan a piece of writing. Many people (dyslexic or not) do this on paper, using coloured pens. There are several computer programs that allow one to do this on-screen; one of the best is called 'Inspiration'.
- Reading: text readers (where a digital voice speaks the words)
- Writing: aural feedback
  In my opinion, the best computer program is called Read and Write. This enables the user to hear what he or she is typing, and to paste in other text for the software to read aloud. It also alerts the user to homophones and has a dictionary and spelling checker that can be heard.
- Voice recognition
  Voice recognition software enables the user to speak into a microphone and the words appear on the screen. It is very useful for those who are good at formulating their ideas by dictation, but it is easier to train it (teach it to recognize your voice) if you have a relatively 'neutral' accent rather than a strong regional one.
- Digital voice recorder
  Dyslexic students use digital recorders to record lectures and other meetings. The sound quality is good and the recordings can be uploaded to a computer.

[3] These are all described at www.dyslexic.com and by Draffan (2009).

- Scanner and scanner pen
- Personal digital assistant.

There are other items that help with personal organization. Accessibility provided by a student's course is covered below.

UK Legislation

These points are from the UK's Disability Discrimination Act (1995, succeeded by the Equality Act, 2010):

- Universities must anticipate students' needs.
- Dyslexia is included under 'disability'.
- It is illegal to discriminate against a dyslexic person.
- 'Reasonable adjustments' have to be made.
- Arrangements have to be explicit.
- There is individual and institutional responsibility.
- A 'level playing field' must be provided, i.e. equity of conditions for all.
- This must be embedded practice rather than 'bolted on'.

As a result of this legislation, universities should implement procedures for agreeing alternative assessment and examination arrangements that:

- are widely publicized and easy for students to follow
- operate with minimum delay
- allow flexibility in the conduct of the assessment
- protect the rigour and comparability of the assessment
- are applied consistently across the institution
- are not dependent on students' individual funding arrangements.

Universities should also make the following adjustments available:

- flexibility in the balance between assessed coursework and examinations
- demonstration of achievement in alternative ways, such as viva voce examinations
- additional time allowances, rest breaks and rescheduling of examinations
- the use of computers, amanuenses, readers and other support in examinations
- the availability of examinations or the presentation of assessed work in alternative formats
- the provision of additional rooms and invigilators for those using alternative arrangements.

The Disability Discrimination Act (2005)

This introduced a positive duty to eliminate discrimination and harassment and a requirement to promote equality of opportunity. It brought about a great deal of change in UK universities. The general equality duty includes the promotion of equality of opportunity. The UK's Higher Education Academy (HEA 2010) has published detailed guidance for academic staff.[4] Specific duties under the DDA included:

[4] http://www.heacademy.ac.uk/resources/detail/inclusion/Teaching_For_Inclusion.

- active involvement of disabled people
- impact assessment regarding disability equality
- a Disability Equality Scheme for the institution.

It is now normal to see physical accessibility features everywhere; these include ramps, automatic doors and accessible toilets (although these are still often labelled 'disabled toilet', which does not inspire confidence in the user). Accessibility in university course design, delivery and assessment, while better than it was, still has some way to go.

In the UK there is now a single Equality Act, passed in October 2010. This brings together a range of earlier legislation, including that on disability referred to above. The associated Code of Practice on Further and Higher Education reached the end of its consultation period on 31 December 2010, and it is due to be laid before Parliament in summer 2011. Meanwhile, the earlier Code of Practice remains available on the Equality and Human Rights Commission website[5] and it is full of useful advice.

Reasons for Inclusive Teaching

Inclusive, accessible teaching improves the retention of students (i.e. they are less likely to drop out), and it improves their attainment. Inclusive teaching benefits everyone, and is usually just good practice anyway.

Course Delivery

Tutors can help students with reading by considering:

- providing a screen reader on web pages
- providing printed materials in advance (or making documents available online)
- making it easy to change the appearance of online material
- using a sans serif font such as Arial, in at least 12 point, and wide spacing
- providing a glossary of terms
- using bullet points instead of sentences
- using diagrams instead of text
- offering handouts on pastel-coloured paper
- avoiding sentences or headings in capitals.

These are things that all lecturers should do anyway. My former place of work uses cream paper a lot now because many students have difficulty reading black text on white paper, although student requirements can be complex in this area. Sentences in capital letters cannot easily be read by assistive software; the words also lack the silhouette offered by ascending and descending lower case letters.

These points can also help students with reading:

- Give annotated reading lists (it is essential to mark the key elements on a reading list for those who are not going to be able to read many items).
- Use non-book source material (e.g. tapes, videos, CDs) where possible.
- Type assignment feedback or make audio files (many dyslexic students cannot read handwritten comments on their work).

[5] See: www.equalityhumanrights.com.

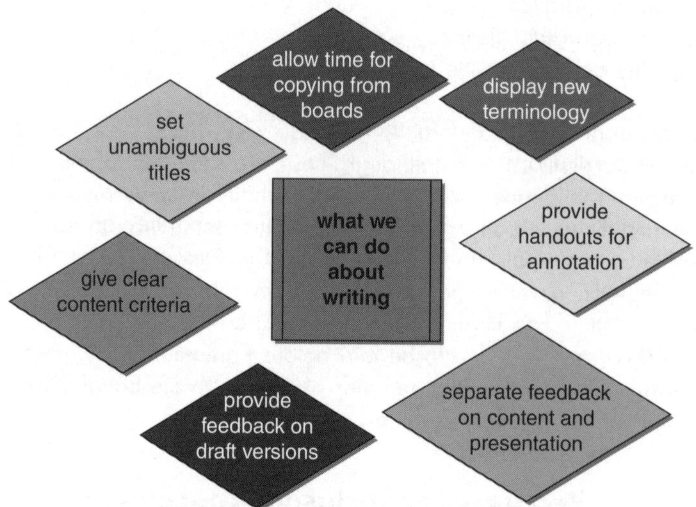

Figure 7.1 Some ways that tutors can help students with their writing.

- Colour-code technical instructions.
- Consider using two columns of text (short lines can be easier to read).
- Align text on the left only (to keep word spacing even).
- Refer students to a student support librarian, if one is available.

Writing for Tutors

The ideas shown in Figure 7.1 are intended to help lecturers support students with writing tasks.

Talking and Listening

Lecturers should bear these points in mind:

- Be patient.
- Be prepared to repeat instructions.
- Use facilitative questioning to help students to test their understanding.
- Encourage use of sound recorders.
- Give clear assessment criteria for presentations.
- Encourage visual communication.
- Consider facilitating video recording.
- Use electronic whiteboards.

Dyslexic students often long to ask for spoken information to be repeated but feel embarrassed about saying so. At the start of a new course, if the tutor says that he or she is happy for students to make sound recordings, this will not only communicate acceptance and awareness of learning difference but also encourage students to disclose that they are dyslexic (it depends on the nature of the session, of course). If participants are going to be talking about personal matters, they will need to be asked for their permission for the recording and an assurance that it will be used only for the person's private study.

Tutors should try to use frequent mind maps and diagrams in presentations. Also, accept mind maps from students, for example if the outline of an essay is requested before it is written.

When delivering group sessions, staff should bear the following guidelines in mind:

- Minimize copying from boards and flipcharts.
- Make reading aloud voluntary.
- Make all handouts on coloured paper, not just the ones for dyslexic students.
- Write up difficult spellings for all, rather than indicating who they are for.
- Leave slides on the screen long enough for slow readers/writers.
- Maintain confidentiality: dyslexic students may not want others to know.

I have never met a dyslexic student who enjoyed reading aloud in public; most have painful memories from schooldays. Dyslexic students should be enabled to prepare for sessions by reading any necessary material in advance.

Ways to Help Students with Their Personal Organization

- Ask the student what will help.
- Use email, text messaging and the like; use the same subject header when emailing to help the student identify the message.
- Provide simple maps, plans or diagrams.
- In signs, use colour and graphics.
- Supplement oral instructions with simple written ones.
- Consider providing information online or on disk.
- Avoid having many assignment hand-in dates close together.

One course at the university where I used to work recently produced information about a course unit in the form of a large folded poster. When the student opens it up, it contains many diagrams and charts as well as text, in clearly labelled groups. When I produced books of conference papers, I liked to have each paper (chapter) printed on a different colour. The contents diagram at the front would use the same colours for each chapter. When one university library was refurbished recently, each floor was given a colour. As students arrive at each floor up the stairs, the colour of the wall is continued in the colour of the carpet on that floor; library maps and guides use the same colour scheme.

Be Aware of Emotional Issues

- Avoid public discussion of dyslexia.
- Aggressive behaviour by a student may mask anxiety.
- Supporting students does not mean allowing them to hand over responsibility; students should not blame dyslexia for everything.
- Demonstrate awareness and acceptance of dyslexia, particularly the stress aspects.
- Refer to counselling and learning support services.
- Above all, be sensitive to a student's self-esteem.

It still sometimes happens that lecturers say 'Put your hand up if you are dyslexic'. This is of course embarrassing and unnecessary. Ideally, inclusive practices should be adopted for all; if not, dyslexic people should be invited to speak to the lecturer separately.

My doctoral research (Pollak 2005) showed that there is a strong link between self-esteem and the adoption of a medical model of dyslexia. The Americans call it 'learning disabled' and we in the UK tell students that they must apply for something called the Disabled Students' Allowance, which makes some students uncomfortable. While staff should not imply that 'disabled = bad', language needs careful thought in this sensitive area. The social model of disability does not deny that impairments exist; it states that the disability arises from a lack of accessible arrangements. We can help students by explaining that they are entitled to have a critique of the current official vocabulary.

I believe that learning support tutors need counselling skills. They should listen carefully to the student and show empathy. They should help the student to build on his or her strengths, and to see their difficulties less as the result of their intrinsic deficiencies and more as resulting from the nature of traditional academic practices.

That point raises another significant aspect of the current situation, namely the nature of traditional higher education. For centuries, students have been expected to read large numbers of books, attend many lectures and express their ideas by means of essays and timed examinations. We are currently in a transitional phase where older academics still see it that way but younger ones are accustomed to virtual learning environments (VLEs), podcasts and groupwork. Alternative forms of academic assessment are slowly becoming more widespread (Attwood 2009). Even in very traditional universities it is possible to modify course specifications to read: 'The assignment for this unit will *typically* be a 3000-word essay' so that variations can be facilitated.

Course materials can be made accessible along the lines suggested by these ideas:

- Make presentations as diagrammatic as possible.
- Encourage the use of sound recording (including in individual meetings).
- Indicate key items on reading lists (and key chapters).
- Provide glossaries of technical terms.
- Provide handouts of PowerPoint slides, or at least make them available on the VLE (see below).
- Use non-book source material (e.g. sound files, videos, podcasts) where possible.
- Use at least 36 point text size in PowerPoint.
- If applicable, remind students that they can reserve books via the online public access catalogue, to save them struggling with the Dewey system. In many universities, extended loans are available to dyslexic students.

The following points should be borne in mind by academic staff with regard to coursework:

- Make expectations very clear.
- Include oral assessment, to cover a wider range of all students' abilities.
- Consider non-linear assignments such as portfolios.
- Allow time-bounded extensions to deadlines, because dyslexic students take a long time to read/write.
- Assess work against learning outcomes that will reflect your subject priorities.
- Correct selected spellings only (e.g. technical vocabulary).
- Use two different pens, neither red: one for the material, one for spelling and grammar. Many students associate red ink with bad experiences at school (in the UK at least – but nowadays some teachers are aware of this in schools).
- Write comments legibly. Many dyslexic students struggle to read handwriting, so you may be wasting your time. Alternatively, consider making an audio file of feedback, which could be quicker for you as well as more accessible for the student.

- Correct English by talking to the student along with word-processed comments. This will contribute to the long-term effectiveness of your feedback.
- Do not say 'please use spell-checker'. The student is probably using it a lot but choosing the wrong options.
- Ask for a skeleton plan (or a draft) first, if time permits.

Arrangements such as the following are frequently made for dyslexic students whose courses include examinations:

- extra time (typically 15 minutes per hour)
- a sound recording of questions
- an amanuensis (a person to read the paper aloud and/or take dictation of the answers)
- questions printed on coloured paper
- questions printed in large font size
- use of a computer
- working in a separate room
- provision of a spelling list
- oral examination.

Student Strategies

1 Reading

Figure 7.2 illustrates questions that students can ask in order to feel a sense of power over a book instead of being intimidated by it.

They are also good study skills for all.

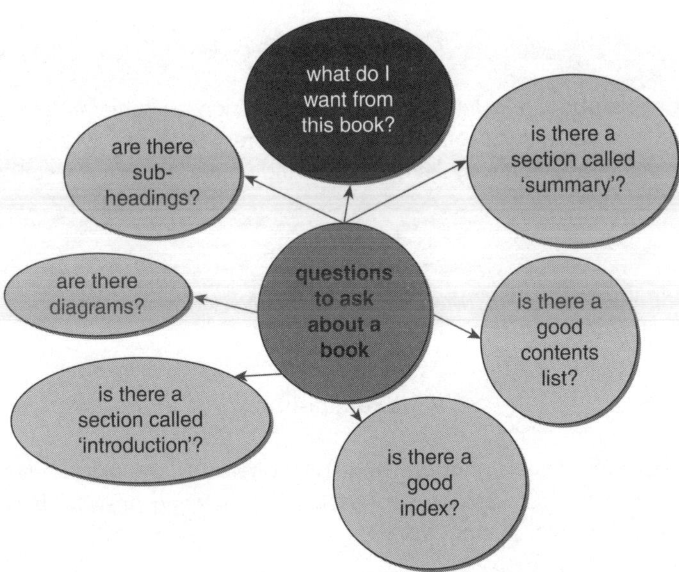

Figure 7.2 Questions that students can usefully ask when reading a book.

Figure 7.3 offers an overview of useful reading strategies.

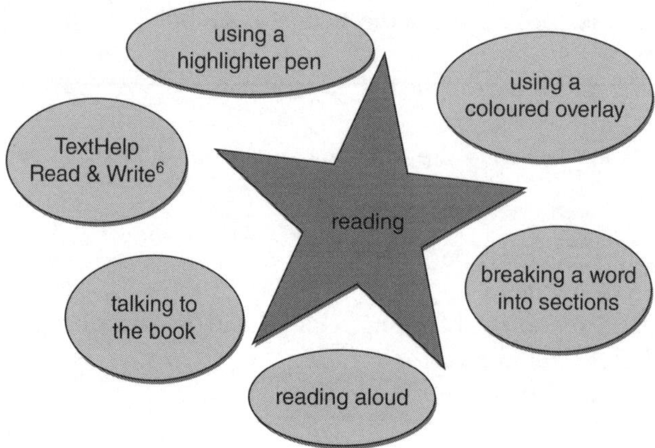

Figure 7.3 Some reading strategies.

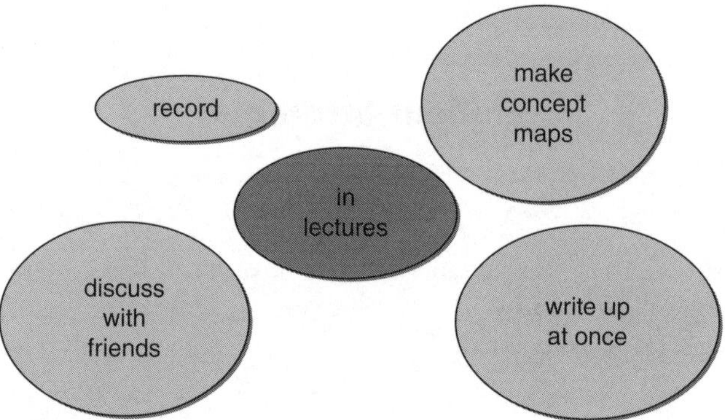

Figure 7.4 Some techniques for dealing with lectures.

2 Dealing with lectures

Talking to other people about a lecture (or any course session, or something they have read) is often helpful to dyslexic students as long it can be done very soon afterwards (see Figure 7.4 for other helpful techniques). Some dyslexic students may have a note-taker funded by the DSA.

3 Writing

'Human support' in this Figure 7.5 refers mainly to one-to-one learning support, which again can be funded by the DSA.

4 Examinations

Figure 7.6 illustrates 'adjustments' that are frequently offered to dyslexic students at UK universities. An amanuensis can also be very useful, but dictating answers is a skill that must be practised if the student is to benefit from it.

[6] TextHelp (also known as Read and Write) is a computer programme. There is information about it at www.dyslexic.com.

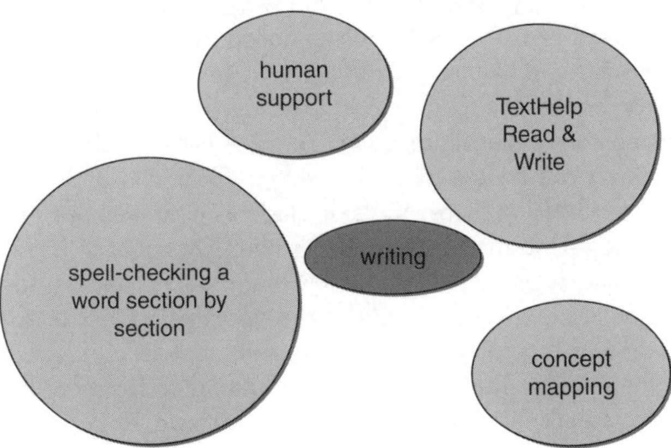

Figure 7.5 Some strategies for dealing with writing.

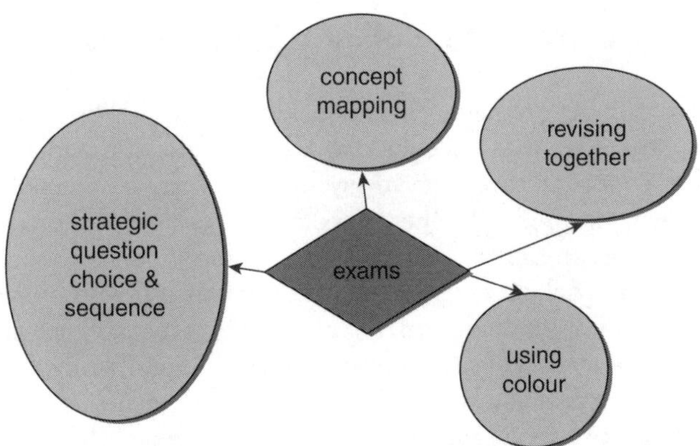

Figure 7.6 Some strategies for dealing with examinations.

There does however, remain a key area of potential tension between conventional higher education practices and many dyslexic people: the concept of linear thought referred to above. It is not just an essay that has to start with an introduction, proceed through points one to (say) six, and end with a conclusion; a presentation must also do this. Many dyslexic students, on the other hand, assemble their ideas in two-dimensional or three-dimensional form; such a preference can also lead to issues with the concept of time (Cooper 2009). Currently, the system provides one-to-one learning support tutors who usually spend a lot of time facilitating students to squeeze their natural thinking style into the narrow confines of a conventional essay. In other words, academic norms are immutable and the student who is 'different' has to be made to conform.

While the latter remains a common situation, there is plenty of inventive work going on in higher education with regard to academic assessment. Some of this is led by dyslexic people and others involved in Art and Design (e.g. WritingPAD[7]). Symonds (2006) is a leading figure in the dissemination of the viva voce (oral examination) revival.

[7] www.writing-pad.ac.uk.

As regards information for dyslexic students, the well-established website 'Dyslexia College'[8] is full of practical tips. Another website, called 'Being dyslexic',[9] is run by and for dyslexic people and includes a community forum as well as education-specific pages.

There are now some books that model good practice by including CDs containing either the full text or supplementary material (or both). Some of these (such as Jamieson and Morgan 2008) are for staff; others are for dyslexic people (e.g. Goodwin and Thomson 2004; and Hargreaves 2007). On accessing these, dyslexic students may well see the suggestions and respond 'I do that already'. Learning support tutors often hear that; it is an indication of the level of self-awareness and sophisticated strategies that dyslexic people have needed in order to get into university. Similarly, dyslexic students are apologising less and less for their use of assistive technology. Sound recording is extremely useful, not only in lectures and seminars but also in one-to-one meetings. There is no need to apologize for recording, but of course common courtesy may require informing people that a recorder is in use. Academic staff are much more accustomed to sound recording then they were; the next stage must be the acceptance of video recording – for example, where complex formulae are being worked out on a board.

A University Policy about Dyslexia

A number of factors are important here. There should be effective liaison with feeder institutions such as further education colleges and schools, and with widening participation practitioners in higher education. Every university should ideally be aiming to be a 'dyslexia-friendly' institution (Pavey *et al.* 2010). There should be a culture of shared responsibility.

Support is best delivered on-course, i.e. not only by a separate tutor, and all staff should be dyslexia-aware. This should include people working in marketing, who promote the university. University websites should not be 'busy', i.e. full of pictures, especially moving ones, lots of jazzy colours, lots of small text. Websites should be easily adjustable by the user, and ideally offer screen reading (although to my knowledge, no British university yet offers this).

It is important that all documents, such as university regulations, should be available in alternative formats. An official university policy on dyslexia is not required; what we need is a policy on neurodiversity – a policy for all learning differences.

When I talk to lecturers about dyslexia, I always say that the kind of practices I call 'dyslexia-friendly' are simply good practice for any lecturer. However, for a university to be a truly dyslexia-friendly place, there should be easy access to spoken versions of books, or at least digital versions so that students can use text-readers. There should be alternatives to exams because these demand speed of information processing, speed of handwriting and the ability to produce good grammar and spelling under pressure. However, if the course is a professional one where these are essential abilities, that is a different matter. There should also be alternatives to the dissertation or other long essays, because these demand linear thought.

The Future

That brings us to looking ahead at the future situation for dyslexic students in higher education. As Cooper (2009, pp. 68–69) points out, inclusive arrangements for such students need to start from the first point of contact with a university:

[8] www.dyslexia-college.com.

[9] www.beingdyslexic.co.uk.

> Rational university entry criteria would identify the skills and abilities that a candidate needs in order to undertake and complete a course successfully, and which will not be taught during the course.

At present, university prospectuses vary widely in that respect. It is unfortunate that the huge increase in student numbers has seen the virtual abandonment of the admissions interview. However, we do have the university open day, and dyslexic applicants are strongly advised to go to those. They afford the opportunity to meet course tutors and discuss accessibility, as well as to meet support staff.

The very first point of contact for many is of course the university website. Why do university sites generally lack screen readers and easy-to-use facilities for changing the background colour, font, font size and font colour? Where are the W3C[10] Web Accessibility Initiative logos, to prove that the sites have been checked for accessibility? It is essential for students to feel able to disclose neurodiversity such as dyslexia (and indeed disabilities), and such features would be a clear indication of a basic level of awareness on the part of the institution – as well as signalling to all potential applicants that this is an inclusive university. Could it be that some universities want to be seen as *exclusive*?

Many universities nowadays insist that all new staff undertake a postgraduate certificate in higher education. Such courses cover best practice in learning, teaching and assessment; much of the standard wisdom overlaps remarkably with dyslexia-friendly practice. Unfortunately, these staff courses usually include a separate session on disability and learning difference, often presented as 'how to accommodate students who are different'. The way forward is for accessible and inclusive practice to be regarded as mainstream, rather than 'adjustments'. The Open University has an excellent online resource designed to enable staff to create a learning environment that is inclusive by design.[11]

Another important part of the way forward is for staff development about inclusive practices to be more strongly supported. Making reference to it in the appraisal process, peer observation schedules and promotion procedures offers meaningful incentives. Academic staff are understandably put off by an emphasis on legal obligations but can be encouraged by reference to improving student retention and attainment (which frequently results from accessible learning and teaching).[12] This chapter includes a number of checklists; lecturers are often understandably resistant to these until they notice that most of the points do not amount to the imposition of extra work, but constitute the kind of good practice that is desirable in any case. A succinct summary of such good practice is provided by Pavey *et al.* (2010).

Staff sometimes suggest that 'alternative' forms of academic assessment lack academic rigour, particularly when they are fundamentally non-linear. Dyslexic students themselves often say that they prefer not to seek adjusted forms of assessment because they want to feel that they have passed the course on the same basis as everyone else. The key point here is that higher education involves, for example, the ability to research a range of sources, explain their ideological stances, critique them and arrive at a synthesis or other form of justified conclusion. It can be seen that the dyslexic brain is often able to shine here – but there must be flexibility in what constitutes an acceptable way to express the outcome. Cooper (2009) quotes several students who are very frustrated by the emphasis on conventional academic writing. Could it be that some of our eminent professors reject the idea of, say, a three-dimensional model as a project because their own cognitive style cannot cope with such a thing?

[10] World Wide Web Consortium.

[11] www.open.ac.uk/inclusiveteaching.

[12] A list of online resources for accessible learning and teaching can be found at www.brainhe.com/staff/methods/index.html.

Professor John Stein often states that, if the dyslexic brain were 'bad news' for the human race, evolution would have removed it a long time ago. The commercial world needs its imaginative thinkers and we have the dyslexic millionaires to prove it. Similarly, universities need what dyslexic students can offer. The system must therefore abandon the current within-person deficit model of dyslexia, and in this regard things have improved. One of the London universities no longer has a 'Dyslexia Clinic' (although an online search for that phrase reveals a depressing number of centres for children that are called exactly that), and another UK university no longer defines dyslexia (on a web page for students) as a 'chronic neurological disorder'. But many students still have to deal with the medical model daily.

A new development from 2011 is that the Office For Fair Access (OFFA) now requires UK universities to describe services for students who are disabled as part of the justification for charging the maximum student course fee.

Conclusion

As Morgan and Klein (2000) put it, we live in a non-dyslexic world, and the challenge remains for academia to offer accessible learning and teaching for all, without lowering academic standards. To this end:

- It is essential to seek the views of dyslexic students.
- We should not be pathologizing this common kind of brain; truly accessible teaching removes the need to do so.
- Learning support should be available to all, with staff available who are trained to support learning differences; dyslexic students should not be referred to separate provision.
- There is no 'dysartistica' or 'dysorientica' – in other words, those who are poor at drawing or have navigational difficulties have not so far been labelled with a learning difference, yet dyslexic people have been.
- One key challenge for universities is finding ways for diverse students to show that they can meet the essential learning outcomes.
- Equality means that both failure and success have to be a possibility for all. Disability is part of the equalities agenda and should be afforded the same respect as other dimensions.

As I retired after 35 years of working with dyslexic people, I was greatly encouraged by the progress being made. I recently examined a PhD thesis by a dyslexic person whose university, after some hesitation, allowed her to make a sound recording of the feedback at the end of the viva. A recording of the whole viva would have been better but it was progress (facilitated by the student's determination). My book on neurodiversity (Pollak 2009) is printed on cream paper in a sans serif font and the text is aligned on the left throughout (see also Brunswick 2009). Again, a CD or online availability of the whole text would have been useful additions but a traditional academic publishing house has been flexible. There are increasingly frequent examples of 'alternative' work for dissertations and theses. Say not the struggle nought availeth!

David Pollak acknowledges support from Professor Alan Hurst and Dr Nicola Martin in the preparation of this chapter.

References

(books marked ** include the text on a CD)

Attwood, R. (2009) Well, what do you know? *Times Higher Education*, 1881, 32–37.

Brunswick, N. (2009) *Dyslexia: A beginner's guide*, Oneworld Publications, Oxford.
Cooper, R. (2009) Dyslexia, in *Neurodiversity in Higher Education* (ed. D. Pollak), Wiley-Blackwell, Oxford.
Draffan, E.A. (2009) Assistive technology, in *Neurodiversity in Higher Education* (ed. D. Pollak), Wiley-Blackwell, Oxford.
Equality Act (2010), Office for Disability Issues, London.
Goodwin, V. and Thomson, B. (2004) *Making Dyslexia Work for You*, David Fulton, London.**
Griffin, E. (2007) *Social anxiety and cognitive behavioural techniques*, www.brainhe.com/students/types/SocialAnxiety.html, accessed March 22, 2011.
Hargreaves, S. (2007) *Study Skills for Dyslexic Students*, Sage, London.**
HEA (2010) *Inclusion*, available at http://www.heacademy.ac.uk/resources/detail/inclusion/Teaching_For_Inclusion, accessed September 28, 2011.
Jamieson, C. and Morgan, E. (2008) *Managing Dyslexia at University*, Routledge, London.**
Morgan, E. and Klein, C. (2000) *The Dyslexic Adult in a Non-dyslexic World*, Whurr, London.
Pavey, B., Meehan, M. and Waugh, A. (2010) *Dyslexia-friendly Further and Higher Education*, Sage, London.
Pollak, D. (2005) *Dyslexia, the Self and Higher Education: Learning life histories of students identified as dyslexic*, Trentham Books, Stoke on Trent.
Pollak, D. (ed.) (2009) *Neurodiversity in Higher Education*, Wiley-Blackwell, Oxford.
Symonds, H. (2006) *The Viva Voce Handbook*, University of the Arts, London.**
The Disability Discrimination Act (1995), Her Majesty's Stationery Office, London.
Wechsler, D. (1981) *Wechsler Adult Intelligence Scale – Revised*, Harcourt Brace Jovanovich/Psychological Corporation, New York.

8

Dyslexia Support at the Royal College of Art

A Symbiotic Relationship

Qona Rankin, Royal College of Art, London, UK

The post of Dyslexia Co-ordinator at the Royal College of Art (RCA) was created in 2002. This was in response to feedback from RCA staff and students indicating that, whilst often demonstrating outstanding talent as artists and designers, students with dyslexia can be considerably disadvantaged in their studio presentations and in their theoretical and written submissions. To address this, the College prepared a dyslexia policy statement in 2000 with the aim of clarifying the support available for dyslexic students in terms of financial assistance, learning and teaching strategies, tutorial support and assessment processes. To support the policy, the RCA's Learning and Teaching Committee agreed to fund a consultative exercise in conjunction with the Dyslexia Teaching Centre in London to identify good practice and to make recommendations to formalize support for dyslexic students. As a result, the post of Dyslexia Co-ordinator was created and I was appointed. I was immediately excited by the potential impact that an efficient and specialized service could have on the dyslexic students' learning experience.

Dyslexia Support Making a Difference to the Students

My initial thoughts were to establish a workable system for the students to be screened, assessed, supported and offered help with applying for the Disabled Students' Allowance (DSA). Thanks to the generous funding, we can pay most of the cost of a dyslexia and/or dyspraxia assessment and, if subsequently required, a Needs Assessment will be arranged. If the student is applying for the DSA, we can help them with that too, and then coordinate and deliver both group and individual support programmes.

When students receive their assessment report we try to explain that there is nothing wrong with them and so we're not looking for a cure. We tell them that, although dyslexia and dyspraxia are defined as disabilities, we see them as different ways of processing. It is the context of school, with its insistence on concentrating on left-brained activity and the rewarding of excellence in traditional academic subjects, that has made them feel disabled. Sometimes students become angry or depressed about the lack of earlier diagnosis and help. We can then refer them to our counselling service, which can help them to come to terms with their feelings. More often than not students are relieved to discover that there is an explanation for their lack of academic achievement and I am frequently asked, 'Does this mean I'm not just stupid after all?'

Supporting Dyslexic Adults in Higher Education and the Workplace, First Edition. Edited by Nicola Brunswick.

I established a dyslexia database that enabled me to keep track of students' progress. I put together a schedule of group workshops which took place once a week and which were available to any student on the database. Clearly, for students, managing the reading and research material for their courses, not to mention putting together a logical and coherent argument in the 6 to10,000-word dissertation, was a real hurdle. So too was the need to write formal reports, fill in applications for residencies and navigate through complicated web sites for potential grants and funding (the Arts Council England web site provides a particularly good example of how complicated these application forms can be). Students are also required to produce professional-looking curricula vitae (CVs) and letters of introduction to galleries. That was where the main focus of these early workshop sessions lay.

I then set about looking at cross-college studio practices. I should explain that, prior to qualifying as a dyslexia support tutor in 1998, I taught 3D design, first on various foundation courses and then on a Product Design BA. Prior to that I was an art student, which added up to 30 years spent in art and design education. I wanted to put my experience, knowledge and understanding about this to practical use. I decided to focus on improving the dyslexia-friendliness of the very particular ways and means of teaching art and design through practice.

The main vehicle for teaching art and design is through projects. These may relate to exploring a particular material or technique, or responding to an abstract concept, or coming up with a practical solution that fulfils a specific set of criteria. Generally, students are given a written brief containing the necessary information to start them off on the creative journey. However, this can be very challenging for students. A ceramics student once told me that she just couldn't understand what the brief was asking her to do. When she explained her confusion to the tutor, he was able to offer physical examples of what he meant and she was then able to see a possible way forward; she produced some stunning pieces in response (for example, see Figure 8.1).

Dyspraxic students could have directional confusion, which might make threading a loom, for example, particularly difficult. Those with short-term memory problems might find it stressful to remember that they have booked a kiln for a specific time on a certain day. Sequencing difficulties can make remembering a complicated set of instructions, as for example during a demonstration of lithography or etching, difficult. Visual perceptual difficulties could make scaling models for the architecture students, or writing a cutting list for the design product students, problematic. Fashion students having to organize their time between three or four concurrent projects may reach a state of complete overload. Slow verbal retrieval can be overcome by rehearsing a presentation, but what happens when you are put on the spot, having to justify yourself, with questions being fired at you during a project presentation or a viva voce examination? It is these areas of professional practice support that particularly interest me.

Figure 8.1 A piece of work produced by a dyslexic ceramics student at the RCA.

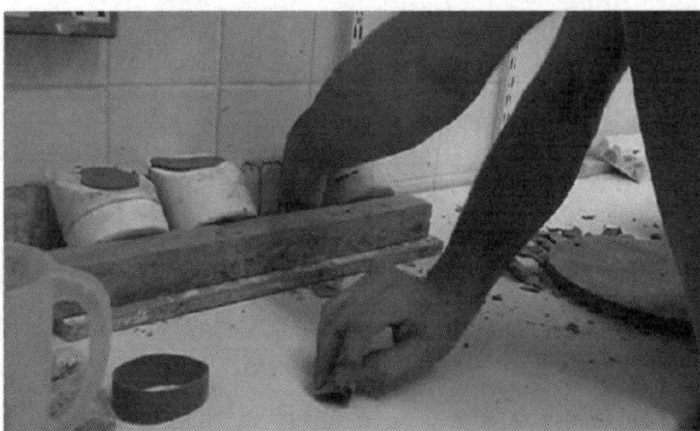

Figure 8.2 A still image from a video recording of a practical ceramics tutorial.

During any particular project the student will have tutorial contact with various members of staff. As a result of the tutorial, the student will receive a tutorial report summing up what was agreed and referencing any material the tutor feels will help. Two years ago a ceramics tutor was concerned about a severely dyslexic student who found it very hard to take the written tutorial advice on board and so to progress. After weeks of experimentation the tutor found a software package called 'Audacity'[1] that would enable him to record the tutorial and save it as an Mp3 file, which the student could then download and listen to as many times as needed.

Last year the RCA's Teaching and Learning committee provided funding for me to make a film that described this (a still image from the film is shown in Figure 8.2). The film is accessible through our web site.[2] I was also flattered recently to be asked by two dyslexia tutors at other institutions for permission to use the film as part of dyslexia awareness raising events they were running.

Often projects will end with a 'critique' where the student presents his or her work to the group and is required to justify it. This experience can be a nightmare for a student with slow verbal retrieval, which is made worse by the stress of being 'put on the spot'. I now run regular workshops to give students practice at talking about their work and I've found that giving them the opportunity to present within a supportive group has enabled them to build up confidence in a more public situation.

Although all subjects at the RCA are taught through projects, some subjects such as architecture may have more seminar- and lecture-based content while others such as ceramics, jewellery, printmaking and sculpture rely quite heavily on students learning through demonstrations. Learning through demonstration has its problems, particularly if a complicated sequence is involved. It occurred to me that having a video recording of the demonstration, which could act as an aide-memoire, would benefit not only dyslexic students but also foreign students and those whose family commitments sometimes prevent them from attending college. Last year I received funding from the Centre for Excellence in Teaching and Learning in Design (CETLD) to make the first of what I hope will become a series of demonstration videos called 'Legendary Masterclasses'. The first ones are on the RCA Virtual Learning Environment and the CETLD web site,[3] and a still image from these videos is shown in Figure 8.3.

When the 'Masterclass' video was presented to the funding organization, it was evident that the need for this type of resource was not clearly understood by a section of the audience. It was suggested that a further film be made explaining what makes a demonstration work well, or what could be done to improve it. In the film 'Learning Through

1 audacity.sourceforge.net.

2 http://www.rca.ac.uk/Default.aspx?ContentID=159535.

3 http://arts.brighton.ac.uk/research/cetld/learning-through-the-design-process/living-legend-masterclasses.

Figure 8.3 A still image from one of the 'Legendary Masterclass' videos.

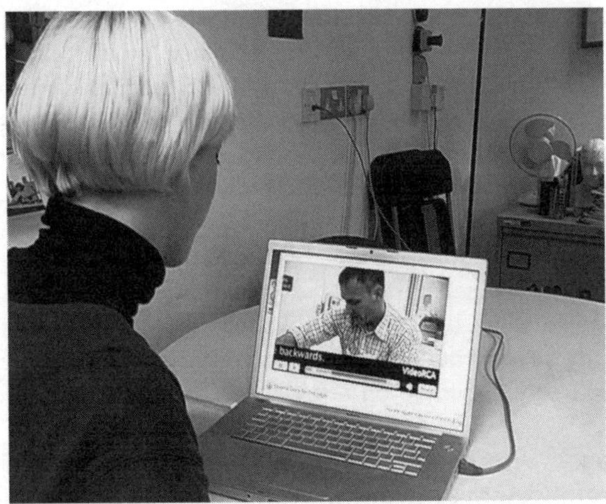

Figure 8.4 A still image from one of the 'Means to an End' videos.

Demonstration', which we are hoping will become part of a series called 'Means to an End: Enhancing Art and Design Teaching Methods for Students with Dyslexia', we interviewed a ceramics student, a jewellery student and a printmaker, and asked them to explain how demonstrations help to support their particular learning needs (this film is shortly to be on our college intranet – see also Figure 8.4).

The ceramics student, who has visual perceptual difficulties, said that he has no difficulty at all if he is trying to produce a positive form of something but that, when he has to make a negative mould, he finds it really difficult to work out which positive part relates to which part of the negative mould. He thought that seeing the product and having it there for the entire demonstration would be helpful. He also made the point that, when learning about working with plaster, demonstrations are often run in tandem so that while one lot of plaster is 'going off' another process can be demonstrated. He said the effect of this is that the two processes 'get all jumbled up' in his brain and he can't remember what sequence goes with what process. His solution was first to have the processes demonstrated in different areas of the workshop, and then to have the plaster in two colours; for instance, you could have the blue demonstration and the pink one. He also made the point that sometimes the vocabulary is very specific and so to have access to a glossary of terms might be helpful.

The jewellery student suggested that demonstrations were meaningless unless she actually got to have a go, so that she could translate the instructions into practice and remember what it felt like. The size of the group needed to be small enough to allow time for everyone to participate actively. The added benefit of this would be that you didn't feel so intimidated about asking questions. She also made the point that, as she had difficulty understanding words, it was much more helpful if the handouts were in picture rather than word format.

The printmaking student talked about how, when software was being demonstrated, she could make meaningful notes that would help her to navigate to a particular menu. She thought one-to-one sessions were vital so that the demonstrator could proceed at the student's preferred pace. She also observed that frequent ten-minute breaks should be built into the demonstration, enabling students to maintain concentration.

The Students Making a Difference to Dyslexia Support

One thing I hadn't considered when I started offering support to dyslexic students at the RCA was the effect that their ingenuity and generosity could have on producing resources for future generations of art and design students, and in some instances on dyslexia in the wider population.

During my second year at the college I was approached by a student called Natascha Frensch, who was developing a font to help with dyslexic reading difficulties. This font, which is now called Read Regular,[4] needed testing. Together we contacted some specialist schools and between us managed to test more then 100 dyslexic children. We gave them a passage from *Harry Potter* to read in different fonts, and it was extraordinary how their fluency improved as they read aloud text written in the Read Regular font.

The following year a dyslexic animation student called Emily Mantel showed her film *Gifted* as part of her graduation show (see a still from the film in Figure 8.5). This four-minute film communicates what it's like to be dyslexic so powerfully that I often find individuals weeping after seeing it. I regularly show it during dyslexia awareness-raising sessions and I know that, since it has been made freely available on our web site,[5] other professionals have used it in a similar context.

As part of the College's Diversity Week in 2009, we organized an exhibition of work made by our dyslexic and dyspraxic students. We had a private view with an invited

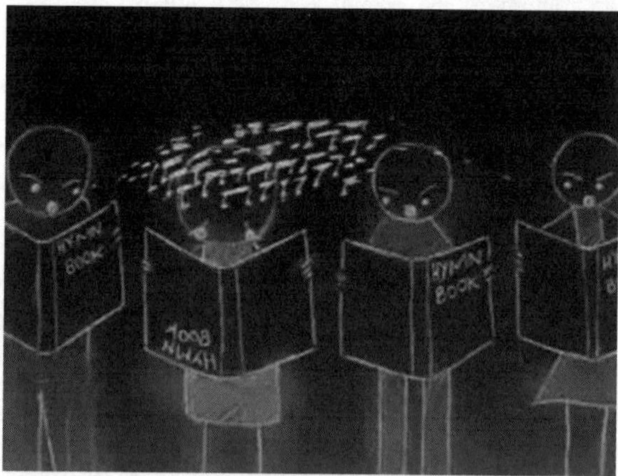

Figure 8.5 A still image from Emily Mantel's animated film *Gifted*.

4 www.readregular.com/english/intro.html.

5 http://www.rca.ac.uk/Default.aspx?ContentID=160532&groupID=160532.

audience of children, teachers and parents from Fairley House School, a specialist school in London for children with specific learning difficulties. Professor Robert Winston introduced the evening with a short address in which he emphasized the importance of encouraging all children to aim for their full potential. We then heard from three dyslexic students at Imperial College London, and three from the Royal College of Music, all of whom gave short presentations about their work. The questions and subsequent letters from the children showed how enthused they had been by the whole event. It has also led to an exciting and mutually rewarding relationship between the RCA and Fairley House.

One project that has developed out of this relationship is part of a new initiative at the RCA, called AcrossRCA. This offers students the opportunity to participate in one of a number of interdisciplinary collaborative projects. I will be running a project called 'Dyslexia, dyspraxia and maths', which I'm hoping will attract, in particular, animation, jewellery and product design students. This project will involve 12 to 15 dyslexic RCA students who will work with staff and pupils of Fairley House to develop materials to help secondary school children get to grips with basic mathematical procedures. The children and staff will comment on the results of the collaboration at the final presentation. I'm hoping that, by using their intimate experience of learning differences to produce practical outcomes, our students will be able to make use of their dyslexia to help future generations learn in ways that make abstract mathematical concepts easier to understand and remember.

Dyslexia and Drawing

I was particularly intrigued when, four years ago, having helped some students with their dissertations, they came back to see me and asked if I could help them with their drawing difficulties. They made remarks such as:

> When I have to draw things on the spot things start to go wrong. I'll try and draw a circle and it's never a circle. What I can see in my head I can't really get down on paper.
>
> *Jewellery student*

> I was doing a perspective drawing and it looked really right to me until I saw the rest of the class's drawings and I realized I'd got the perspective back-to-front if that makes sense.
>
> *Ceramics student*

> On my BA I was told by tutors that I couldn't draw. So I always used to photograph stuff and then photocopy the photographs, which I could then redraw over and work into an illustration, but it all took a long time.
>
> *Fashion student*

> In the life drawing studio I felt like a total idiot. The tears came from the inability to draw.
>
> *Ceramics student*

> If I've got a client and I'm drawing a cross section of a ring, I just confuse people, which can be quite embarrassing, if they're going to give me money for something and they just think she can't even draw it.
>
> *Jewellery student*

The students' remarks started me thinking about how drawing could be made more accessible to these and other students. I discussed this with Professor Alan Cummings, our Pro Rector, who was responsible for establishing Dyslexia Support, and who remains a much valued supporter. Alan encouraged me to establish an interdisciplinary research group to examine some of these issues. Pedagogic research into dyslexia and drawing has also been funded, because the committee appreciates the benefits of understanding and exploring different learning styles and unorthodox ways of teaching essential skills. This has enabled an exciting ongoing research collaboration between the RCA, Swansea Metropolitan University, University College London, and Middlesex University, which has recently produced some interesting findings (e.g. McManus *et al.* 2010; Riley *et al.* 2009).

I am also currently working with a student in Interaction Design on a project concerning learning to read musical notation for aspiring musicians with dyslexia. The Royal College of Music seemed an obvious place to look for collaborators and I believe this is now starting to happen. I can't wait to see what will emerge.

On February 18, 2009, at the suggestion of the RCA Alumni Officer, Mark Parkin, I co-hosted an alumni/dyslexia support evening called 'Dyslexia in the Workplace and the Classroom'. As part of the presentation I invited five dyslexic or dyspraxic alumni who are all working successfully in the fashion, textile, ceramics and sculpture professions to show slides of their work and to talk about how they had overcome aspects of professional practice that had been difficult for them because of their dyslexia or dyspraxia. The examples of customized strategies they shared with the audience was a testimony to the enormous creativity, perseverance and determination to succeed of the individuals involved and, as I later discovered from emails, was a source of tremendous inspiration to many in the audience.

The first alumni speaker was Ian Scott Kettle (Fashion Womenswear 2007), a practitioner for 18 years. As a practitioner, teacher and student, Ian had realized that, although his creative activities remained unaffected by his dyslexia and dyspraxia, it was establishing the 'structure' that went round them that was the problem (especially as he had also suffered from epilepsy from the age of 13).

Ian felt that the key step was to understand exactly what dyslexia and dyspraxia are and to deal with them as an individual. He had started working in the fashion industry in the early 1990s, and he found himself not just producing his work but having to present it to clients, and this was when things became difficult for him. Ian then gave his tips for teaching, selling, doing and working. He said that, in all these situations, he tries to find ways of explaining that he has this issue. He also takes photographs of all his students, clients and manufacturers, and puts their names with them. He tries to make a linear understanding of his day by colour-coding his activities.

When it came to reading material (Ian was also doing his teacher training), he read only the first paragraph and the last paragraph of every chapter (i.e. the Introduction and the Summary) and found that this had worked for him so far. He had also started doing something similar with the lectures he attends, getting all the available handouts beforehand, reading them through, then attending the first 20 minutes and last 10 minutes of an hour-long lecture. It sounds rude, but he knows he won't process the information if he doesn't leave the lecture for this period. When it comes to reading fiction books, he knows that he has a problem with structure so he creates 'family trees' to plot all the characters in the book. For meetings he 'sounds out' the area beforehand to make sure there will be no distractions and he makes sure that he sits in a place in the room that he finds conducive to concentration.

Finally, Ian said that he felt many people treated dyslexia as if it was a bit of a joke, but that it was of course a serious issue for which you have to develop a coping mechanism. He always tells people about his 'condition' and how it affects him – he is 'out and proud'. He finds, if he does that, be it with clients, manufacturers or 16-year-old students, they are perfectly happy with it and give him the space in which to function.

The next speaker, Vanessa Rolf (Constructed Textiles 2004) confessed that 'lack of preparation' was one of her issues, and that this would be reflected in her talk. Vanessa is an artist with her own studio who takes part in residencies and who also works as part of one of our projects, called ReachOutRCA (this is the College's outreach scheme for secondary school pupils). In this role Vanessa has to fundraise, project manage, write reports, and also complete funding applications. So she understandably felt she had possibly given herself the worst job she could as someone who is both dyslexic and dyspraxic!

She had been diagnosed only when she came to the RCA, however, as the environment of the College made her question how she coped with things such as the pressure of study. Unfortunately it was too late for her to obtain help during her studies, but Vanessa did receive help after she became Student Union President, receiving a year of 'counselling' on how to deal with her dyslexia/dyspraxia issues. What she found particularly invaluable was having someone to help her identify which of her problems related to her own personality, and which were due to her dyslexia/dyspraxia.

As her short-term memory was very poor, Vanessa said she felt that her coping mechanisms were inefficient; she is very easily distracted, does not prioritize jobs well, and has various time-management issues. However, now that she knows these problems are due to her dyslexia/dyspraxia, she can begin to address them. Plus, her job is helping her to deal with them: if she can write a funding proposal for ReachOutRCA, then she can write one for a Residency.

Next, Alex Metcalf (Design Products 2007) wanted to discuss how dyslexia affected his work, particularly his RCA graduation project; this was a device that allows people to hear water moving inside trees. Since graduating he had been travelling to different parts of the country – to parks and botanical gardens – to put in place an installation that allows the public to do the same, using hanging headphones. In relation to this, Alex wanted to talk about a particular aspect of his dyslexia: his poor short-term memory. The example he gave of this was that, although he had been able to grasp the quite complex details of how a tree functions, he wasn't easily able to identify the trees he was studying, which could be quite embarrassing. Alex revealed that he had a particular problem with trees with similar leaves, such as an elm or a lime, but had managed to learn the more general types. It seems that the very simplicity of the problem makes it difficult, with Alex finding it much easier to remember the more complex things. He is currently trying to find ways of dealing with this.

Stephen Graham (Ceramics and Glass 2007) had just started work as a part-time lecturer at Liverpool Hope University and found that certain aspects of his dyslexia had become apparent again. He had struggled with reading and writing for as long as he could remember, muddling through until he came to the RCA and was assessed for dyslexia. Stephen said the dyslexia support team had given him very useful advice regarding organization, such as keeping everything within small, manageable time brackets, and not letting pride stop him from acknowledging that he needed help. He had particular trouble with grammar and the written word, but obtained help from his cousin, a proofreader, when it came to checking his dissertation.

However, when Stephen left the RCA, he felt that he had lost the 'security' of the RCA dyslexia support and became more reliant on his friends for competitions and applications.

When he was appointed as a part-time lecturer in Liverpool, initially everything was fine – he had no problem doing the project briefs for example, but he came unstuck when he had to write down tutorials and give feedback about them, then 'panic-mode' set in. He sought advice from friends, including Ian Scott Kettle, which helped. Stephen concluded by saying that it was an ongoing struggle with new problems being thrown up that required the development of new coping strategies.

The final alumnus speaker was Kate McGwire (Sculpture 2004). She arrived at the RCA aged 38, but had suspected throughout childhood and early adulthood that she was dyslexic. In particular she had experienced numerous problems with writing, and she avoided written work whenever possible. She had become very adept at hiding her secret as she grew up, without realizing how much she was holding herself back. When she left school she did various jobs but, whenever things became difficult at work, she just left. So, being assessed when she arrived at the RCA, and actually acknowledging she had a problem, was very enlightening. Openly sharing with people who had similar problems was an incredible release, although she found the amount of additional work she had to put in to improve her problem areas was really daunting. However, some of the techniques she was taught really helped her to work on gaps in her work and in her personal life.

Kate said she was fortunate that at the 2004 RCA Graduation Show her piece 'Brood' was bought by the Saatchi Collection and displayed in their gallery. At the time she thought she was made, but soon realized after leaving College that having good work was not enough. Although she could talk about her work confidently, when she had to write about it, that confidence ebbed away. Fortunately, in 2006 she met an arts journalist who agreed to help her with the written side of her work. So now, whenever Kate has to write a proposal, she brainstorms, then meets with the journalist, shows her drawings, explains what she is trying to do, and gives her a list of words from her 'brainstorm'. The journalist forces her to articulate her ideas, then goes away to create a piece of writing that is invariably spot on. Their collaboration keeps Kate on her toes, and being able to discuss her ideas with someone regularly is incredibly beneficial to her. Luckily, the journalist likes Kate's work enough to take it in lieu of payment!

Kate is currently working on her web site, which she finds to be an invaluable tool. It means that prospective buyers have immediate access to images of her work and written statements, and therefore she doesn't need to send them out.

Kate tries to be disciplined with regard to filling in the necessary forms for her work; she knows that they won't be completed otherwise. In fact, she has to spend a lot of time on administration, which she finds frustrating, especially as she has a phobia of filling in forms and hasn't yet taken up the challenge of filling in an Arts Council England application (though she believes it is now possible to obtain individual help with that).

Finally, Kate said that her teenage son is now showing signs of dyslexia, and would be tested for it soon. She is determined that he will receive the help that she didn't receive at that age, and that he will be proud and self-confident in whatever he chooses to do.

The alumni stories about individuals' creative ways of overcoming their difficulties, my experiences of working with the RCA students, and a book called *Proust and the Squid: The Story and Science of the Reading Brain* (Wolf 2008) combined to propel me towards setting up a charity to help year 7 and 8 schoolchildren with dyslexia and dyspraxia. The charity trains dyslexic/dyspraxic arts graduates in a basic awareness and understanding of the issues to enable them to build on their own experiences and offer alternative teaching strategies to dyslexic/dyspraxic children. The graduates are then placed within the Art, Design and Technology departments of secondary state schools to work alongside existing staff. The aim is to help them to develop their own strategies with individual students, leading to a much more inclusive approach to teaching their specialist subjects. In addition to working within the arts curricula, the graduates also work alongside Special Educational Needs tutors to give dyslexic children additional help and encouragement over lunchtimes and after school. The charity is now in its second year.

Conclusion

It seems to me that within dyslexic art and design students there is a huge untapped potential. There is also clear willingness amongst staff and students to develop support strategies that will make the ways and means used to teach and work within art and design even more accessible and inclusive. This will, I hope, complement the tried and tested techniques already employed to help with reading and writing difficulties. Certainly, at the RCA, this spirit of innovation and trying new approaches seems to be paying huge dividends. It's not so much a case of:

↔ 'give and take' but more a case of:

⟳ 'give and take and then give back.'

Acknowledgements

Images in this chapter used with kind permission of the Royal College of Art.

References

McManus, I.C., Chamberlain, R., Loo, P.-W. *et al.* (2010) Art students who cannot draw: An exploration of the relations between personality, dyslexia, perceptual problems and drawing skills. *Psychology of Aesthetics, Creativity, and the Arts*, 4, 18–30.

Riley, H., Rankin, Q., Brunswick, N. *et al.* (2009) Inclusive Practice: Researching the relationships between dyslexia, personality, and art students' drawing ability. *Include 2009 Proceedings: Conference on Inclusive Design*, Royal College of Art, London.

Wolf, M. (2008) *Proust and the Squid: The story and science of the reading brain*, Icon Books, London.

9

Dyslexia, eLearning and eSkills

E.A. Draffan, University of Southampton, UK

eLearning

At one time the use of computer-based or digital technologies was considered marginal to many learning and teaching practices, with most materials being produced on paper. Now in the UK most institutions offer a mix of environments with face-to-face situations complementing electronic learning (elearning) or technology enhanced learning (TEL). The problem for those of us trying to understand elearning is that this type of teaching and learning varies enormously. Although usually computer-based, it can range from the use of complex virtual learning environments (VLEs) with course information, timetables, discussion forums, lecture or class notes and web links all in one place, to a series of different types of materials collected together on a teacher's home page or the school intranet, with the use of portable technologies as part of the mix.

Increasing numbers of students are accessing their learning via their mobile phone, a device that is always to hand, well used and almost 'a must have accessory'. For students, the small screen of a smart mobile phone is 'a window to an infinite space' (Prensky 2004), and an enhanced communication device through which they are able to watch videos, listen to podcasts, initiate discussions, question tutors, reflect on their learning at any time and in any situation. This means that those developing learning materials are destined to take into account the fact that they are working in a rapidly changing technological environment. These changes require flexible use of multiple and alternative formats wherever possible to encourage and engage all learners. Developers and teachers need to be aware of the increasing number of presentation platforms regularly used by students that may better suit their personal preferences allowing for colour, font, text to speech and other adaptations. Not everyone will have technology with accessibility settings built in – they may have to be added to the learning materials.

Virtual learning environments and Content Management Systems tend to be hosted on a network of computers made up of a variety of different software services and applications containing files and folders; some of these can be reached only via a secure intranet at school or on the college or university campus. Most learning environments are viewed via a browser such as Internet Explorer, Mozilla Firefox, Opera, Chrome or Safari, whether on a computer, netbook or smartphone. The learning environment would have its own navigation system as well as that of the browser. This can be quite confusing for some students, with secondary menus and additional home or back buttons. Not all systems allow for customization of the format such as colour changes to backgrounds, font resizing, and enhancements such as increased white space to improve readability. The area containing the

Supporting Dyslexic Adults in Higher Education and the Workplace, First Edition. Edited by Nicola Brunswick.

course materials can appear cluttered and may even lack good search facilities. It is important to be able to search for courses as well as the documents within the courses.

Course leaders are often unaware of these issues and fail to allow time for training to set up personal preferences alongside the best way to use the system. Students may receive a quick session on the main features of the system at the beginning of a term and then not use it for many weeks, which can make it hard for them to remember some aspects of the set-up. It is important to make sure that features that allow for changes to be made to the look and feel of the VLE are available to all users, whether via the specific application or the desktop settings on the laboratory or library computers.

The use of multimedia content such as podcasts with audio presentations or videos can lead to a wider take-up of online learning materials. Some students find the alternatives complement their text-based learning, while others find the audio versions provide essential 'overlearning'. Uploading course slides alongside documents and journal articles, plus web links to other information, can also aid note-taking and encourage further research. However, some dyslexic students can find the sheer volume of online materials a concern and need guidance as to how to prioritize their reading and make best use of essential materials.

As has been mentioned, elearning can be a mix of face-to-face learning with time spent online, also known as blended learning, or totally based on a distance learning arrangement where the entire course is carried out online, often in a similar fashion to the way Open University courses are run. These courses require considerable text input, with online forums and discussion groups. Text to speech can help with the reading but good spell-checking features and speech recognition software may be required to speed input and assist with fluency of writing.

The complexities of enabling students to initiate and enjoy the discursive nature of collaboration within an elearning environment can be daunting for all involved. In discussion forums, students may unwittingly 'go off subject' or use inappropriate language without realizing the possible outcomes, which may impact on the group as a whole. Negative feelings can creep in, with the more vulnerable students lacking the courage to engage. Others may be so used to the unstructured nature of their web-based 'chats' or messages in a social context that it is hard for them to use more formal language and follow guided themes. Some find the type of discussion forum that has many different subject lines within the topic threads unfolding down a web page both muddling and hard to read. There is a need to define clearly each topic space, with guidelines as to how subject lines will evolve and content remain directed to the subject matter. One idea that may help is to have a main topic or group inserted in brackets before the subject line, for example Re:[History] Research Project for the summer.

There are, however, many advantages to enhancing knowledge through the use of online or web-based resource materials as long as they are accessible. Accessible, in this case, refers to the flexibility of use and personalization of presentation, as has been mentioned. When working on a computer or handheld device where the actual text or graphics contained in a book, document or web page are accessible, the content can be separated from the display. This means that the content displayed can be changed in many ways, which is not possible when reading from paper (other than by using an external magnifier, or coloured overlays for changing the overall look). Learning support features such as summaries and keyword highlights can be added, and links to more information or discussion opportunities can lead to further interaction.

Accessibility also includes the chance to make the most of additional assistive technologies, which may include productivity tools such as spell-checkers, as well as free and open source applications that work with specific browsers or provide unique services such as conversion of audio files to Mp3 format for playing on portable devices.

The more sophisticated assistive technologies, such as text to speech, allow for minutely controlled screen reading or text to speech with pausing, different rates of reading, a wide range of voices and word highlighting, where the user can decide what is read aloud and the colours needed. Magnification can be used to clarify text, and scanning with optical character recognition to allow access to digital text that appears as an image.

Some portable document formats (pdfs) are saved as pictures, which means that, although they can be seen on both a computer screen and mobile device such as a smartphone, they may not be used with a text to speech application without virtual scanning and recognition, which takes time. Some students like to be able to dull the glare of black text on a white background with the use of a pale coloured background such as pink, cream or pale blue, and to add wider line spacing.

It is also possible to save texts in digital talking book formats such as 'Daisy', which works with the chapter and subheadings, page numbers, bookmarks and other navigational aspects provided by style sheets. When users want to have the book read back, they can jump to the desired chapters and pages for easy reading. Key elements can be found and the contents table can act as an interactive series of links to further areas within the book. As mentioned, it is also possible to have text read with highlighting, to help users follow the words as they listen. There are the commercially available Dolphin EasyConverter and EasyPublisher with EasyReader[1] software applications that offer the user a way of converting books and texts into navigable interactive files. Freely available macros for Microsoft Word document conversion and open source players also make it possible to enjoy digital talking books or simple audio Mp3 files for listening on portable digital players.

Technology-enhanced learning, which is now the term used by many rather than elearning or online learning, can allow for review and revision with formative assessment for feedback during a course. It enables those who are used to working in a digital world to take examinations in a format that matches their daily experiences rather than handwriting in an unfamiliar environment. Students can engage with others across the world on subjects of shared interest and often work with learning materials that come from other educational institutions, provided in alternative formats that may not be available within their own virtual learning environment.

eSkills

The rapid increase and complexities of elearning platforms have resulted in escalating training implications for us all when it comes to making the most of elearning environments. Most teachers and lecturers will be using applications such as Microsoft Word, Excel, PowerPoint, and web-based quiz tools along with Adobe Acrobat PDF documents. These programs are being used in very exciting ways, but are now seen as adjuncts to the world of online environments that include terms such as 'Web 2.0' (O'Reilly 2005) where immediate interaction and collaboration can take place. The virtual learning environment of the enclosed Blackboard[2] or Moodle[3] domain has moved into the wiki, blog and social networking world. Wikis allow for information to be developed in collaboration with others, and blogs are like a diary or journal that encourages comments as feedback between readers. Instant access to more collaborative forms of learning is also possible with the sharing of online documents, calendars and journal articles with short instant messaging about topics, such as is seen on Twitter,[4] and conversational messages in FaceBook.[5] However, not all the assistive technologies work so well within the user's browser environment, and not all browsers react in the same way when they present content. Some students may find they are composing using Microsoft Word and then cutting and pasting their work into a blog for fear of losing the work and to make use of Word's

[1] See: www.yourdolphin.com.
[2] www.blackboard.com.
[3] moodle.org.
[4] www.twitter.com.
[5] www.facebook.com.

better spell-checking features, despite the extra time this takes. Others express concern about editing wikis for fear of making mistakes or peers criticizing their additions.

The problems of skills linked to successful elearning engagement are myriad but, for those developing the materials, there is a need to be very aware of accessibility requirements. Students also need to know how to make the most of the available assistive technologies and which choice of technology best suits a given situation.

There are numerous guides on how to make online documents accessible, such as the JISC TechDis Accessibility Essentials and the LexDis guides,[6] but the important thing to remember is that it is so much easier to include aspects of good design that aid accessibility at the outset rather than trying to retrofit. Perhaps the most important features that make documents easier to read are:

- Use **styles and templates** provided by the application. Create headings and subheadings (Heading 1, 2, 3, etc.) using styles, not just bolded, enlarged or centred text. Use easy-to-read templates offered in PowerPoint. Make sure your fonts are readable, preferably size 12 or 14, or 44 down to 32 for presentations. When working directly online such as in a blog or wiki, white space and clear layout are essential.
- Use **picture descriptions known as 'alternative (alt) text tags'** for all graphics including graphs and clip art. Use simple one- or two-word explanations that can be seen when the mouse lands on the image or heard by the screen reader. Try not to use background images that add clutter to text.
- Use **page numbers** for easy navigation, and **bulleted or numbered lists** using the menu button and built-in styles, *not* just symbols and spaces, so that quick navigation is possible. Web pages need clear menus, good search features and clarity of content.
- Make sure all **tables have headers** across the top. Table row and column titles should be concise and, if possible, provide a summary of important elements so they make sense when text is read aloud.
- Ensure **good colour contrast** within charts and images and for text, if this is important for explaining items. Check this by printing out in black and white. Texts that can reflow easily and contain graphics that resize are a bonus on mobile technologies when it comes to easy reading.

Developers who provide web pages and documents with the above elements will help assistive technology users. However, students need to know when and how to use the different features within their assistive technology programs in order to make the most of each option. Just comparing two well-known applications sometimes found on institutional networks illustrates some of the differences. The TextHelp Read and Write[7] speech button works with Word, PowerPoint, Excel and web page reading, but PDFAloud needs to be used for Adobe Acrobat documents. You can choose to have single words read, or sentences or paragraphs. When using ClaroRead,[8] you can have the text read within the document or load Accessible PDF reader, and then you can change the colour of the text background, fonts, etc. Complex documents that appear as pictures or diagrams may need to be accessed using the TextHelp Screenshot Reader that copes with small samples of text, or optical character recognition systems providing text output from virtual scanning systems within the applications.

When using the latest version of TextHelp Read and Write it is possible to set up a 'screen mask' to colour-tint the whole screen or just the sections that are being read. This can be very helpful to mask out distracting areas on web sites or when reading down a long page. It is also possible to achieve this with Claro Screenruler, or with settings in ClaroRead that allow for underlining, and for different sections to be highlighted as they are read aloud. Again,

[6] www.lexdis.org.uk/guide.

[7] www.texthelp.com.

[8] www.clarosoftware.com.

this can help concentration and to maintain position on a page whilst reading. ClaroView allows for the entire screen to be colour tinted.

It should be noted that there are many other software programs that offer similar features, such as Don Johnston's Solo collection,[9] which has word prediction software (Co:Writer) and read/write software (Write:Outloud) and Dolphin's EasyTutor. There are also free alternatives such as WordTalk,[10] working with Microsoft Word and ReadPlease,[11] which can be used online. There are also applications that can be held on a USB pen drive – many can be found on the JISC Regional Support Centre Scotland North and East 'eduapps'[12] web pages but, once again, support may be needed to put together an appropriate assistive technology toolkit. The advantage of having assistive technologies on a pen drive is that they are available for use with any computer across an organization (as long as a USB port is available).

There are times when students need to learn how to find information online using the equivalent of a Boolean search. This was used by librarians as a card indexing system, long before modern computers were linked to the internet, with words such as 'and', 'not' and 'near'. Rather than using words, it may be easier for students to substitute mathematical symbols such as '+' and '-' for 'and' and 'not', or inverted commas on either side of a query for 'near'. This method for searching has become as important as learning the ramifications of the Dewey system for finding books on the shelves in a library.

The most commonly used online search engine is Google[13] but, if you just type in a keyword for a project or essay, the likelihood is that you will have millions of results to work through. This is difficult enough for someone who can scan-read, but even harder for those who have difficulties reading large amounts of information. Using the advanced search with any search engine usually offers the Boolean logic mentioned above. Google has some very helpful instructions (see Google Advanced search support[14]) but it can also be useful to try specialist search sites – these are listed by Wikipedia[15] under specified subject areas. Some general examples used by university students include Google scholar for academic journals. Others are Google books, when students want to use text-to-speech with the books they have online, and Google maps when they need to find a place they wish to visit or view as part of a project.

When developing strategies for organizations using elearning, it may be helpful to create a 'Statement of Technology', addressing the issues of computer skill levels. This can help to provide a process for coping with the differing levels of expertise that staff and students have for learning technologies, the use of assistive technologies and the development of online learning materials. The statement may include guidelines related to each elearning environment, with information about accessibility, for instance whether it is possible to use text-to-speech or change any elements within the learning materials or application to suit the learner. It may also be essential to provide checklists for students' technology skills as frustration can creep in when access is not easy and valuable learning time is lost.

Ideas for Making Working Online Easier

Many students with dyslexia experience difficulties related to the processing of written language. These problems are sometimes compounded by short-term memory difficulties, a

[9] www.donjohnston.com.
[10] www.wordtalk.org.uk.
[11] www.readplease.com.
[12] www.eduapps.org.
[13] www.google.co.uk.
[14] www.google.com/support/websearch.
[15] en.wikipedia.org/wiki/List_of_search_engines.

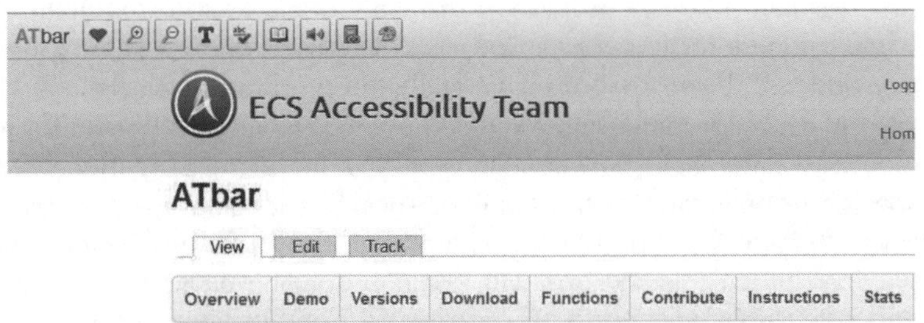

Figure 9.1 The ATbar toolbar.

lack of organizational skills, and time management issues, which all impact on learning within an online system.

The clear presentation of materials is vital, with good navigational assistance and a variety of multimedia options to tap into both visual and auditory skills. The interaction with learning materials can also help memory. Being able to watch a YouTube video[16] on a topic, as well as read notes and make comments as reminders, can all help learning. YouTube has an easy to use player[17] with larger coloured buttons that may be useful. The free open source project Synote[18] allows for synchronized transcriptions to be uploaded or to be linked automatically with videos and audio, as well as annotations that can act as synchronized bookmarks for finding information when it comes to revising.

Viewing web pages that have black text on white can be difficult for some, and it may help to use a quick way of changing colours such as Accessibar, a Mozilla Firefox add-on[19] that also allows magnification, increased line spacing and items read aloud when the text-to-speech addition has been added. Internet Explorer has similar features within the tools menu, and 'My Web My Way' offers easy instructions for changing the look of accessible web pages.[20] The freely available open source ATbar toolbar[21] works with most browsers as a bookmark and offers similar options, including text to speech and a dictionary. The code for the toolbar can be embedded into any web site or learning environment, as demonstrated on the ATbar web site[22] (see Figure 9.1).

Some elearning includes collaboration, for example having a discussion online in a synchronous way rather than being able to write, think about it and then send a note, as with email. This immediacy tends to lead to concerns about writing skills. There is always the option of composing in a word processor package like Microsoft Word, and copying the text into the online editor, then using a chosen spell-checker, or using a free program such as Windows LiveWriter that has a built in spell-checker and works directly with several messaging and blogging services.[23]

Many online text editors that are used for uploading text to the web have what looks like a word processor menu bar but some come without a built-in spell-checker. When using a browser such as Internet Explorer or Mozilla Firefox it is possible to use TextHelp Read and Write Gold to spell-check, but some students seem to forget about their specialist assistive

[16] www.youtube.com.
[17] icant.co.uk/easy-youtube.
[18] www.synote.org.
[19] https://addons.mozilla.org/en-US/firefox/addon/4242.
[20] http://www.bbc.co.uk/accessibility.
[21] http://access.ecs.soton.ac.uk/projects/toolbar.
[22] http://access.ecs.soton.ac.uk/projects/toolbar/demo.
[23] http://explore.live.com/windows-live-writer.

technologies at this stage. It is also possible to use the Google toolbar[24] with the spell-check button added. Internet Explorer has a free download ieSpell,[25] and for Firefox there is a British dictionary add-in.[26] These spell-checkers will turn errors red when the checker is started, or underline them in a similar manner to Microsoft Word. However, it should be noted that there are considerable differences between the quality of the browser spell-checkers and those available as specialist applications with phonic or specialist spelling lists available to users. Examples such as TextHelp Read and Write, ClaroRead, EasyTutor and Oribi VeritySpell[27] have been developed specifically to cope with complex spelling errors rather than simple letter transpositions or single-letter errors. These specialist applications are often able to correct over 70% of the errors made, whereas the browser spell-checker may reach only around 50% accuracy.

Google has offered other ways of collaborative writing with Google docs, and a calendar that can be synchronized with Outlook and mobile phone calendars to help with organization. There are also free online mind-mapping tools such as Mindmeister[28] or Gliffy.[29] Neither is as powerful as their desktop counterparts, such as MindManager,[30] Mind Genius[31] or Inspiration,[32] but they can help when working in an elearning situation if you want to share maps with others in the same way that you can share pictures on Flickr[33] or videos on YouTube. Of course, you can share your thoughts in 140 characters with a quick tweet using Twitter,[34] and there is an accessible version of this service[35] that looks less cluttered and works well with screen readers. All too much? Jane Hart has a very useful web site that follows the latest trends in Web 2.0 and elearning from an educational perspective – the latest news can be sent to you via email if you follow her Pick of the Day.[36]

There are so many ways of sharing and learning online that this chapter can only scratch the surface of this subject but, if you want to see some of the strategies, productivity tools and assistive technologies that students at the University of Southampton are using to help with their elearning, visit the homepage of the LexDis project at www.lexdis.org.uk.

References

O'Reilly, T. (2005) *Design patterns and business models for the next generation of software*, available at oreilly.com/web2/archive/what-is-web-20.html, accessed September 21, 2011.

Prensky, M. (2004) *What can you learn from a cell phone? Almost anything!* Available at http://www.marcprensky.com/writing, accessed September 21, 2011.

[24] http://www.google.com/intl/en_uk/toolbar/ff/index.html (for use with Firefox); http://www.google.com/intl/en_uk/toolbar/ie/index.html (for use with Internet Explorer) accessed September 28, 2011.

[25] www.iespell.com.

[26] https://addons.mozilla.org/en-US/firefox/addon/3366.

[27] http://www.dyslexic.com/itemMatrix.asp?GroupCode=VetitySpell&eq=&MatrixType=1.

[28] www.mindmeister.com.

[29] www.gliffy.com.

[30] www.Mindjet.com.

[31] www.mindgenius.com.

[32] www.inspiration.com.

[33] www.flickr.com.

[34] www.twitter.com.

[35] www.accessibletwitter.com.

[36] janeknight.typepad.com.

10

Reading Comprehension in Adult Students with Dyslexia

Areas of Weakness and Strategies for Support

Rob Fidler, University of Surrey, UK and John Everatt, University of Canterbury, New Zealand

Introduction

The present chapter focuses on text understanding amongst students with dyslexia in tertiary education contexts, though the issues covered should have similarities in the workplace. Students in higher education (HE) will form the main group from which the present conclusions were derived. From an educational perspective, this is an important group to consider (see Du Pre, Gilroy and Miles 2007). Increasing numbers of students with dyslexia are entering HE within the UK. Government statistics indicate that the number of known first-year students with a specific learning difficulty on entry was 10,430 in 2000/1; 21,000 in 2004/5; and 30,415 in 2008/9.[1] This group, along with those who are assessed while at university/college, requires strategies to enable successful course outcomes, to gain academic qualifications consistent with their ability in the topic studied and to enter the workforce as graduates with skills that should enable them to attain and retain employment.

Literacy is the focus of the present discussion due to its being the main area of difficulty for students with dyslexia that leads to poor educational success, but which appropriate education-based strategies can go a long way to overcome. Text understanding is the literacy skill that adult education students need to use frequently in their studies in order to access course material. Although HE students are the focus of the work discussed in this chapter, low levels of literacy skills are a potential problem in the workplace also. A 1993 government report estimated that 60% of all jobs required a reasonable level of literacy, and that the cost to the economy of illiteracy within the UK workforce was estimated at over £10 billion per annum (Stainthorpe 2002). Over the past 17 years this cost has continued to rise and those who experience difficulties in developing literacy skills, for whatever reason, find themselves at a disadvantage compared to their literate counterparts. Therefore, the present discussion will focus on strategies that may be useful for adults with dyslexia when studying at college/university level and which should also support dealing with text in a work environment. Specific reference will be made to both learning strategies and technological solutions; though, for clarity, the chapter will start with a brief discussion of the view of reading that underpins the current work, and data describing the reading characteristics shown by tertiary-level students with dyslexia.

[1] www.hesa.ac.uk (accessed 2010).

Supporting Dyslexic Adults in Higher Education and the Workplace, First Edition. Edited by Nicola Brunswick.

The Reading Process

Reading is a complex skill and problems can occur at different points in the decoding, assimilation and interpretation of text. Many current theories of reading have adopted an interactive approach that suggests that a strength or weakness in one sphere of reading can have an impact upon another. Stanovich (1980) states how individuals with reading difficulties in one domain can overcome weaknesses by being more reliant on another level in the reading process, as he says:

> Higher-level processes can actually compensate for deficiencies in lower level processes. Thus a reader with poor word recognition skills may actually be prone to a greater reliance on contextual factors because these provide additional sources of information. (*Stanovich 1980, pp. 35–36*)

Additionally, many theorists in the field of reading research contend that, despite the multitude of factors affecting reading acquisition and development, the process can be divided into two key spheres: decoding and comprehension. This is often referred to as the simple model of reading (Gough, Hoover and Peterson 1996; Hoover and Gough 1990). Dyslexia is associated with decoding deficits that may be due to poor phonological processing skills (see Gillon 2004; Snowling 2000). However, poor reading can also be due to other factors such as weak comprehension skills (see discussions in Cain and Oakhill 2007; Snowling and Hulme 2005). Such weak comprehension skills can occur for several reasons. For example, Oakhill and Yuill (1996) state that comprehension difficulties arise from weaknesses in inference making, understanding text structure and comprehension monitoring, whereas Stothard and Hulme (1996) argue that weaknesses in decoding, global comprehension difficulties and weak metacognition are the main culprits of reading comprehension failure. Cornoldi, De Beni and Pazzaglia (1996) highlighted three factors that warranted further scrutiny when understanding reading difficulties: (i) working memory (a form of short-term memory that allows the concurrent retention and processing of information); (ii) metacognition (the idea of the individual thinking about how to perform the task in hand); and (iii) listening comprehension (the ability to draw meaning from spoken language). Each of these areas may need to be considered when developing reading comprehension support packages for HE students with dyslexia.

An important assumption of the simple model of reading has been that as readers gain in knowledge and experience they become more fluent and efficient in their decoding skills and can concentrate their energies on comprehending texts. Hence, poor decoding can impact on comprehension in several ways. If the reader is unable to decode a word, the meaning of that word will not be available to assimilate with other words, thereby reducing understanding. However, the interactive nature of the reading system may support decoding through the processing of the meaning of words around the word that is presenting difficulties: i.e., the context within which a word is written may allow the meaning of a non-decoded word to be inferred. This, though, may relate to a second source of reduced comprehension. Resources that can be used to help determine a correct interpretation of text are absorbed by inefficient decoding processes. Non-decoded words in a text may also have to be reread once context has been processed, leading to slowed reading that may impact on comprehension if storage is time-limited. Basically, some information may be forgotten if reading is very slow, leading to understanding being incomplete or to the recall of details being limited (and, possibly, to the need to reread). Strategies that can be used to reduce the reliance on time-limited storage, which typically relate to storage via meaning, may prove helpful to negate this impact. Finally, a focus on decoding may mean that comprehension strategies are not practised, leading to lower skills in these areas of reading (i.e., a form of Matthew effect in which poor reading leads to a lack of practice that makes reading levels fall even further behind expectations; see Stanovich 1986), and to the need for such strategies to be taught. How these differing factors interact within a particular individual will determine success of comprehension and influence the way reading is performed (i.e., its characteristics).

Literacy Characteristics Related to Adult Dyslexia

Dyslexia has been seen as a problem with acquiring accurate and/or fluent word reading and spelling despite adequate learning opportunity (see working definition of the British Psychological Society 1999). The main characteristics of dyslexia in childhood are problems with word-level literacy that are associated with weak word decoding (i.e., translating between a written word and its verbal language equivalent) and poor phonological processing (the ability to process efficiently sounds within words). Similar dyslexia-related weaknesses can be found in adulthood during further education (Beaton, McDougall and Singleton 1997; Patton and Polloway 1996; Ramus *et al.* 2003) and these may impact on employment when performing a job search or completing an application form. They can also become a problem when the individual is required to process written text as part of a change of job specification, an upgrade, or a promotion (see discussions in: Fitzgibbon and O'Connor 2002; McLoughlin, Leather and Stringer 2002; Reid, Came and Price 2008).

Therefore, some of the basic features of childhood dyslexia can characterize dyslexia in adulthood, though the specific manifestation of literacy problems presented in adulthood may be different from, or more variable than, that found in children. For example, Miles (1993) has argued that reading accuracy may not be as reliable an indicator of dyslexia in adults as spelling ability, and this may be particularly the case amongst those who reach tertiary education. Whereas some individuals with dyslexia continue to perform poorly on tests of word reading accuracy throughout their life, others can score reasonably well on such measures but show evidence of slow reading speeds or lack of confidence in literacy tasks (see Brooks, Everatt and Fidler 2004; McLoughlin, Fitzgibbon and Young 1994).

As discussed above, those with continued poor reading accuracy are likely to show poor reading comprehension levels whereas those with reasonable accuracy scores may show good comprehension levels, particularly when ease and speed of basic reading processes are not vital (see Lesaux, Pearson and Siegel 2006; Simmons and Singleton 2000). Hence, there is likely to be variability in word reading accuracy between adults with dyslexia but differences may be found also in the ability to comprehend text – and this will be the case whether the comparison is across students or the performance of the same individual across different reading contexts.

Research also suggests that children with dyslexia, on average, show evidence of relatively larger effects of word meaning compared to their peers (Nation and Snowling 1998). This is consistent with the findings in adulthood suggesting that those with reasonable accuracy levels may compensate for poor word decoding skills by determining the gist of a text; this allows them to infer the meaning of words with which they are struggling. Therefore, it seems the case that, if ease of reading is not exceeded too much, and adult dyslexic readers are given enough time to use context-based strategies to support decoding and improve identification of the meaning of individual words, then their reading comprehension may be at a similar level to that of their non-dyslexic peers (Elbro, Nielsen and Petersen 1994; Jackson and Doelinger 2002). Although this semantic-based reading strategy may not be the most efficient way of processing text (see also Stanovich 1980), it may be sufficient in many cases. Hence, the literacy problems associated with dyslexia in adults would be more likely to be identified via measures of:

- reading rate rather than accuracy
- continued poor spelling
- inefficient decoding (i.e., in non-word or pseudo-word reading tests, as in pronouncing an unfamiliar letter string, such as 'sploog'), and
- comprehension problems under time pressure or when ease of reading is reduced.

In the case of reading, the latter may be the most important to consider when determining appropriate support plans. Adults are rarely required to read out loud and accuracy may be a problem only when it interferes with comprehension. Therefore, strategies to support reading among adults with dyslexia, particularly those studying for further education qualifications, may need to focus on improving comprehension so that the adult can recognize the benefits. Similarly, if adults with dyslexia use the strategy of slowing reading (and rereading text) to allow context to aid decoding, and thereby increase understanding, this would support arguments that extra time in timed assessments is an appropriate accommodation for HE students (Singleton 1999; see also Runyan 1991).

For the purposes of educational support (in HE support services, for example), reinforcing this slowing reading strategy or replacing it with a more effective alternative are important issues to study. For example, it may be that reducing decoding problems and increasing reading speed are the best ways to improve text understanding and retention for adults with dyslexia (although the association between reading fluency and comprehension reduces with age as more complex reading material is experienced: Paris *et al.* 2005). Alternatively, focusing on ways to support understanding specifically may be more beneficial. The following section, therefore, considers strategies to support comprehension levels amongst adult students with dyslexia.

Strategies for Success

Comprehension as a skill in itself is seldom taught (Bell 1991). Many people learn how to comprehend incidentally, probably through appropriate practice, and it may be that a consideration of self-acquired strategies can inform support methods. Riddick, Farmer and Sterling (1997) outline a number of case studies where UK higher education students detail their experiences of being dyslexic and how this has had an impact upon their learning throughout the education system. One participant, Andy, noted that his reading:

> is very slow . . . you'll be looking at a page of text and you may be jumping ahead, or skipping a line . . . then I realise I'm reading a line I've already read and that produces a sense of absolute rage and frustration. You have to read a page two or three times before you extract anything . . . it's difficult, it's a slog. (*Riddick* et al. *1997, p. 37*)

Another student, Janet, confirms the need to reread text, but also seems to indicate that, if she is given sufficient time, her comprehension is adequate, as she says:

> I always find comprehension hard and I really need to read it twice to actually grasp it – then I can answer the questions, no problem. (*Riddick* et al. *1997, p. 51*)

Further testimony from Jenny confirms this trend:

> . . . I'm still the same now, it's trying to read quickly and taking in what I'm reading. I can read a page and not actually take in what I have read . . . If I want to read and take

anything in it takes a long time and I sort of stop and highlight something or underline it really. (*Riddick* et al. *1997, pp. 135–136*)

The main point here is the need to slow reading down for understanding. Similar evidence has been gathered in a recent study involving nine UK university students with dyslexia (full details are reported by Fidler 2009). Consistent with the self-reports in Riddick, Farmer and Sterling (1997), most of the participants reported that they had to read slowly, they experienced some decoding difficulties, would reread information once or several times, and they needed strategies to support their understanding or recall of texts. One notable participant stated that by the time she has started reading a second sentence, she has already lost understanding/recall of the first sentence read, leading her to have to reread several times to break down the overall semantic structure of the text. She reported that she sometimes rereads more complex material 15 times or more. This level of rereading may reflect major decoding problems, lack of confidence in abilities, slow processing or inefficient strategies to support understanding. It may be, for example, that reducing decoding problems or improving comprehension strategies will lead to a reduction in the level of rereading necessary for the individual.

In order to assess the potential effectiveness of different interventions on comprehension levels, the nine university students with dyslexia mentioned above were given training in different strategies that might improve their understanding of written text. These students showed levels of reading comprehension that were worse than those of their non-dyslexic peers, and all had received a recognized UK-based assessment of dyslexia.

Of the five interventions used in the work, one involved text being spoken to the participant via text-to-speech software that the student could manipulate to an appropriate rate of speaking. The hypothesized rationale behind this intervention is that the text-to-speech system will remove decoding problems from the task of understanding text.

A second involved teaching the student keywords within the text. The hypothesis here was that if the student had to read slowly (or reread) to use context around a word to decode it or infer its meaning, then teaching these words prior to reading the text should reduce decoding resources and allow these resources to be used for text understanding.

A further three methods focused on comprehension skills rather than decoding problems. These required the student to focus on thinking about the text. In one, training was given to produce a simple mind map about the text, with colour highlighters being used to structure and review information. Another required the student to read the text and at the same time to highlight main/important sections while making summary notes simultaneously. The final method could be described as a pre-reading task in which headings and sentences in the first paragraph of text were read prior to the whole text being seen. This was used to build a model of what the whole text was about so that further information in the text could be considered in relation to this pre-existing knowledge. The latter three methods are more consistent with metacognitive methods within the literature (Bereiter and Bird 1985; Glover, Ronning and Bruning 1990; Thiede, Anderson and Therriault 2003).

Reading comprehension level was assessed prior to training in the five methods via the Adult Reading Test (ART; Brooks *et al.* 2004), which required the answering of comprehension questions following text reading. Text processing levels were assessed after training in each intervention by requiring the student to read text using the intervention method, then answer comprehension questions about the text and write a summary of the text (these are referred to as 'report' and 'question' in Figure 10.1). Different texts were used for each intervention to avoid practice effects produced by reading the same text several times. Comprehension questions were scored based on the number correct, and summary reports were marked on a

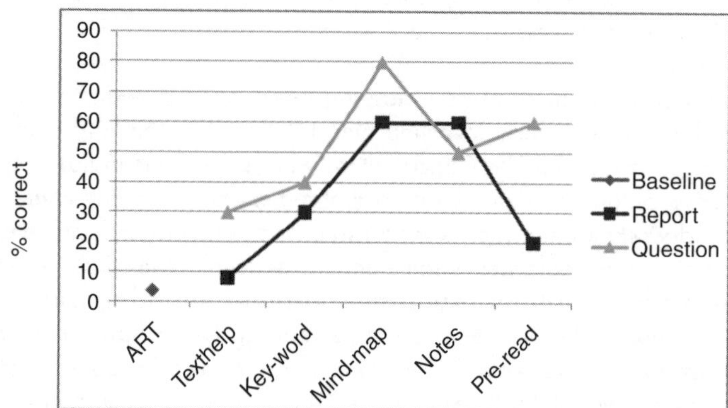

Figure 10.1 Average scores on measures of reading comprehension questions and text report for nine adult students with dyslexia across five training conditions.

scale by two different markers who showed a high level of reliability (r > .9). Scores on these measures are presented as percentages in Figure 10.1 to allow comparison.

The results of this study indicated that the strategies that produced the greater gains in understanding and recall of text were those that incorporated the use of mind-mapping techniques and the writing of summary notes (the third and fourth methods described above). These two strategies can best be described as online metacognitive strategies, as they enable the reader to think about the text during the actual process of reading.

Feedback from all the students indicated that it was the process of engaging with the text and being forced to think about the content that was of crucial importance. The argument here is that students with dyslexia will need more time to process information; therefore slowing down reading can show positive benefits, particularly in comprehension. Hence, although slow reading speeds are a key characteristic of the reading performance of most adults with dyslexia, this may be to support the comprehension of textual information.

Although decoding can be a problem for many students with dyslexia, the evidence here is that strategies focusing on improvements in decoding, so that good comprehension can be achieved, may not be the primary solution for all. If this were the case, strategies used in the intervention study that focused on decoding skills (i.e., the use of text-to-speech software and learning key words) should have produced benefits to comprehension as large as, if not larger than, methods that focused on skills following word recognition. It may be the case that many older students with dyslexia have learned to decode most commonly-used words effectively, or are able to rely on context when reading to decode reasonably well.

Despite the evidence in favour of the metacognitive strategies in Figure 10.1, individual differences in reading characteristics clearly need to be taken into account when deciding whether decoding or comprehension strategies should be the focus of intervention/training. For example, research by Higgins and Zvi (1995) assessed the contribution that optical character recognition software and text-to-speech software might have in supporting adult learners with reading difficulties. They concluded that this type of technology helped students' reading comprehension where their reading was severely impaired, but it potentially interfered with understanding when students had good reading scores.

Those who have reasonable decoding skills, including a significant number of adults with dyslexia, may not be best suited to this strategy, consistent with the data reported in Figure 10.1. However, even within the nine cases reported in Figure 10.1, there were those who benefited more from strategies that focused on decoding skills. Therefore, it may be the case that those adults who find printed material inaccessible, possibly due to severe difficulties with decoding, may need more wide-ranging support (Kitz and Nash 1992) or will have to rely more on their listening comprehension skills by hearing the text. This should lead to a technological approach proving the more successful intervention (see discussions in Gregg and Banerjee 2009).

Having time to read documents can also support workplace competency. Good time-management and organizational skills, an area that many adults with dyslexia find problematic, can aid workplace preparation: for example, factoring in sufficient time to read documents prior to meetings could prove beneficial, particularly with practice in the comprehension strategies discussed above. Ensuring that documents are available for scrutiny prior to meetings will also aid the employee to obtain both an overview of the subject material and give time to assess relevant detail.

A number of workplaces offer mentoring schemes for new staff that may provide appropriate support with the organization of work responsibilities. However, support from a mentor on organizational issues may require disclosure regarding the specific learning difficulty, and this is an issue that the individual needs to consider. On the other hand, a lack of disclosure is likely to lead to a less supportive or understanding response from work colleagues, as well as reduced access to support mechanisms. Applications to the UK-government-funded Access to Work scheme for support would also require disclosure to an employer (see also Fitzgibbon and O'Connor 2002; McLoughlin, Leather and Stringer 2002; Reid, Came and Price 2008).

In addition to individual differences in reading characteristics, different tasks may require different strategies. Although text understanding may be the most important reading skill for most adults, another important aspect of reading, especially in a number of office-based workplaces, is that of proofreading. Proofreading can be a difficult task for most adults with dyslexia, and often it can feel inappropriate to ask others to check reports or letters in a workplace. Here, the use of text-to-speech software can be particularly useful, as listening back to what has been written enables the reader to identify more easily errors with grammar, punctuation and sentence structure. Software that is able to check confusable words such as homophones (their/there for example) can alleviate considerable concerns or anxieties related to workplace competence (for discussions of different types of technology that may prove useful for adults with dyslexia see Draffan 2008, and her chapter in this book).

Other technological solutions are available to support adults with dyslexia in the workplace, not just with reading but with a host of literacy-based tasks. For example, trainee nurses may find portable medical spelling checkers useful when reading medical terms or writing care plans. Standard spelling checkers and reading pens can also be used to identify words when reading; these can be used alongside standard technology such as online dictionaries and checking definitions on search engines. Voice-activated software, used to assist writing skills by dictating text directly on to a computer screen, can be used to dictate research notes when reading, either when studying or within the workplace to summarize documents. Dictating a summary of what has been read is a strategy that actively engages the reader and therefore should facilitate comprehension and recall of information. This software relies on a good level of verbal articulation and the development of dictation skills. Such skills require practice and, therefore, take time to master. However, once a reasonable level of proficiency has been attained, such tools can lead to efficient working practices in both the education and employment environment (Smythe 2010 provides an excellent discussion of the potential benefits of technology, though within the framework of considering the training needs and potential pitfalls that should be taken into account prior to use.)

The use of visual imagery to recall information from text is another strategy advocated by some professionals (see discussions in Mortimore 2003). Such an approach, which a number of dyslexic learners seem to like, can be translated into the creation of mind maps whilst reading. Although not the preference of all (e.g., not all the nine student whose results are reported in Figure 10.1 found mind maps to be beneficial), graphic organizers also may prove useful to support understanding (see review in Kim *et al.* 2004). Similarly, it can be useful to adopt a more visual approach to summary writing; for example, the use of colour to coordinate key points was reported as beneficial by many of the nine students in the study represented in Figure 10.1.

Colour, in the form of overlays, has also been reported to be helpful for those readers who experience visual stress or movement of print whilst reading, and the background colour of computer screens can be altered either by changing the preferences within the display settings on Windows, or by purchasing software that enables background colour changes with all applications, including online material (for discussions of visual stress in adults, see Singleton and Trotter 2007). Again, these may be subject to individual preference or individual differences and, therefore, may not be appropriate for all. However, anything that makes a literacy practice easier or more comfortable for the individual may be worth exploring.

Conclusion

Adult readers with dyslexia tend to have persistent difficulties with literacy and some of the skills underlying reading and writing. Adults assessed as severely dyslexic may find screen-reading software helpful. Others who have a reasonable ability to decode words are possibly better advised to focus their attention on becoming active readers. Developing strategies to enable the monitoring of text, the reinforcement of understanding, and the integration of new with existing knowledge are likely to be of particular benefit. Clearly, for many adults with dyslexia, support in reading individual words can be useful. However, for many, the task of reading requires a good level of comprehension, particularly in work or adult education environments. Technology can be used to support aspects of reading, particularly proofreading, but it is argued here that the key is to engage actively with text via metacognitive strategies. Writing summaries whilst reading, the use of highlighter pens to identify relevant information, and using mind maps to structure and organize information all seem to aid comprehension and recall. These strategies, it can be argued, are time-consuming. Therefore, effective planning of tasks and time management are important skills required to supplement reading and other literacy-based strategies. Finally, the lack of reading practice that often results from reading difficulties means that many adult dyslexic readers, even those who have acquired reasonable decoding skills, will not necessarily have learned comprehension strategies that support the required level of understanding. Support in this area of literacy would seem as vital for adult dyslexic readers as it is for the younger reader learning to decode.

References

Beaton, A., McDougall, S. and Singleton, C. (eds) (1997) Special issue: Dyslexia in literate adults. *Journal of Research in Reading*, 20 (1).

Bell, N. (1991) *Visualising and Verbalising*, Gander Educational Publishing, San Luis Obispo, CA.

Bereiter, C. and Bird, M. (1985) Use of thinking aloud in identification and teaching of reading comprehension strategies. *Cognition and Instruction*, 2, 131–156.

British Psychological Society (1999) Dyslexia, literacy and psychological assessment. *Report of a Working Party of the Division of Educational and Child Psychology of the British Psychological Society*, British Psychological Society, Leicester.

Brooks, P., Everatt, J. and Fidler, R. (2004) *The Adult Reading Test*, Roehampton University of Surrey, London.

Cain, K. and Oakhill, J. (eds) (2007) *Children's Comprehension Problems in Oral and Written Language*, Guilford Press, New York.

Cornoldi, C., De Beni, R. and Pazzaglia, F. (1996) Profiles of reading comprehension difficulties: An analysis of single cases, in *Reading Comprehension Difficulties: Processes and interventions* (eds C. Cornoldi and J. Oakhill), LEA, Mahwah, NJ.

Draffan, E.A. (2008) New technology to support adults with dyslexia, in *BDA Dyslexia Handbook 2008/9* (ed. C. Singleton), British Dyslexia Association, Bracknell.

Du Pre, L., Gilroy, D. and Miles, T. (2007) *Dyslexia at College*, 3rd edn, Routledge, London.

Elbro, C., Nielsen, I. and Petersen, D.K. (1994) Dyslexia in adults: Evidence for deficits in non-word reading and in the phonological representation of lexical items. *Annals of Dyslexia*, 44, 205–226.

Fidler, R. (2009) *The Reading Comprehension Skills of Adult Students with Dyslexia*. Unpublished doctoral dissertation. University of Surrey, UK.

Fitzgibbon, G. and O'Connor, B. (2002) *Adult Dyslexia: A guide for the workplace*, John Wiley & Sons Ltd, Chichester.

Gillon, G.T. (2004) *Phonological Awareness: From research to practice*, Guilford Press, New York.

Glover, J.A., Ronning, R.R. and Bruning, R.H. (1990) *Cognitive Psychology for Teachers*, Macmillan, London.

Gough, P.B., Hoover, W.A. and Peterson, C.L. (1996) Some observations on the simple view of reading, in *Reading Comprehension Difficulties: Processes and interventions* (eds C. Cornoldi and J. Oakhill), LEA, Mahwah, NJ.

Gregg, N. and Banerjee, M. (2009) Reading comprehension solutions for college students with dyslexia in an era of technology, in *The Routledge Companion to Dyslexia* (ed. G. Reid), Routledge, Abingdon.

Higgins, E.L. and Zvi, J.C. (1995) Assistive technology for postsecondary students with learning disabilities: From research to practice. *Annals of Dyslexia*, 45, 123–142.

Hoover, W.A. and Gough, P.B. (1990) The simple view of reading. *Reading and Writing: An Interdisciplinary Journal*, 2, 127–160.

Jackson, N.E. and Doelinger, H.L. (2002) Resilient readers? University students who are poor recoders but sometimes good text comprehenders. *Journal of Educational Psychology*, 94, 64–78.

Kim, A.-H., Vaughn, S, Wanzek, J., and Wei, S. (2004) Graphic organizers and their effects on the reading comprehension of students with LD: A synthesis of research. *Journal of Learning Disabilities*, 37, 105–118.

Kitz, W.R. and Nash, R.T. (1992) Testing the effectiveness of the Project Success Summer Program for adult dyslexics. *Annals of Dyslexia*, 42, 3–24.

Lesaux, N., Pearson, M. and Siegel, L. (2006) The effects of timed and untimed testing conditions on the reading comprehension performance of adults with reading disabilities. *Reading and Writing: An Interdisciplinary Journal*, 19, 21–48.

McLoughlin, D., Fitzgibbon, G. and Young, V. (1994) *Adult Dyslexia: Assessment, counselling and training*, Whurr, London.

McLoughlin, D., Leather, C. and Stringer, P. (2002) *The Adult Dyslexic; Interventions and outcomes*, Whurr, London.

Miles, T.R. (1993) *Dyslexia: The pattern of difficulties*, 2nd edn, Whurr, London.

Mortimore, T. (2003) *Dyslexia and Learning Style*, Whurr, London.

Nation, K. and Snowling, M.J. (1998) Individual differences in contextual facilitation: Evidence from dyslexia and poor reading comprehension. *Child Development*, 69, 996–1011.

Oakhill, J. and Yuill, N. (1996) Higher order factors in comprehension disability: Processes and remediation, in *Reading Comprehension Difficulties: Processes and interventions* (eds C. Cornoldi and J. Oakhill), LEA, Mahwah, NJ.

Paris, S.G., Carpenter, R.D., Paris, A.H. and Hamilton, E.E. (2005) Spurious and genuine correlates of children's reading comprehension, in *Children's Reading Comprehension and Assessment* (eds S. G. Paris and S. A. Stahl), Erlbaum, Mahwah NJ.

Patton, J.R. and Polloway, E.A. (1996) *Learning Disabilities: The challenges of adulthood*: Pro-Ed, Austin, TX.

Ramus, F., Rosen, S., Dakin *et al.* (2003) Theories of developmental dyslexia: Insights from a multiple case study of dyslexic adults. *Brain*, 126, 841–865.

Reid, G., Came, F. and Price, L.A. (2008) Dyslexia: Workplace issues, in *The Sage Handbook of Dyslexia* (eds G. Reid, A. Fawcett, F. Manis and L. Siegel), Sage, London.

Riddick, B., Farmer, M. and Sterling, C. (1997) *Students and Dyslexia*, Whurr, London.

Runyan, M. (1991) The effect of extra time on reading comprehension scores for university students with and without learning disabilities. *Journal of Learning Disabilities*, 24, 104–108.

Simmons, F. and Singleton, C. (2000) The reading comprehension abilities of dyslexic students in higher education. *Dyslexia*, 6, 178–192.

Singleton, C. (1999) Dyslexia in higher education: Policy, provision and practice. *Report of the National Working Party on Dyslexia in Higher Education*, University of Hull, Hull.

Singleton, C. and Trotter, S. (2007) Visual stress in adults with and without dyslexia, in *Visual Factors in Reading* (eds P.L. Cornelissen and C. Singleton), Wiley-Blackwell, Oxford.

Smythe, I. (2010) *Dyslexia in the Digital Age*, Continuum, London.

Snowling, M.J. (2000) *Dyslexia*, 2nd edn, Blackwell, Oxford.

Snowling, M.J. and Hulme, C. (eds) (2005) *The Science of Reading: A handbook*, Blackwell, Oxford.

Stainthorpe, R. (2002) Learning and teaching reading. *British Journal of Educational Psychology Monograph Series II*, British Psychological Society, Leicester.

Stanovich, K.E. (1980) Towards an interactive compensatory model of individual differences in the development of reading fluency. *Reading Research Quarterly*, 16, 32–71.

Stanovich, K.E. (1986) Matthew effects in reading: Some consequences in individual differences in the acquisition of literacy. *Reading Research Quarterly*, 21, 360–364.

Stothard, S.E. and Hulme, C. (1996) Comparison of reading comprehension and decoding difficulties in children, in *Reading Comprehension Difficulties: Processes and interventions* (eds C. Cornoldi and J. Oakhill), LEA, Mahwah, NJ.

Thiede, K.W., Anderson, M.C.M. and Therriault, D. (2003) Accuracy of metacognitive monitoring affects learning of texts. *Journal of Educational Psychology*, 95, 66–73.

11

Dyslexia Support at University and on Work Placement

Pauline Sumner, Middlesex University, UK

Working in the dyslexia support service of a large London university, I am delighted to see the continual development of understanding and awareness of dyslexia within higher education (HE) institutions. Individuals with dyslexia are becoming more aware of the raised levels of understanding and what is available in the way of dyslexia support and, consequently, they are more confident about coming to university to study. Once at university, students assessed with dyslexia may be eligible for the Disabled Students' Allowance (DSA). This is funding for one-to-one dyslexia support tutorials, specialist equipment and assistive software such as a digital recorder, text-to-speech and mind-mapping software, with specialist IT training provided to assist with learning how to use the software. Special arrangements, such as additional time, can also be put in place to assist with exams, which are often a concern.

A key element of what is available for students is the one-to-one dyslexia support provided by specialists who have been trained to help students with their courses of study. Interestingly though, it would seem that the extent and content of the support tutors' work with their students, and the professionalism of their work, are not fully understood or recognized by those working outside the dyslexia milieu. In an attempt to redress this situation and raise awareness, the first part of this chapter will provide an overview of the specialist work that dyslexia support tutors do (see Figure 11.1).

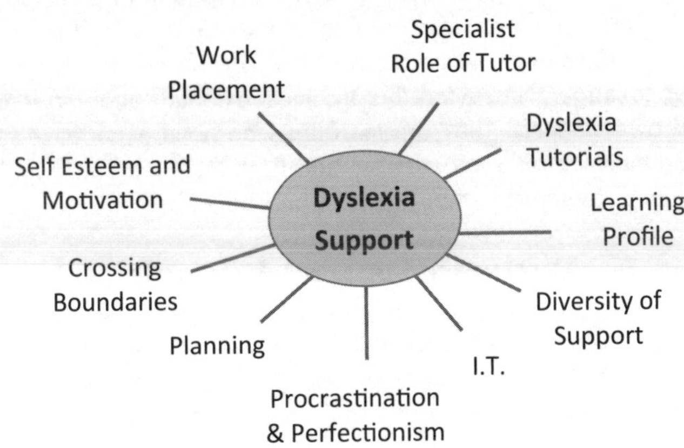

Figure 11.1 Overview of chapter.

Supporting Dyslexic Adults in Higher Education and the Workplace, First Edition. Edited by Nicola Brunswick.

As well as looking at the way that study skills are incorporated within an individualized student learning programme, an additional focus will be on how tutors work with students to help them to believe in themselves as learners, considering the all too common issues of low self-esteem and confidence. As work placements form an integral part of many HE courses of study, the second part of this chapter will consider ways in which students with dyslexia can be supported in their professional practice learning by their dyslexia support tutors working together with placement staff.

It is impossible to reflect in one chapter the wealth of dyslexia support practice occurring across higher education, but I hope that the scenarios included will demonstrate the flexibility of practice which reflects the very individual needs of students with dyslexia. Whilst the scenarios are drawn from experience, to respect issues of confidentiality they are not representative of work done with any one particular student, and in some cases a blend of experiences is used; all names have been changed.

The Specialist Role of the Dyslexia Support Tutor

To explore the role of the dyslexia support tutor, I would like to start by introducing the 'Guidelines for Quality Assurance in Specialist Support for Students with Specific Learning Difficulties (SpLD)' produced by the Association of Dyslexia Specialists in Higher Education (ADSHE, 2009).[1] The work was carried out under the auspices of two key objectives of ADSHE:

1 to share knowledge and disseminate good practice, including promoting and developing the understanding of all aspects of dyslexia; and
2 to clarify and promote students' entitlement to dyslexia support within individual institutions and throughout the sector.

The Guidelines cover the range of specialist support including identification, assessment and best practice regarding delivery of one-to-one tutorials, raising dyslexia awareness and understanding across institutions, and administrative procedures. The appended colour-coded mind map (which can be downloaded from the ADSHE web site[2] as a poster) provides an excellent visual overview of the breadth of work that tutors carry out with their students.

Specialist tutors work with students with any of the SpLDs, including dyspraxia, Attention Deficit (Hyperactivity) Disorder (AD(H)D), Asperger's syndrome and dyscalculia, but they are usually referred to as dyslexia support tutors as dyslexia is the most common form of SpLD. The British Dyslexia Association web site[3] provides a list of recognized training courses that dyslexia support tutors are required to undertake to work with adults. However, I feel that I can safely speak for colleagues in saying that the most essential ongoing learning that tutors receive is from their own students. They are the ones who have experienced the repercussions of their difficulties on their learning experience, and from them we can gain knowledge and understanding of what is required in their tutorials and beyond.

Dyslexia Support Tutorials

A student-centred focus is an essential element of a tutor's work. Each student demonstrates a very individual and complex profile of learning strengths and weaknesses. The nature of their requirements will vary considerably according to the subject, type and assessment demands of

[1] Further information about the work of ADSHE, how to become a member, the Guidelines for Quality Assurance in Specialist Support for Students with SpLD and other useful resources can be obtained directly from the ADSHE web site.

[2] http://adshe.org.uk/wp-content/uploads/specialist_support.pdf.

[3] www.bdadyslexia.org.uk.

the course they are studying, be it at foundation, undergraduate or postgraduate level. It cannot be ignored that the educational background of the individual student will have a significant impact on the work carried out in tutorials. Importantly though, students will bring with them talents with, for example, their creativity, communication skills performing arts or practical hands-on abilities, and computer skills. Usually there is a strong desire to prove that they are able to study and a solid determination to work hard. Reinforcement of such attributes plays an essential part of tutorial support in working with the more challenging literacy and numeracy elements that students have to address in achieving the required level of academic status.

Learning Profile

Dyslexia support tutors start to build a holistic overview of their student's learning profile through initial discussions about their educational background, their concerns and personal goals. Where a student has undertaken a diagnostic assessment, the quantitative and qualitative information about the specific learning challenges and needs of the student can be used to underpin and guide the tutorial support. The profile can be developed further if the student has applied for DSA and undertaken a Needs Assessment; this provides a useful breakdown of the practical needs of the student whilst studying at university, as well as the recommended assistive software and equipment that the student may be eligible to receive.

The 'safe space' of the tutorial offers the perfect environment to facilitate learning. The tutor works with individual students to identify their preferred strategies within an individual learning programme; this will focus on helping them to develop a metacognitive understanding of their preferences in accessing information and how they learn best. Based on the student's particular strengths and style of learning, a range of multi-sensory teaching methods is developed to assist the student to use alternative approaches and to develop compensatory strategies, drawing on resources and assistive software as appropriate.

Diversity of Support

Regular tutorials are provided with the overall aim of working to achieve independent student learning. However, the increasingly demanding requirements at each level of a course, and the need for frequent reviews of learning, means that long-term goals must be flexible.

Whilst the breadth of work covered is diverse, it is always based on the priorities brought by the student to each tutorial. The following provides an idea of the type of work that may be covered:

- time management and organization
- essay-writing skills, including written expression and use of academic language, grammar, syntax, punctuation, spelling, sentence, paragraph and essay structure
- active reading strategies to deal with complex texts and identify key concepts
- assisting with verbalizing ideas/concepts and developing a narrative for assignments
- brain-storming/mind-mapping ideas to initiate the writing process and plan an essay
- IT skills, use of assistive technology and specialist equipment
- use of library and electronic resources
- paraphrasing and referencing
- research methods
- dealing with lectures, note-taking, etc.
- exam preparation and memory/revision techniques
- presentation skills
- preparing for employment.

Embedding Information Technology

Most of the areas covered in one-to-one tutorials can benefit from embedding the use of assistive technology and specialist equipment. Consideration should also be given to the wealth of free or low-cost online educational applications that are becoming available to enhance the student's multi-sensory learning milieu; these are particularly useful for students who are not eligible for DSA funding. In respecting individuality, however, the level of ability and interest in using information technology must be measured and support adapted according to each student. There may still be anxieties for students when having to use computers, sometimes for the first time when they come to university. One example of this is provided by Steve:

Steve

Steve, a part-time Fine Art student, had no interest in using a computer before he attended university. When commencing his course he found it impossible to access the online resources such as timetables and lecture notes, and he could not send emails or access the internet for his research. Although he was given some basic computer training, the nature of his dyslexia and associated poor short-term memory meant that he could not remember the instructions. By the time I met Steve for tutorials, he had become extremely anxious about missing his lectures and practical sessions which, by the nature of his part-time degree status, were rather irregular. He had been advised to email his lecturer for clarification but this had just increased his levels of stress and further blocked his ability to think of logical ways to deal with his IT difficulties.

A priority in the tutorials, therefore, was to teach Steve how to use a computer, to guide him to the requisite information, and to make it easily accessible for him. For example, we downloaded and adapted his timetable within a personal planner by colour-coding the relevant times and dates when he had to attend and by adding in other commitments. In working to the ethos of independent learning, it was essential to increase Steve's confidence to become proficient with the computer in a way that suited him. This was achieved by setting aside a time in each weekly tutorial where I employed a modelling strategy (see Figure 11.2). To start, I showed Steve how to access his email account and open an email; Steve made notes and drew visual representations of toolbars, icons, etc; he then practised the activities until he was able to do them independently. The next week we reviewed the first tasks and then repeated the process, adding a new activity. For Steve this took a lot of time out of the tutorials, but it enabled him to take ownership of using his technology and to become proficient in emailing lecturers and others, researching on the internet, typing his essays, cutting and pasting images, and eventually getting to grips with his assistive software.

Procrastination and Perfectionism

Procrastination and perfectionism are common problems brought to tutorials, and both have major implications on the most precious commodity for students – their time. If we were to analyse the conversations we had with our students during tutorials, the most frequently recorded are likely to be:

- 'I just don't seem to be able to get started.'
- 'I have everything in my head but I just can't write it down.'
- 'I have so much to do but don't know how I am going to get it all done in time.'

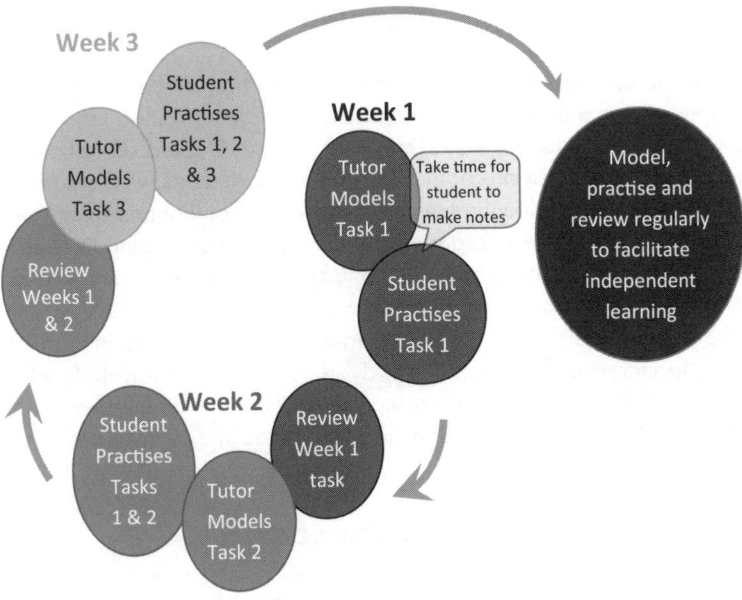

Figure 11.2 Model, practise, review cycle.

- 'I am so worried about this essay as I really want/need to get a good mark.'
- 'I am frightened of failing/plagiarizing.'
- 'I know I can do better but something is holding me back.'

It is a vicious circle: as the pressure of overload increases so too does the fear and anxiety about starting the work; as the stress levels increase so too will the dyslexia difficulties, thus increasing the negative impact on the student's ability to read and write. Added to this is the frequently seen desire of students to be 'perfect' in whatever they do, with a fear of any criticism about work they have done. This is exemplified by Kim:

Kim

Kim was a very capable postgraduate student who was struggling to complete a lengthy report for her Business Studies course. She had extensive subject knowledge, she was already working as a manager in the business milieu, and she was putting many additional hours in to her research and writing. Despite all this, Kim had little confidence in her abilities and would frequently redraft the report and seek reassurance about the standard and content of her work. I found it difficult to reassure Kim that her work was very good and that she did not need to push herself so hard in her desire to perfect her writing.

One week Kim came to the tutorial very upset. It transpired that her lecturer had praised her about another assignment she had submitted and provided constructive criticism on how she could improve her work even further. At the time, as an inexperienced tutor, I could not understand why she was so upset, trying to emphasize how well Kim had done. I have since seen this happen with other students and have learnt from them that criticism, be it constructive or otherwise, can return them to earlier educational experiences of being heavily ridiculed or criticized about their literacy abilities. These are powerful emotions of which all of us working with students with dyslexia need to be aware.

Planning

A particularly effective element of one-to-one tutorials is helping students to become aware of why they are experiencing difficulties such as procrastination or overworking, and then plan how they can work in a less stressful way. This usually comes back to organization, time management and collaborating with students to prioritize their workload, create task lists and time planners. Teaching them how to break their workloads down into smaller, more manageable, 'chunks' enables them to attach their own personal deadline to each smaller piece of work, which will be more easily achievable. This provides the necessary reassurance that personal goals can be achieved, and motivation to progress through heavy workloads to meet official deadlines. Further assistance can be provided by electronic time management resources which are becoming increasingly popular and 'dyslexia friendly', particularly where they can be downloaded to mobile phones. These strategies won't always be the answer, but it is up to the tutor to help students to navigate through such difficulties in their own preferred way.

Crossing Boundaries

Whilst a tutor's role is not to provide subject-specific support, working with course materials provides the necessary relevance to ensure that learning is more meaningful to the students. A common scenario presented by students with dyslexia is where they have become lost in the tangle of sorting out subject handbooks, reading lists, online virtual learning environments and timetables. As a result, the all-important understanding of the subject knowledge has often been abandoned. Chris demonstrated these difficulties from the first time we met:

Chris

Chris started tutorials halfway through his first year; by this time he had 'lost his way' on the course and was thinking about leaving as he felt that he 'just did not understand what the lecturers were talking about'. He had read only a few of the recommended weekly texts and had missed coursework deadlines. In our initial discussions it became apparent that Chris had severe difficulties with reading and, although he had tried to read the teaching materials, he had become demoralized and given up, allowing the work to pile up.

In this situation it was useful to go back to basics, helping Chris to access the relevant information from the subject handbook and online materials, and provide the necessary overview of what was required of him. Referring to lecture handouts, I encouraged Chris to talk about what he remembered from the lectures and I started to 'doodle' key points on a large piece of paper using coloured pens. It soon became apparent that Chris knew a lot more than he thought and he started to add his own notes to what was now becoming a rough mind map. He went away from the tutorial motivated with the knowledge that he had taken control of his learning. Over the following weeks it was evident that he had become more confident in his reading ability, accessing and understanding his lecture notes and more complex texts; this was further reinforced by his learning to use text-to-speech software to download reading material to listen to on his Mp3 player.

In similar situations it has sometimes been necessary to go even further back to basics (please don't tell the lecturers!) by using A-level reading materials or internet resources such as Wikipedia. This empowers students to get to grips with their subject and to gain the confidence to move forward with their own learning by reading the appropriate-level texts and writing essays. It may be felt that tutors are crossing the line of working with subject-specific knowledge, but I would argue that this is, in fact, just enabling students to see their way through the mire and showing them how to learn.

Self-Esteem and Motivation

As has been seen throughout this chapter, emotions cannot be ignored when working with students with specific learning difficulties. Dyslexia support tutors are well aware of the limits of their professional practice and the importance of referring students on to counsellors where necessary. From personal experience this is becoming a more regular occurrence and we work closely with our university counselling team. It is still the case, however, that some students will come to tutorials with issues that need to be dealt with before we can progress with the session: they may be upset and crying, very anxious or just in need of 'letting off steam' to clear their way to concentration. A box of tissues is useful to have at hand!

As a result of negative and demoralizing experiences within their past education, students' lack of self-esteem and confidence can result in considerable anxiety, linked with their learning at university. It is astounding that students are still reporting historical experiences of being called stupid, thick or lazy, being embarrassed by school teachers in front of the class, and deplorable stories of bullying. The one-to-one tutorial offers a 'safe space' in which the student can relax and not feel embarrassed about discussing their problems with learning, with students frequently saying that it is the first time they have been 'allowed' to talk freely about their dyslexia. Working with students in discussing these experiences can be a useful, facilitative approach towards moving them forward in a more positive and empowering fashion.

As tutors, we develop a toolbox of resources. Some of these can be likened to life coaching skills,[4] which are particularly effective in motivating and empowering students to establish realistic goals and to take control of their own learning. And yes, this is still working within a study skills remit but with the understanding gained from experience that it is only when students attain a confident sense of self-worth in their ability to study that they will be able to read effectively, write essays, prepare for exams or give presentations. As students begin to realize that they are able to achieve their targets, their motivation, confidence and self-esteem increase, anxiety levels fall and their pathway to learning becomes clearer.[5] An excellent example of this is provided by Jay:

Jay

Jay ran his own successful complementary health practice, but returning to study was proving to be very stressful. Despite his extensive subject knowledge and experience, Jay was finding it impossible to understand the complex theories he was expected to

(*Continued*)

[4] See, for example, the Association for Coaching's web site: www.associationforcoaching.com/home/index.htm.

[5] A comprehensive insight into these important issues is provided by Robert Burden in his book *Dyslexia and Self-Concept: Seeking a dyslexic identity*.

relate to practice, and frustrating that on some days he was able to study but on others he could hardly read or write. Although usually an organized person, he was 'drowning' within his heavy study commitments and was putting off the inevitable reading and writing.

During tutorials we talked about his concerns and used his diagnostic assessment as a 'way in' to provide him with a self-understanding of his learning difficulties. By reflecting on the fluctuations in his concentration, he realized that this usually depended on his ability to get what was being taught 'into his own framework'. Amongst other things, this included having the time to draw on his skills of using visualization in his learning.

This was a turning point for Jay in planning his workload and developing his learning programme. We were able to integrate more visual strategies within which we linked theory with visual images of his patients, or created 'friends'. He designed mind-mapped templates that could be adapted for different patient scenarios/treatments, and created collage-type posters and index cards for remedies using pictures, diagrams and pressed herbs, etc. The practice of carrying out this work helped him to focus and remember the important theoretical elements for forthcoming exams. Once Jay had received his assistive technology, he designed interlinking mind maps on his laptop, developing an ever-evolving electronic resource that could be used for both his studies and practice.

By establishing and understanding his personal learning framework, Jay was able to move forwards more confidently with his coursework preparation. This does not represent the only work covered in tutorials, and certainly his course of study was not all plain sailing, but he had the motivation and self-esteem to know that he was able to work through the challenges and return to tutorials if necessary.

As has been emphasized throughout this chapter, each student is very different. There are students with dyslexia/SpLD who are able to get through university without tutorial support at all, using compensatory strategies that they have already developed. Students who have been recognized at a young age with dyslexia tend to be more confident about their abilities and more proactive in talking to their lecturers should they need to. Some will come for a short programme of dyslexia tutorials, gaining adequate skills to see them through their course or until they come across more complex work. Students who are assessed with dyslexia or another SpLD later in life, however, may have a greater number of issues to contend with in coming to terms with learning about themselves and their dyslexia, whilst also having to cope with an intensive university course.

The overview provided here is not intended to delve into the complexities of dyslexia, which are well-documented elsewhere (for example, see Brunswick 2009; and the ADSHE Guidelines 2009, for further information and references). Nor could it provide an exhaustive picture of the extensive work of the dyslexia support tutor (which is summarized in Figure 11.3), but I hope it has provided a useful insight into the individualized and student-centred work that is carried out within the ethos of dyslexia/SpLD practice in empowering students with dyslexia to work effectively towards their goals.

The role of the dyslexia support tutor does not stop, however, with the academic elements of the course within the university setting. There is also an important requirement to support students with advice and guidance during their practice learning whilst on work placements, and this will be explored in the next section.

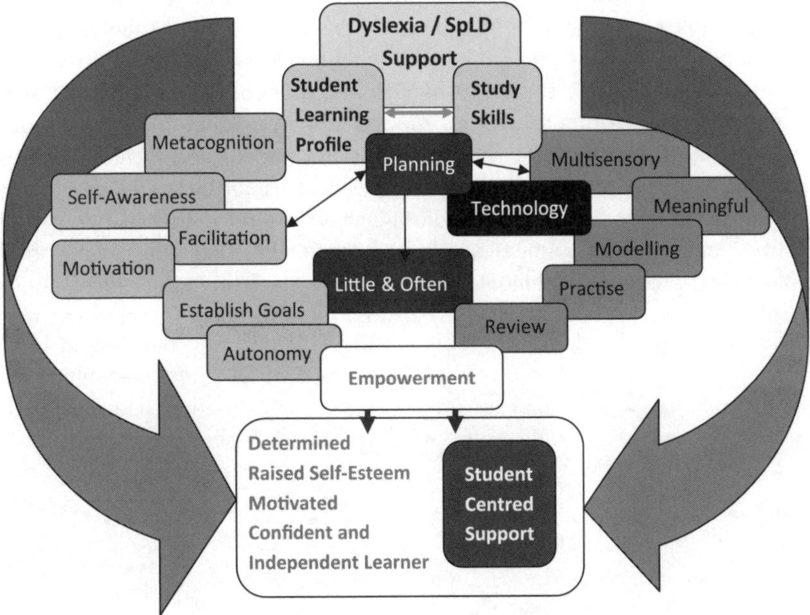

Figure 11.3 Visual representation of dyslexia support in higher education.

Dyslexia Support on Work Placement

In consideration of the Equality Act (2010) and Disability Discrimination Act (1995), Higher Education Institutions need to liaise with work placement providers to promote disability equality; the essence of the anticipatory nature of the Disability Equality Duty is to be proactive in creating a more inclusive workplace.

From personal experience of working with students with dyslexia who are training to become teachers, social workers, nurses and midwives, it is evident that work placements raise many concerns for our students; there is often a reluctance or fear about talking to mentors or other staff about their dyslexia. If a student does not disclose their dyslexia, it makes it difficult for placements to be proactive in providing support or putting in place reasonable adjustments where necessary. Dyslexia support tutors can help their students to consider the various aspects of disclosure.

Disclosure

Some students may feel it is not necessary to disclose as they have developed good coping strategies; others may be unsure of the procedure or concerned about possible repercussions. It is, however, important for students to recognize the positive reasons for disclosure, such as to:

- open up communication channels
- encourage a clearer understanding of dyslexia and related issues for all staff
- enable the implementation of support, and
- reduce students' anxieties about hiding their dyslexia.

There are a number of examples of good practice across the HE sector with regard to encouraging students to feel more confident about disclosure. Our dyslexia support service has worked with nursing and midwifery staff to introduce a disclosure booklet and form that provide information about dyslexia for both the student and the mentor. Limited knowledge regarding dyslexia is frequently reported as being the reason that mentors/supervisors are unsure about how best to support their dyslexic students. The simple colour-coded dyslexia form links suggestions from both mentor and student for support to the particular placement requirements.

It is hoped that the disclosure form will encourage the student and mentor to discuss the student's strengths, weaknesses and challenges as well as useful strategies previously employed by the student, and reasonable adjustments where necessary. Of course, fitness for practice must be demonstrated by meeting all the proficiencies and requirements of the student's professional practice placement; however, a 'dyslexia-friendly' placement, where students feel at ease about disclosing their dyslexia, will assist them in achieving their full potential. This was the case with Gina:

Gina

Gina, a first-year mature nursing student, was assessed with dyslexia prior to her going on her first work placement. This left her with negative feelings about her abilities, and she was concerned that anyone would 'find out about her dyslexia' as she felt it would be seen as detrimental to her becoming a nurse.

Gina came along to her first tutorial demoralized with tales of woe about her work placement mentor, who had become impatient about repeating instructions (for example to set up equipment) and annoyed with her about her poor handwriting, and spelling mistakes. We unpacked Gina's concerns about her abilities and reflected on her impressive practical skills and attributes built up from past experiences of working in the caring community. As well as promoting positive thinking, we developed a reflective framework that could be used within her assessments. The reflective framework also provided us with the vehicle to plan how Gina would prepare for her next clinical placement, considering issues of disclosure and discussing her dyslexia with her mentor, and developing practical strategies.

Gina's second placement proved to be far more successful. The disclosure booklet gave Gina the confidence and guidance to discuss her difficulties 'officially' with her mentor who was then able to implement practical solutions and a few simple reasonable adjustments. For example, a 'quiet' time and place was provided for Gina to write up a daily reflective diary for her Professional Portfolio; Gina used a notebook to record instructions and got into the practice of repeating back the instructions to her mentor to check understanding. The self-directed learning process re-established Gina's commitment to continue her training to become a nurse. By talking about her difficulties, she was also able to raise dyslexia awareness for her mentor and other staff, who sought suggestions from Gina to improve future mentoring practice.

Work Placement Strategies

The dyslexia support tutor is ideally suited to work with the student to develop strategies that can be transferred into work practice, according to personal and placement requirements. Whilst it is a tutor's role to empower the student towards independence, it may be necessary to review strategies in accordance with the increasingly complex and diverse work placement experiences. A few suggestions for useful strategies are provided below:

- design templates for administrative procedures using colour-coded sections
- use diagrams, flow charts and mnemonics to aid memory
- develop colour-coded daily/weekly planners and daily prioritized task lists
- prepare frameworks that can be used for examples of work practice and procedures, e.g. what I should do if I am called on to do a) . . . or b) . . . ?
- carry out role-play exercises of specific scenarios to enhance communication skills
- adapt the use of the student's assistive technology to workplace tasks, e.g. produce templates using mind-mapping software; consider use of dictaphone and note-taker software in meetings.

Good Work Placement Practice

Where required, dyslexia tutors can provide guidance to mentors or supervisors regarding useful support and simple adjustments that can be put in place for students on placement. There are many examples of good practice, some of which are provided below:

- allow extra time for planning and completing reading and writing tasks
- provide a quiet space for reading and writing
- offer support with checking written work for spelling and grammar
- check understanding of verbal instructions
- allow students to use a notebook or dictaphone to record information
- produce work rotas in advance and be flexible regarding work hours to assist with continuity of dyslexia support tutorials
- encourage students' involvement in the development of placement programmes, consideration of necessary support and dyslexia awareness training
- work to encourage individual strengths and abilities
- encourage and support the use of assistive technology such as text-to-speech, speech-to-text and mind-mapping software.

When making reasonable adjustments, a balance has to be reached between the level and cost of the support required and compromising standards. However, support and adjustments can usually be implemented fairly easily and cost-effectively, and these are frequently employed as good practice anyway. Where there is a need for more intensive support, there is no doubt that this could be a draw on resources, but to leave a student to struggle and possibly fail could result in severe ramifications at both an institutional and personal level. All reasonable efforts should be made by dyslexia support tutors, lecturers and placement staff to be proactive in working with students to meet the necessary criteria and to empower them to work towards the required standards of professionalism in their future employment.

References

ADSHE (2009) *Constitution for Association of Dyslexia Specialists in Higher Education*, available from www.adshe.org.uk.

ADSHE (2009) *Guidelines for Quality Assurance in Specialist Support for Students with SpLD*, available from: www.adshe.org.uk.

Brunswick, N. (2009) *Dyslexia: A beginner's guide*, Oneworld Publications, Oxford.

Burden, R. (2005) *Dyslexia and Self-concept: Seeking a dyslexic identity*, Whurr, London.

HMSO (1995) *The Disability Discrimination Act 1995*, Her Majesty's Stationery Office, London.

Office for Disability Issues (2010) *Equality Act 2010*, Office for Disability Issues, London.

12

Preparing for Work

Dyslexic Undergraduates Making the Transition into Employment

Fiona White, Richard Mendez and Rosanne Rieley, all from the University of Leicester, UK

In the past, dyslexic people may have been worried about applying to university or any branch of adult education. Fortunately, many dyslexic people now study at university and have the opportunity to fulfil their potential and become graduates. The UK Higher Education Statistics Agency (HESA) figures for 2008–2009 cite 30,415 dyslexic students in Higher Education (HE). This represents 3.2% of the whole student population. In 1994–1995 there were just 2,359 dyslexic students in HE, representing 0.4% of the student population. This chapter focuses on how dyslexic students can be supported as they move from university into the world of work and outlines the award-winning programme entitled Access to Employability,[1] which has been running for three years at the University of Leicester. All the illustrative quotations included were made by students who took part in focus groups or in the programme itself.

Transition Stages

School/college to higher education

There is a positive emphasis on transition from school/college to university with many institutions offering different events, including prospective student taster days, open days, summer schools and interactive workshops. There is also a widening participation team within the Higher Education Funding Council for England (HEFCE).[2] There is considerable support in HE for dyslexic students whilst they are studying, via the Disabled Students' Allowance,[3] which finances study support and assistive technology. Students will often receive many hours of study support throughout their degree, and their primary focus is understandably on their assessment and success in this sector. There are many dyslexic students in HE who are constrained by the little time they have left after assessment priorities have been met, and therefore feel they do not have the time or the energy to pursue activities that might enhance their employability. However, as graduate numbers increase, the need to be as employable as possible becomes even more important.

[1] Times Higher Education Award: Outstanding Support for Students 2009.
[2] http://www.hefce.ac.uk/widen.
[3] http://www.direct.gov.uk/en/DisabledPeople/EducationAndTraining/HigherEducation/DG_10034898.

Supporting Dyslexic Adults in Higher Education and the Workplace, First Edition. Edited by Nicola Brunswick.

Higher education into work

Support for the transition into work for dyslexic students in HE is less apparent than support for their transition from school/college into the HE sector, although there is a growing industry that provides assessment and support in the workplace (Kindersley 2008; Moody 2008). General careers programmes are well advertised in HE institutions but anecdotal feedback and other sources suggest that many students do not necessarily access these services (DfEE 2001).

There seems to have been limited provision in HE that specifically targets dyslexic students in preparing them for the job market. This may be intentional in line with an inclusive agenda. However, when they come to address their futures, students may want support from dyslexia support staff who know them well and who understand their strengths and concerns. They may also want information about support in the workplace and how disability legislation and adjustment works through schemes such as Access to Work.[4]

It is tempting to dwell on the immediate difficulties and concerns of dyslexic students, but of equal interest to those working with dyslexic students in HE should be their longer-term aspirations. To appreciate the whole transition cycle for students, we need to know more about:

- how dyslexic students perform in the job market and whether they remain in employment
- dyslexic students' main concerns about employability and employment, and
- how HE institutions and students might address these concerns.

What Happens to Dyslexic Graduates when they Leave University?

From the publication of the Robbins Report (Committee on Higher Education 1963) to the report by the Confederation of British Industry Higher Education Task Force (2009), *Future Fit: Preparing graduates for the world of work*, the focus on student/graduate employability has gained momentum and prominence within HE and also in wider forums.

This focus has permeated through to other agendas such as those relating to access and widening participation. In their 2010 report, *What Happens Next? A report on the first destinations of 2007/2008 disabled graduates,* the Association for Graduate Careers Advisory Services (AGCAS) Disabilities Task Group (2010, p. 5) claims that:

> Support to disabled students . . . has long been a part of careers provision. Many services have provided mentoring schemes, leadership programmes, employer-sponsored projects and web-based resources specifically for disabled students.

Whilst acknowledging the work of HE staff in supporting disabled graduates, assessing the direct impact of such interventions can prove difficult. The AGCAS report (2010, p. 20) illustrates relative parity between the employment outcomes of 2007–2008 UK/EU full-time first degree graduates with dyslexia compared with their non-dyslexic counterparts. The research identifies that 50.4% of graduates with a specific learning difficulty (including dyslexia) were in full-time paid work six months after graduation. This compares well with non-disabled graduates, as 51.9% of these entered full-time paid work in the same period.

The findings also suggest that a higher proportion (23.3%) of 2007–2008 UK/EU full-time first degree graduates with a specific learning difficulty (SpLD) entered professional careers

[4] http://www.direct.gov.uk/en/DisabledPeople/Employmentsupport/WorkSchemesAndProgrammes/DG_4000347.

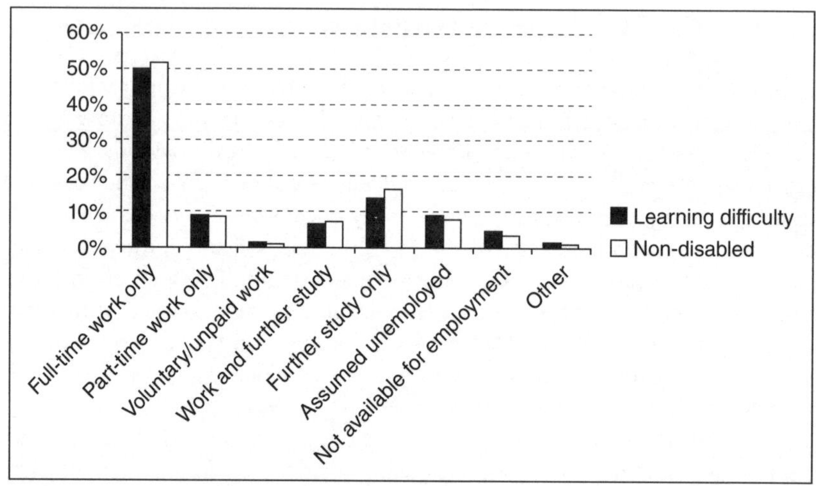

Figure 12.1 2008 destinations of graduates with a specific learning difficulty compared with non-disabled graduates (in percentages).

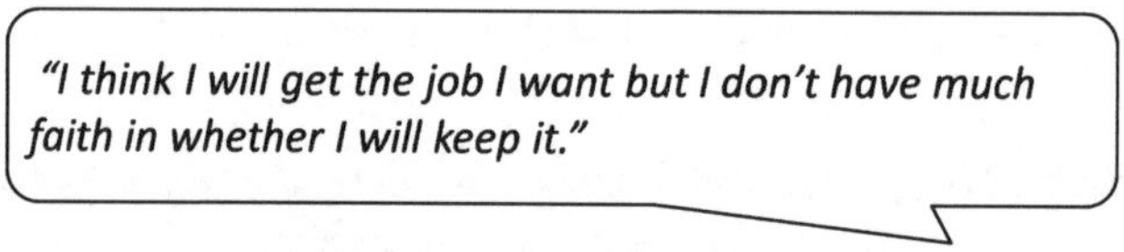

"I think I will get the job I want but I don't have much faith in whether I will keep it."

Figure 12.2 Student apprehension on retaining a job.

compared with those from 2006–2007 (22.6%). In contrast, 9.9% of 2007–2008 UK/EU full-time first degree graduates with an SpLD were assumed to be unemployed; this is a 2.3% increase compared with their 2006–2007 counterparts. Figure 12.1 is adapted from the AGCAS (2010) report entitled *What Happens Next?* and summarizes the AGCAS findings pertaining to graduates with SpLDs.

Whilst some of these statistics give cause for optimism, they may not reflect some of the realities of employment in the longer term. The information does nothing to inform us of job retention, i.e. what percentage of graduates with an SpLD retain their jobs after 12 months' employment (see Figure 12.2).

The survey also does not indicate why a higher number of students with SpLDs are 'not available for work' or 'assumed unemployed'.

When local statistics for the University of Leicester from the 2007 *Destination of Leavers from Higher Education survey* (DLHE)[5] were analysed, it was found that while Leicester's non-disabled graduates outperformed the national average (i.e. in avoiding unemployment), Leicester's graduates with a disability were twice as likely to be unemployed than their non-disabled counterparts. They were also underperforming when compared with other graduates with a disability at a national level. Whilst the analysis above does not scrutinize statistics relating solely to dyslexic graduates, it provides sufficient evidence to challenge HE staff to consider what else can be done to improve the employment prospects of dyslexic graduates and, indeed, graduates with disabilities in general.

[5] Available at: http://www.hesa.ac.uk/index.php?option=com_collns&task=show_colln&Itemid=232&c=C07018&s=3&wvy=any&wvs=3&isme=1.

What are the Key Concerns of Dyslexic Undergraduate Students about Employment and Employability?

Two focus groups (with first-, second- and third-year students with dyslexia) were conducted at the University of Leicester in 2008; all students were asked a series of questions relating to employability and they were encouraged to discuss their thoughts openly. The 11 students came from different degree disciplines.

Most of the students had not undertaken significant work experience although a few had engaged in limited work-shadowing opportunities or vacation work. When pressed about why they had not acquired more work experience, many cited time management issues associated with their disability. Additionally, most students had not compiled a curriculum vitae (CV).

Students were then asked about their prior knowledge of, and engagement in, existing employability provision open to all students at the University. The majority had limited knowledge of work experience and employment-related opportunities. The students were asked to think about how their extra-curricular activities (e.g. part-time work, Students' Union society work) could be valuable evidence in terms of employability skills. All but one of the students admitted that they had not previously appreciated the linkage between their extra-curricular activities and employability skills. Many had thought that if their extra-curricular activity had nothing to do with their degree, it would not be worth mentioning to a future employer.

None of the students taking part in the focus group had ever used the Careers Service. Most of the students expressed anxiety about obtaining a job and about workplace demands. Views expressed included concerns about:

- employers' perceptions of disabilities
- obtaining a job
- how to manage dyslexia in the world of work
- adhering to deadlines and meetings in the workplace
- being misunderstood
- having to write things down
- having to give presentations.

Students were unsure how to address such anxieties.

Third-year students in particular were concerned about obtaining a job, fearing that their disability would be a barrier. Others also cited concerns relating to employers' perceptions about their disability, and they anticipated that negative stereotyping was likely amongst employers. Interestingly, the same views were expressed by students with disabilities in research by Houghton (2006), who commented that, 'the fear of discrimination and a negative response based upon ignorance was voiced by all students' (p. 6).

How should Higher Education Institutions Respond?

Most universities have a wide range of opportunities available for undergraduates to take up work experience and develop employability skills; these opportunities include careers services, specialist careers tutors, work experience programmes, volunteering centres, careers fairs, skills workshops and personal development planning. However, the Department for Education and Employment (2001) suggested that, 'from research undertaken for the review, it was clear that those who appear most in need are often those least likely to use their Careers Service' (p. 26).

The findings from the focus group, coupled with the University of Leicester's 2007 graduate destinations data, led to the establishment of the Access to Employability programme in 2008. However, in an educational climate where inclusive education is paramount, making the decision to offer specialist provision was a difficult one. For example, in his work, Hirst (2008) discussed the need for inclusive learning for students with disabilities. This philosophy was recognized by Chapman (2008) who stated that, 'disabled students should not be treated as a separate category with distinct and totally different needs' (p. 70).

However, the focus groups suggested that there is value in providing an exclusive forum in which students can have full and frank conversations about their disabilities with staff and peers who know them and who understand the concerns they may have. Understandably, students might choose not to discuss sensitive issues if they were part of an all-inclusive programme that also included non-disabled students.

The programme needed to address some of the specific concerns identified from the focus group results, namely: lack of work experience (a major disadvantage in graduate employment) and anxieties regarding graduate employment and disclosure.

The Access to Employability Programme

The programme is a collaborative venture between the Career Development Team and the AccessAbility Centre. It is designed to support dyslexic students and other students with disabilities in making the transition from university into work. The programme is open to any student in the University who uses the AccessAbility Centre. At the beginning of each academic year students registered with the AccessAbility Centre, including all undergraduates and postgraduates, are invited to sign up for the programme. Students who are assessed by an educational psychologist whilst on course are given information about the programme when they have their post-assessment interview. It is interesting that a significant number of international postgraduate students who do not have a disability also attempt to sign up for the programme, perhaps indicating the desire for small-group support across the University's diverse population.

The programme helps students to think about their academic and extra-curricular skills. Activities facilitate students' identifying and rehearsing their employability skills. Morley and Aynsley (2007) suggest that, 'professional scientific and technical employers place greater emphasis on graduates' subject knowledge' (p. 232). Academic skills and knowledge are important but students are sometimes unsure how they can demonstrate these in a way that appeals to an employer. The Access to Employability programme offers an opportunity to discuss openly what being dyslexic means in terms of employability and employment. Students can prepare for the challenges they face and share the diverse ways that they reach their goals.

How the Programme is Structured

Workshops

The main aims of the workshops offered are to empower and increase student confidence, and to provide experiential learning. Each workshop is tailored for a specific academic year group, addressing student issues such as skills, disclosure, work experience and applications (see Figure 12.3). The workshops include a range of short interactive activities, open discussions in small groups, video podcast footage and employer talks to engage the students. Some examples of these workshops are given below.

Showcasing skills

Some employers recognize the particular skills/abilities that dyslexic people can bring to their business: creativity, persistence and problem-solving to name just a few. Many disabled people have become 'serial innovators' in the sense that they are constantly finding new ways to overcome the challenges they face, and this can be seen as a valuable asset to employers (Employers' Forum on Disabilities, 2010). The Access to Employability programme tries to help students to identify and articulate what they have to offer an employer (see Figures 12.4 and 12.5).

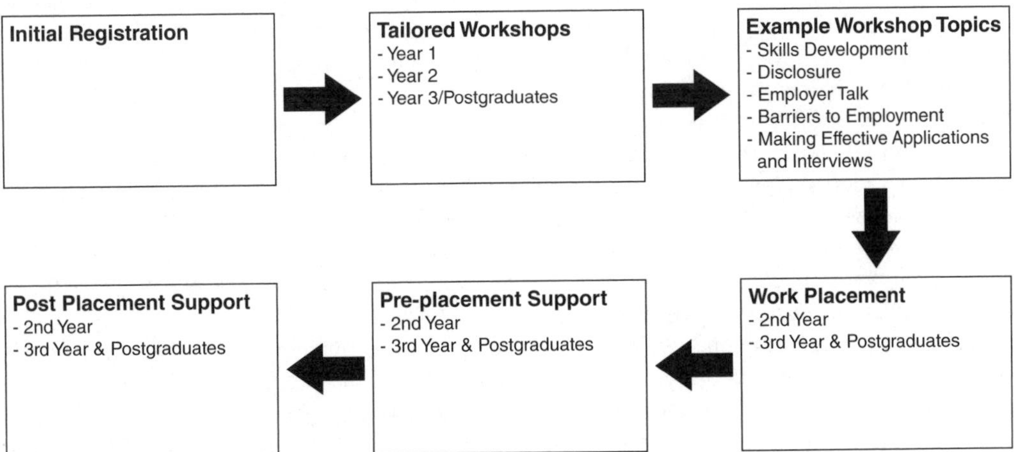

Figure 12.3 How the Access to Employability programme is structured.

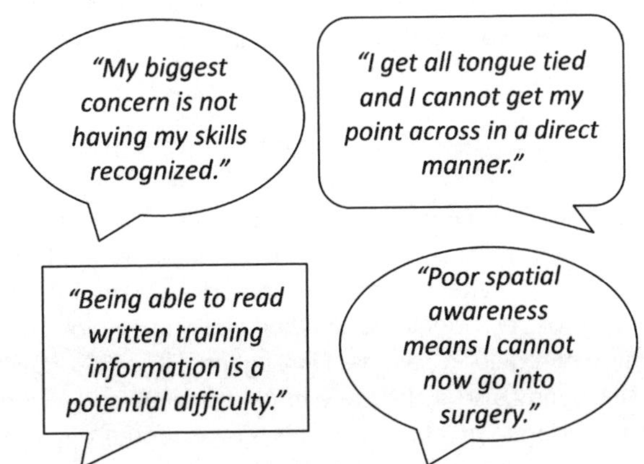

Figure 12.4 Student perceptions of their skills.

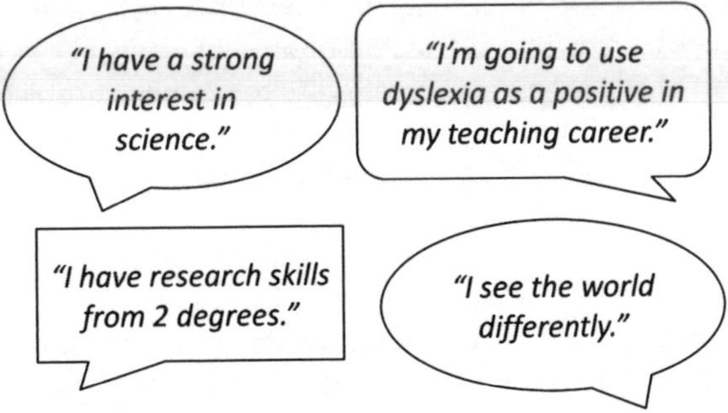

Figure 12.5 Student strengths.

First-year students attend two workshops focusing on transition to higher education, maximizing their time during their studies and CV building. This helps them in the second year to build up both academic skills and work experience. There is evidence that there are 'statistically significant relationships between extra-curricular activity and the transition process' (Tchibozo 2007, p. 54).

The other focus for first years is to develop a process of talking about dyslexia comfortably and in a positive way with different audiences, including an employer. One student wanted to share and practise ways of presenting to an employer both the difficulties and solutions of being dyslexic. The group decided that the best approach was to be open about a problem but immediately follow up with a suggestion of how it could be overcome on the basis of: 'I find x hard but this is what I do to get round it'.

Madriaga (2007), when referring to dyslexic students, suggests that, 'life after higher education worried students . . . it was difficult for them to see future employers being accepting of their impairments, let alone valuing them' (p. 408). The application and interview processes alone pose a number of dilemmas for dyslexic students and may cause anxiety. Increasingly, the application process begins online with small boxes or tick options, which can be a frustration for dyslexic students.

Second-year students attend two workshops covering skills auditing, work placements and issues surrounding these, and making effective applications. The programme also offers one-to-one assistance with the application process. Students can then sign up for a work placement/taster day during the term. Students also have access to video podcasts of dyslexic students who have graduated and are in work. Feedback suggests that students have appreciated both the work experience and the workshops.

Final-year and postgraduate students attend two workshops focusing on work placements, exit strategies and making effective applications and interviews. They are also offered work placement opportunities.

Disclosure

At the British Dyslexia Association's International conference in 2008, interesting questions were highlighted around disclosure of an SpLD to a prospective employer, both in the UK and the USA (McLoughlin 2008; Price 2008). Students are usually prepared to disclose dyslexia whilst studying in HE but appear to be reluctant to do so when entering employment. This may be because, once the pressure of regular assessment throughout HE is no longer there, students adapt to the workplace very well. It may also be because there is anxiety and uncertainty about the timing and outcome of disclosing to an employer. This is even more likely with students following professional courses such as nursing, medicine, teaching and pharmacy. There is considerable literature on dyslexic employees in healthcare professions that highlights some of the challenges they experience (Illingworth 2005; Harriss and Cooper 2005), but it is not so clear what specific strategies they may have learned in preparation for their future employment whilst in HE.

Through the use of e-resources and discussion groups, students in our programme are encouraged to consider whether they agree with disclosing their disability (see Figure 12.6 for some representative comments) and to consider any circumstances when they would not disclose. This provides peer support and a forum for airing any concerns and issues.

Employer talk

A dyslexic employee representative of a large graduate recruiter discussed his own experience of disclosing a disability in the recruitment and selection process before going on to have a successful career. This provides a positive role model and an opportunity for students to talk about their own concerns.

"I would not disclose to an employer because I would be worried that they would think I'm not capable of doing the job."
"I will disclose to an employer because people will allow for small grammatical errors if they know you are not being lazy."
"I will disclose to an employer, otherwise this will always be standing in the way of my work relationships and my performance."

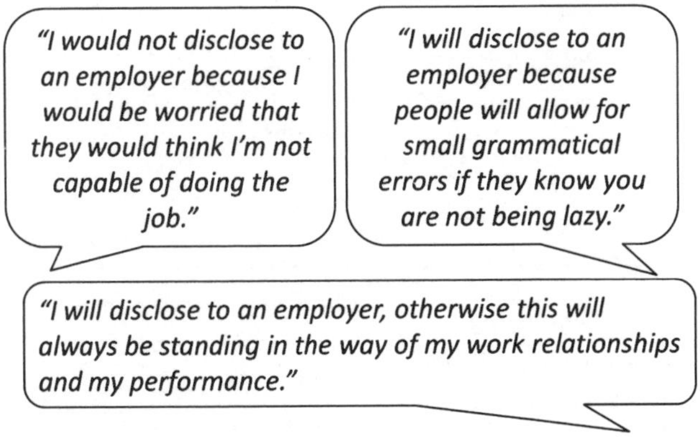

Figure 12.6 Students on disclosure.

"Being able to read written training materials for the vocation is potentially a difficult obstacle"
"I cannot get my point across in a direct manner"
"My inability to visualise in 3D meant that surgery would be a bad idea"

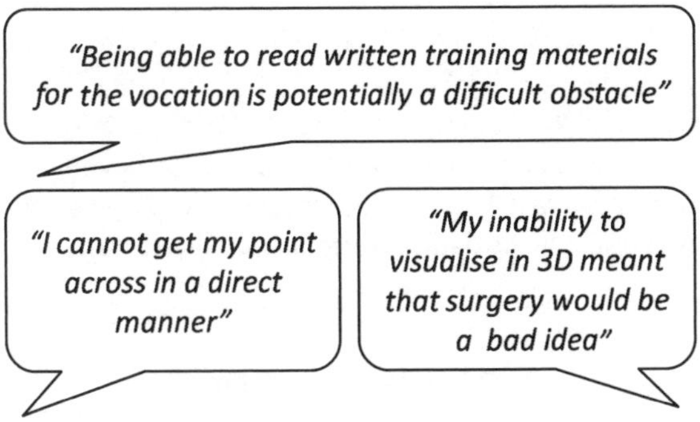

Figure 12.7 Barriers to employment.

Barriers to employment

Through group discussion, students were encouraged to think about possible barriers to employment that they might face (see Figure 12.7), and then to suggest ways to overcome these. This allowed students to share views and offer solutions to each other.

These comments suggest that students may welcome an opportunity to focus in detail on what they may need to discuss with a future employer. Relevant issues might be:

- how to make information exchange as accessible as possible
- providing additional training, and
- using assistive technology, such as that provided through Access to Work.

Work Placement

Students will have different reasons for wanting to undertake work experience (see, for example, Figure 12.8).

They are provided with an overview of the nature of each placement and have the opportunity to sign up on the day of the workshop for short pre-arranged work placements and taster days from a range of local employers. Placement opportunities span business, teaching and the voluntary sector. Supportive work placements can be very valuable as students get a chance to 'try out' disclosing, asking about adjustments, whilst learning about

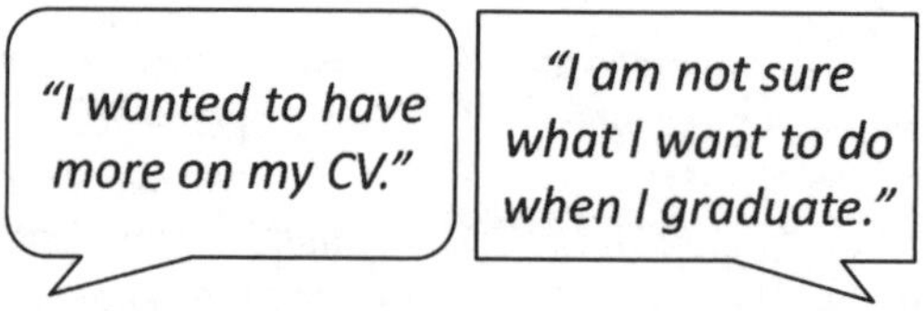

"I wanted to have more on my CV."

"I am not sure what I want to do when I graduate."

Figure 12.8 Reason for wanting a work placement.

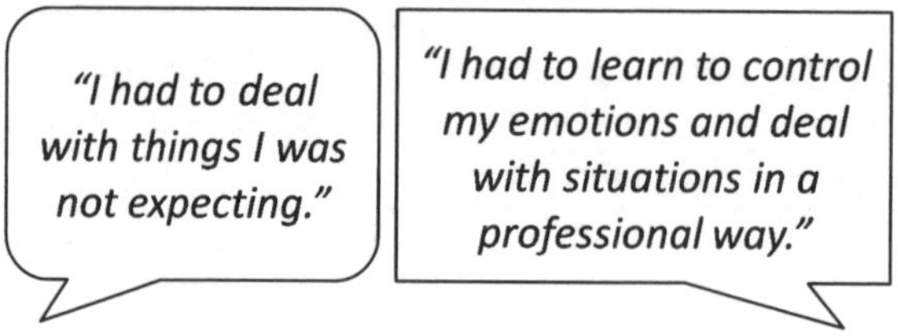

"I had to deal with things I was not expecting."

"I had to learn to control my emotions and deal with situations in a professional way."

Figure 12.9 Learning whilst working.

themselves in a variety of situations. Students work one or two days a week for a total of 15 days; alternatively, there is the option of one-day work-shadowing. It is the students' responsibility to negotiate with the employer the days and times they will be working.

Students valued the work placement opportunities (some comments about this are shown in Figure 12.9). One student who was initially frustrated by being given what she perceived as menial tasks, later admitted to having learned useful techniques for negotiating more effective mentoring.

Placement Support

Prior to going on work placement, students have access to a one-to-one consultation to help them gain the most from their placement and to provide them with guidance notes for skills and reflection purposes.

Students then commence their work placements and have access to e-resources. To help reduce the anxieties that students had previously highlighted, resources have been produced and are available on the University's Virtual Learning Environment. These resources will be further enhanced with more input from graduates and employers in the future. Sanderson (2008) and Draffan (2008) have provided useful information on technological adjustments in the workplace. Students are also encouraged to attend a post-placement consultation with a work experience team member for help with evidencing skills.

Currently, employers are made aware of the programme's aims and they interview students for the placements. They have an opportunity to give feedback both to the students and to the University, and this has generally been positive, with only one student not completing the placement.

Evaluation of the Programme

Evaluation is currently under way and involves employers, students and staff. Initial feedback from students is positive, as is shown in Figure 12.10. It seems that providing opportunities to talk freely about dyslexia in the workplace are welcomed but students also wish to know more about practical ways of presenting their skills to an employer.

For example, dyslexic students across all year groups highlighted the need to be more confident in written communication and presentation skills. For the next academic year, dyslexia support staff will pilot specific workshops that address this and complement the

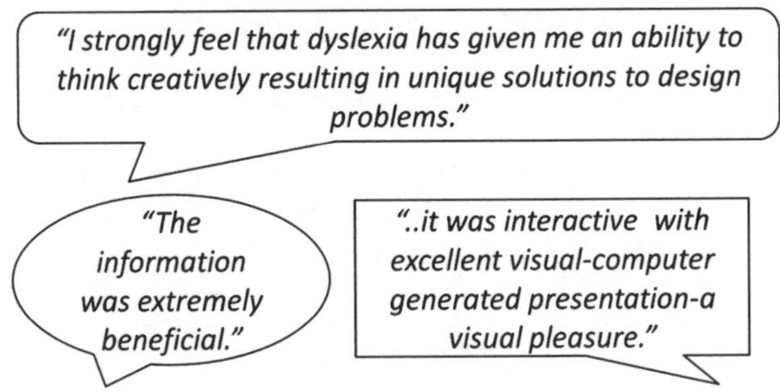

Figure 12.10 Student feedback on the programme.

one-on-one sessions students have with the careers adviser. More opportunities to practise interviews and presentations will be offered because, during the workshops, it was observed by the dyslexia support staff that some of the students did not do justice to themselves when presenting in short activities. Similarly, in the work placement part of the programme, although most students did very well, one dyslexic student was unable to take part because she was too anxious; this student has recently graduated with a first class degree. Confidence-building remains a key priority in all stages of the programme.

Evaluating the impact of the programme in the longer term presents significant challenges because of contact systems, data protection issues and passage of time. However, students who have participated are asked if they could provide onward contact details and it is hoped that these students can be tracked and contacted on up to two occasions in the next three years.

Conclusions

Employability is now a Key Performance Indicator for all HE institutions (HEFCE 2009) but institutional responses across the sector will vary. From the experience at the University of Leicester, it seems that the following key points should be taken into consideration when planning activities to increase the employability of students in such a widely diverse population:

- Students with SpLDs may welcome a forum to discuss sensitive areas of the whole process of applying for, obtaining and retaining a job.
- Students with SpLDs value the opportunity to gain work experience whilst at university as their opportunities to do so elsewhere may have been limited.
- Students with SpLDs do succeed academically but that does not necessarily mean that they are confident about the skills they have to offer an employer.
- More information is needed about how students fare in the jobs that they get, and about the many skills and strategies they develop in managing dyslexia in the workplace.

In summary, the success of the programme is driven by the creativity, persistence and diverse skills of the students who took part in the programme outlined in this chapter. Practitioners should also bear in mind Whitehead's (2008) comment that:

> When unsupported, dyslexic thinkers can become fearful individuals who may invest a lot of energy in avoiding or deferring challenging tasks and finding excuses why they cannot be done. When supported, however, dyslexic thinkers can be among the most innovative and original contributors to a firm's success.

The authors would like to acknowledge the support of Matthew Mobbs in the production of resources in the programme.

References and Resources:

AGCAS (2010) *What happens next? A report on the first destinations of 2007/2008 disabled graduates*, AGCAS, Sheffield.

Chapman, V. (2008) Developing inclusive curricula. *Learning and Teaching in Higher Education*, 3, 62–89.

Committee on Higher Education (1963) *Higher Education: Report of the committee appointed by the Prime Minister under the chairmanship of Lord Robbins*, HMSO, London.

Confederation of British Industry (2009) *Future Fit: Preparing graduates for the world of work*, Confederation of British Industry Higher Education Task Force, London.

Department for Education and Employment (2001) *Developing modern higher education careers services, Report of the review led by Sir Martin Harris*, DfEE, London.

DLHE (2007) *Destination of Leavers from Higher Education Survey*, HEFCE, Bristol.

Draffan, E.A. (2008) New technology to support adults with dyslexia, in *The Dyslexia Handbook 2008/9* (ed. C. Singleton), British Dyslexia Association, Bracknell, pp. 204–212.

Employers' Forum on Disabilities (2010) *Disabled graduates* (online), http://www.realising-potential.org/news/disabled-graduates/, accessed January 6, 2010.

Harriss, A. and Cooper, R. (2005) Dyslexia in the workplace. *Occupational Health*, 57, 25–32.

HEFCE (2009) *HEFCE strategic plan 2006–2009*, updated June 2009 (online) http://www.hefce.ac.uk/pubs/hefce/2009/09_21/, accessed August 8, 2010.

Higher Education Statistics Agency (2008) *Destinations of leavers from higher education, comparative report* (online) http://www.hesa.ac.uk/dox/dlhe_longitudinal/Destination_of_Leavers_from_HE_Comparative_Report_Feb08.pdf, accessed August 12, 2010.

Higher Education Statistics Agency (2010) *Students and qualifiers data tables* (online) http://www.hesa.ac.uk/index.php?option=com_datatables&Itemid=121&task=show_category&catdex=3, accessed April 5, 2010.

Hirst, A. (2008) The changing legal context, continuing professional development and the promotion of inclusive pedagogy for disabled students. *Learning and Teaching in Higher Education*, 3, 49–61.

Houghton, A. (2006) Disability effective inclusive policies: Student and staff perspectives on experiences throughout the student lifecycle, *The 36th Annual SCUTREA Conference*, Trinity and All Saints College, Leeds, July 4–6, 2006.

Illingworth, K. (2005) The effects of dyslexia on the work of nurses and healthcare assistants. *Nursing Standard*, 19 (38), 41–48.

Kindersley, K. (2008) Dyslexia at work, in *The Dyslexia Handbook 2008/9* (ed. C. Singleton), British Dyslexia Association, Bracknell, pp. 195–203.

Madriaga, M. (2007) Enduring disablism: Students with dyslexia and their pathways into UK higher education and beyond. *Disability and Society* 22, 399–412.

McLoughlin, D. (2008) Employment and adults with dyslexia: Making 'goodness of fit' good, *British Dyslexia Association International Conference 2008*, Harrogate, Yorkshire, March 28, 2008.

Moody, S. (2008) Dyslexia and dyspraxia assessment for adults, in *The Dyslexia Handbook 2008/9* (ed. C. Singleton), British Dyslexia Association, Bracknell, pp. 189–194.

Morley, L. and Aynsley, S. (2007) Employers, quality and standards in higher Education: Shared values and vocabularies or elitism and inequalities? *Higher Education Quarterly*, 61, 229–249.

Price, L.A. (2008) Secrets, stigmas and self disclosure for adults with learning disabilities, *The British Dyslexia Association International Conference 2008*, Harrogate, Yorkshire.

Sanderson, A. (2008) Reasonable adjustments in the workplace: the role of information technology, in *The Dyslexia Handbook 2008/9* (ed. C. Singleton), British Dyslexia Association, Bracknell, pp. 213–219.

Tchibozo, G. (2007) Extra-curricular activity and the transition from higher education to work: a survey of graduates in the UK. *Higher Education Quarterly*, 62, 37–56.

Whitehead, R. (2008, April 21) Letter of the week: Dyslexia in the workplace: disability or talent? *Personnel Today* (online) http://www.personneltoday.com/articles/2008/04/21/45469/letter-of-the-week-dyslexia-in-the-workplace-disability-or-talent.html, accessed June 10, 2010.

Section 2

Supporting Dyslexic Adults in the Workplace

13

Disclosing Dyslexia

An Exercise in Self-Advocacy

Alan Martin and David McLoughlin, both
University of Buckingham, UK

Introduction

One of the ways in which the success of disability legislation and the understanding of specific learning difficulties is reflected in society is the disclosure rate; that is, the extent to which individuals inform employers and colleagues that they have a learning difficulty. Research in the United States and Canada has suggested that individuals with learning disabilities are reluctant to disclose, despite the existence of disability legislation that is supposed to prevent discrimination. The authors found that the majority of adults in the samples of individuals interviewed did not ask for accommodations (adjustments) in the selection process, did not tell their employers during an interview, and did not ask for adjustments in the job (Gerber and Price 2003; Gerber *et al.* 2004; Madaus *et al.* 2002).

Some of the reasons given reflect much misunderstanding surrounding dyslexia, both in terms of the stereotypes held by non-dyslexic people as well as the lack of understanding dyslexic people have of themselves. These included:

- I never thought it would apply to work.
- I was afraid to be found out – they might have taken the job away.
- They would think I couldn't do the job.
- People would look down on you.
- I was embarrassed.
- I didn't think it was my place to ask for those things.
- I would feel like a burden if they gave me anything extra.

There seems to be little, if any, published European research conducted in this important area of disclosure.

Rationale

It may be reasonable to assume that individuals who have experienced the benefits of adjustments are among those most likely to disclose to their employer that they have a learning difficulty. On the basis of this premise one might predict that graduates who had been in

Supporting Dyslexic Adults in Higher Education and the Workplace, First Edition. Edited by Nicola Brunswick.

receipt of accommodations, such as extra time to complete examinations during their student years, would be prepared to tell employers that they have a specific learning difficulty. This study was designed to develop a methodology that might assist with testing this assumption.

It is useful to know what proportion of people with diagnosed learning difficulties disclose these to their employers. However, this study was designed to probe further their reasons for disclosure or non-disclosure by using a combination of demographic data collection, psychometric measures and qualitative open questions. It was also important as part of the methodology to enable participants to express their reasons for disclosure or non-disclosure to an employer; there are two reasons for this. First, there is sometimes an overreliance on psychometric measures or those involving closed questions devised by experts, which limit the ability of participants to describe their individual experiences more fully. Second, given the exploratory nature of this research, it was important to have a facility for participants to express themselves because the research base is relatively limited.

Instrumentation

The questionnaire was compiled by the authors on the basis of the experience of working with dyslexic adults in higher education, and content validity was established by ensuring that the issues covered were also reported in the existing literature. The first aim of the questionnaire was to establish whether the sample of former students disclosed to their employers that they are dyslexic. In addition, and more importantly, it was necessary to discover why they did or did not disclose and what factors were important to them in deciding whether to disclose. The questionnaire also included questions about their perceived strengths, the value of learning support, and their reported self-efficacy (i.e. belief in their own competencies).

The questionnaire was designed to be distributed online using Survey Monkey, a web-based survey design and distribution service. Many of the potential participants were based outside the UK and an online questionnaire was thought to be the most effective means of communicating with them.

Method

The sample

Using the records available from the Student Welfare department at the University of Buckingham, a small private university in the United Kingdom, alumni who had been in contact with the Student Welfare department were asked if they would participate in the research. They were asked if they would be prepared to complete an internet-based questionnaire exploring their experiences as students and, subsequently, while at work.

The initial sample consisted of 153 alumni for whom email addresses were available. The online service used to administer the questionnaire was able to track which email addresses were viable because invalid emails bounced back to the sender. It was discovered immediately in the first email sweep that 30 (19.6%) of the initial sample of contacts consisted of invalid email addresses. This is a significant problem when conducting research using email contacts; people are more likely to stop using their email address and therefore disappear without trace than they are to move from their residential address without leaving forwarding details. However, it is generally thought that this problem is more than compensated for by the relative ease with which people can complete an internet-based survey and provide an instant response rather than return postal questionnaires. It was assumed, therefore, that the remaining 123 emails were delivered, although there was no way of knowing how many of these emails were read.

In total 44 participants completed the questionnaire (35.8% of the viable email contacts). Just over 2/3 (68%) of the final sample were male, and the sample had an average age of 34 (ranging from 25 to 61). The respondents had graduated from the University as long ago as 1985, but 2/3 had graduated within 10 years of the survey being conducted. Therefore, most of the participants were in their first decade of the graduate jobs market.

This response rate, of just over 1/3 of the viable sample, is relatively good for questionnaire research as it is notoriously difficult to encourage adults to participate in research. Several sweeps of the email lists were required in order to gain this number of participants; as expected, each message sweep resulted in fewer returns. A balance must be struck between the frequency of these sweeps and the inconvenience that it might cause to recipients who feel that they are being 'spammed' (i.e. bombarded with unsolicited emails). This sample may have been more motivated to take part due to the personal relevance of the questionnaire subject matter and their link with the University.

Results

Background experience

Participants were asked which SpLD or related conditions they were diagnosed with. The most common diagnosis received by the participant sample was for dyslexia (95.5%) with relatively low proportions of other SpLDs (e.g. 6.8% with Attention Deficit Hyperactivity Disorder and Visual Stress).

Participants were asked at what level of education their specific learning difficulty had been identified, and the majority (86%) reported that their SpLD had been identified only at university.

Participants were asked to report the problems they experience and were able to click multiple items from a list of 14 items. Figure 13.1 indicates the percentage responses to each of the seven most commonly selected items.

Figure 13.1 illustrates that the problems experienced by the sample are relatively evenly distributed among the seven categories. Analysis revealed that, on average, participants reported experiencing five problems associated with their dyslexia.

Participants were also asked to report particular strengths they believe they have, and again they were able to click multiple items.

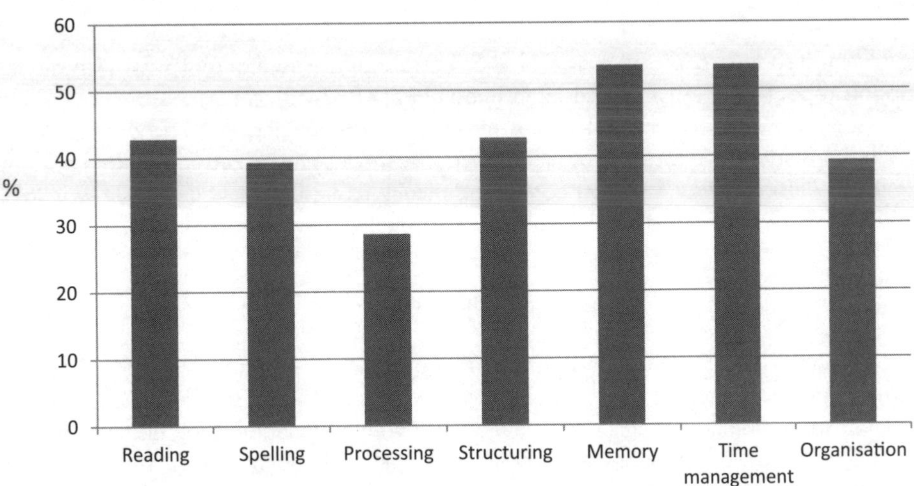

Figure 13.1 Most common self-reported problems experienced by participants with SpLD.

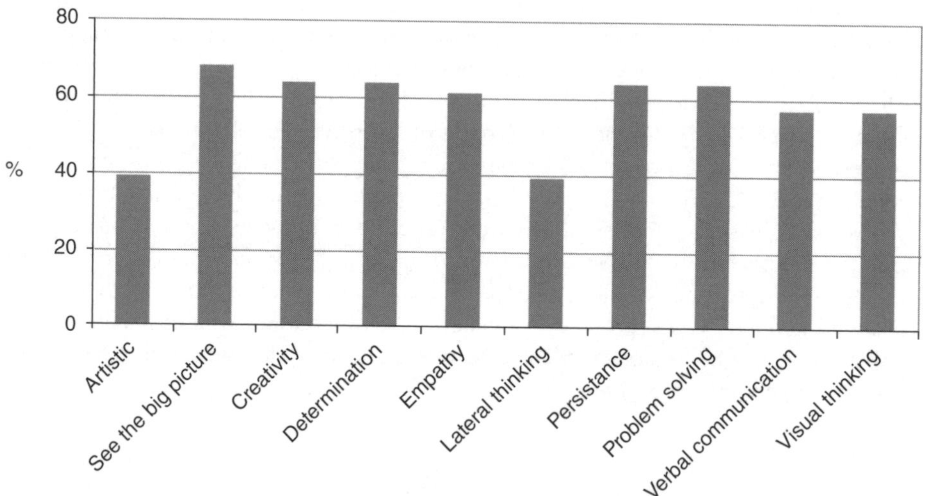

Figure 13.2 Self-reported strengths experienced by participants with SpLD.

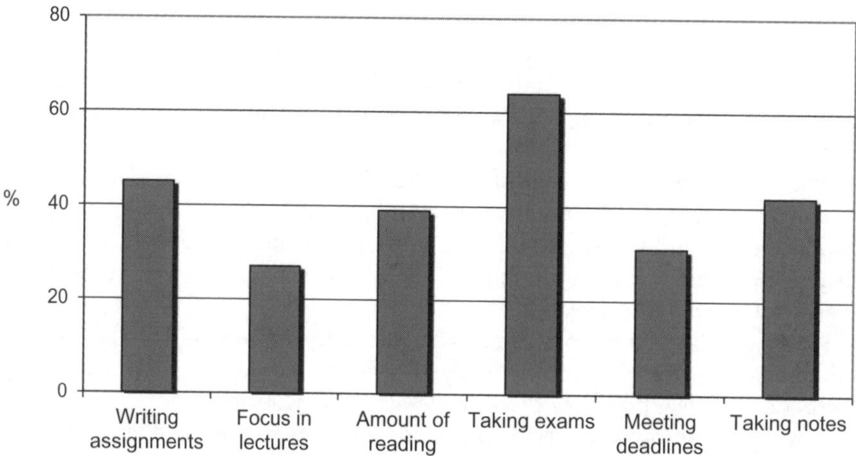

Figure 13.3 Reported difficulties that resulted in participants approaching the Student Welfare department.

The sample reported a broad range of specific strengths (see Figure 13.2), with all participants reporting at least one strength (mean = 5.4 ± 2.48).

Participants were asked what difficulties they were experiencing that had caused them to approach the Student Welfare department. Responses are summarized in Figure 13.3.

This figure illustrates that the most common difficulty experienced at university was taking examinations. However, the other difficulties were relatively evenly distributed.

Employment

It was found that 95% of respondents were working at the time of completing the survey, and were working across a broad range of employment sectors. The most common sectors of employment were manufacturing (13.6%) followed by environmental, food chain and rural occupations (11.4%), accountancy and business (9.1%) and health (9.1%). This demonstrated that the sample was following a diverse range of career paths since graduating from university.

Participants were asked how many jobs they had had since leaving university and over half of the sample (54.5%) reported that they had had more than three jobs, with one person reporting that they had had 13 jobs since leaving university.

Disclosure

The primary aim of this research project was to ask former students whether they had disclosed their SpLD to their employer and, if they had, at what point they had done so. In order to do this effectively it was thought important to divide the sample into those participants who were resident in the UK (45% of the sample) and those who were not (55%). The non-UK resident group comprised individuals from 18 countries, so did not form a geographically coherent group. It was found that, overall, less than 1/5 of the sample (16.7%) had disclosed any details of their SpLD to their employers. In addition, it was found that UK resident participants were statistically no more or less likely than non-UK resident participants to disclose details of their SpLD to their employers. Given that the non-disclosure group was the larger group, it will be analysed first.

Participants were first asked why they had not disclosed their SpLD to their employer; they were able to give multiple explanations from a defined (closed) list but were also given the opportunity to provide their own explanations.

Figure 13.4 shows that the most common response was that participants felt that their dyslexia was not a relevant factor at work (35%). This choice was supported by several answers provided by the participants to the open responses; for example, one participant responded that 'I don't think it was that important to mention it, and I don't think it impacts my work'. Another wrote that 'there is no reason, providing the job gets done as it should'. This indicates that a significant proportion of the participants believe that dyslexia is associated with education and is not applicable to the workplace.

The second most common response was that participants felt their employer would discriminate against them (32%). The next response was that participants felt that, if they disclosed, their employer would feel they are not able to do the job as effectively as someone else (30%). In addition, 27% of participants reported that they felt they would not even be

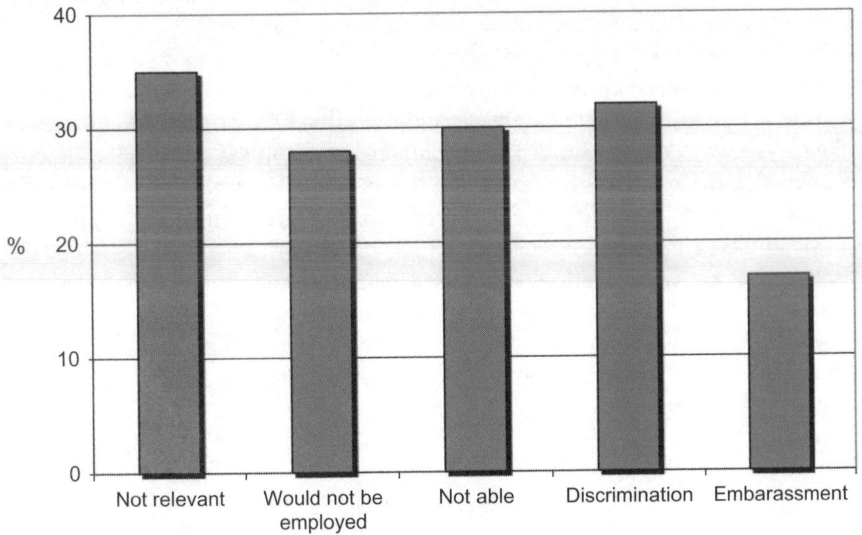

Figure 13.4 Reasons given for not disclosing dyslexia to an employer.

considered for a job if they disclosed upon application. Finally, the least common response from the range offered was the embarrassment of having to disclose their SpLD (reported by 16% of respondents).

The open responses revealed some other reasons for non-disclosure. These included, for example, that the respondent ran his or her own business, as one said: 'Fortunately as a landlord I am self-employed'; another, in a relatively senior position, said: 'I am the director of the manufacturing unit'; while a third revealed that he worked for his family: 'I work on my family business so no need of [*sic*] telling them, because they already know.' These responses indicate varied circumstances, however, all these participants are fortunate to have a relatively high degree of autonomy in their workplaces.

A group of participants added to the closed response 'I did not think it would apply to work' by giving responses such as: 'I did not see the need', 'it was not necessary', 'there is no reason, providing the work gets done' and 'I thought there was no need and I've never been asked'. These are all subtly different from the closed response option and none of the participants had selected this option in conjunction with these. All these open responses indicate that the participants could not see the benefit of disclosing, particularly, as some state explicitly, because they report that it was not necessary to do so within their workplace.

Other participants indicated that they felt less pressure at work than they did at university, thereby indirectly noting that their dyslexia has its greatest impact upon their functioning at times when they need to process large amounts of new information.

Some participants talked about coping strategies, in a broad sense, so that the impact upon their work was limited. For example, one participant reported that 'I know that I am able to over come [*sic*] problems at work through planning, preparations, self improvement and educating my self [*sic*]' while another reported that they have 'learnt to cope with it and manage better'.

Two African participants (based in Nigeria and Ghana) reported that there is little understanding of dyslexia in their countries; one claiming that 'There is little or no understanding of such issues out here' while the other reported that 'They [employer] would not understand what dyslexia is all about.'

One participant who had selected all the closed options except the 'not relevant to work' option also elaborated by stating that they 'did not want to stand out' and that during the recruitment exams within their company they 'didn't want to stand out'. This participant was demonstrably, and possibly justifiably, concerned that their dyslexia would be seen by their employer as a weakness that would hinder their career development.

This section will explore the responses of those who did disclose to their employers. However, it should be remembered that this is a very small sample of participants and great care should be taken when interpreting these findings. The 17% of participants who did disclose their dyslexia to employers did so at different points in the application process: 43% disclosed upon application; 14% did so during the interview and 43% did so once they were in employment. The participants did not consistently report their dyslexia to a particular individual within their employer's institution.

The disclosure group was asked why they had disclosed to their employer. They reported that they disclosed in order to be better understood, and to highlight potential performance issues. However, none of the participants said that they reported their dyslexia in order to be given adjustments at work and none of them asked for adjustments beyond an awareness of their strengths and weaknesses.

Discussion

The majority of the sample was diagnosed with SpLD at university and there are some reasons why this figure may be so high. First, students who had been diagnosed with SpLD at an earlier level of education may have already developed alternative learning strategies and therefore did not feel the need to report to the student welfare department at university. Second, a relatively large proportion of the students at the University of Buckingham are from countries outside the UK and EU. Recognition of SpLDs outside the EU zone is patchy to say the least. Some countries, such as those in North America and Australia, have a relatively good record of recognition and provision, while others, such as many African countries, are less effective at identification and accommodation. Finally, we should recall that most of this sample had progressed through university within the past decade and would have been attending school at least a decade prior to this. It is hoped that in the future many more individuals will be identified at earlier levels of the education system. However, it remains the case that today a large number of individuals are still referred to educational psychologists for a first assessment for SpLD by university learning support departments. This indicates that the identification of adult dyslexic readers is likely to remain an important task for some years to come (McLoughlin, Leather and Stringer 2002).

Most of the sample was in employment and there was a range of experience with employment variability (over half the sample had had three or more jobs since leaving university). The subject of how dyslexic people find an appropriate career path, what Gerber, Ginsberg and Reiff (1992) call 'goodness of fit', was not the main aim of this research but is worth investigating in future. It may be the case that it takes dyslexic adults longer to find an appropriate 'goodness of fit' between their specific skills and those required in various career fields. This is something that careers advisers and practitioners working with dyslexic individuals in academia may need to consider when giving advice, which of course requires the dyslexic person to disclose his or her problem to those concerned.

The suggestion that dyslexia is not a problem within the workplace was the largest category of response given by those who did not disclose to their employer. While these participants were within the education system they would have, by definition, been learning new information all the time so this attitude can be understood. However, unless they have a job that has a very rigid routine, there will still be a need to process new information within the workplace, and it may be important to raise awareness among people with SpLDs of the kinds of problems they may face in the workplace. This is difficult because workplaces vary a great deal but giving them a generic description of how their difficulty can affect day-to-day life, and how these difficulties can be overcome, will help them to develop a flexible approach to problem-solving in the workplace.

The second most common response was that participants felt their employer would discriminate against them. This discrimination could be personal, in the form of a manager who does not care or understand, or it could be institutional discrimination in that there was a feeling that disclosure could limit promotion within the company.

The next response was that participants felt that, if they disclosed, their employer would feel that they were not able to do the job as effectively as someone else. This may potentially be related to the previous response in that participants may feel that they would be discriminated against because their employer believes they are not up to the job. However, this response is more specific because it deals with the employer's perception of dyslexia and other SpLDs, and their perception of its impact upon the work required. It would take a great deal of confidence for someone who has a specific learning difficulty to feel that they can both disclose their difficulties to their employer and educate them about these difficulties at the same time.

In addition, 27% of participants reported that they felt they would not even be considered for a job if they disclosed upon application. This again is probably due to perceptions of competence on the part of the employer, and the feeling that disclosure would put the participant in a weaker position compared to other job applicants.

Finally, the least common response selected by participants from the range offered was the embarrassment of having to disclose their SpLD. In a way, the fact that this is the least common response is relatively positive because it indicates that some of the stigma surrounding SpLDs has been reduced. It may be the case that the 'normalization' of dyslexia and other SpLDs within the education system has filtered through into everyday life. In addition, the work that advocacy organizations do to promote understanding has helped to reduce this stigma. Yet some of our participants were still reluctant to disclose due to embarrassment. It may have been expected that most of those who were embarrassed would be foreign participants, but in fact there was an even split between UK and non-UK participants in reporting embarrassment.

A number of themes emerged when we asked whether there were other reasons for non disclosure. Some participants reported that they were self-employed or ran their own businesses so there was no need for disclosure. It will be important in future for us to establish whether our participants are more likely to become self-employed because of issues of disclosure in the workplace. Other participants felt that they had developed strategies to overcome their problems and were therefore able to function without the need to disclose.

The 17% of participants who did disclose did so at different points in the application process: most did so either upon application or once they were in employment, while a minority did so in the interview. We then asked these participants why they had disclosed, and the most common responses were that they felt it was important to do so and they could be better understood if they disclosed. None of the participants who had disclosed to their employer said they did so in order to be given adjustments at work.

The sample in this study is small and not representative of a solely UK-based population so few broad conclusions can be drawn at present. The University of Buckingham is also not typical among UK universities in that it is an independent, fee-paying institution. However, the UK and non-UK students come from a range of backgrounds and cannot be said to be from privileged or wealthy backgrounds.

The use of an online survey method allows participants to complete the survey and return it quickly. However, some participants may have had a problem with completing the survey online given the nature of the questionnaire. During the design process the potential difficulties of the participants was considered. The number of questions per page was limited so that the whole question could be seen on the screen without scrolling. This enabled participants to focus on the task in hand with as much information as was needed to answer the question, which was visible at all times. In addition, the presentation of the questionnaire was carefully considered: a choice of dark blue background and white or yellow writing was chosen for maximum contrast. Unfortunately, it is not possible for participants to choose their own colour combinations for ease of reading within the Survey Monkey system but this would have been an ideal solution and one that survey software designers may wish to include in future as part of their accessibility package. A progress bar was added to the survey so that participants could see how much of the survey they had completed; this limits the frustration that participants may feel when they are asked to complete an online survey but they are unaware of how much of the survey remains to be completed.

Participants may not have disclosed their SpLD to friends or family (and we know most had not disclosed to employers) so they may not have been willing to complete an online survey which could be observed by others while it was being completed. Despite this concern, the benefits of the online method outweigh the limitations because it is possible to reach a large number and wide range of participants via the internet. There are many special interest groups and societies that have active web forums from which to recruit participants. However, this does run the risk of attracting the 'noisy minority' among these populations. Internet use is increasing year on year among people from all age groups and so the scope for surveying adults in the workplace is increasing. It is hoped that the questionnaire outlined here can be refined and promoted to adult samples of dyslexic readers more broadly.

The findings of this exploratory survey are consistent with some of the conclusions outlined by Gerber and Price (2008). To begin with, their point that self-disclosure is driven by context and the management of personal information is supported by some of the responses received in this study. As outlined above, some of our participants felt comfortable enough to disclose to their employers while others felt there were too many barriers to disclosure. Gerber and Price (2008) point out that the hidden nature of specific learning difficulties means that individuals have greater choice over whether or not to disclose; we found that the majority of our sample was choosing not to disclose but for a variety of different reasons. They also point out that part of the process of disclosure involves educating the person to whom one is disclosing. The small number of participants who had disclosed gave some indication that they had a duty to disclose and educate their employers. However, they did not always do this prior to employment.

It was found that only 15% of graduates who had been provided with accommodations during their university years had revealed that they were dyslexic when applying for a job. The findings of this research were consistent with the work carried out by researchers in North America, who make the point that self-disclosure is driven by context and the management of personal information. As outlined above, some of our participants felt comfortable enough to disclose to their employers while others felt there were a variety of barriers to disclosure.

A significant minority of the participants expressed the view that dyslexia is a problem within the education system and not within the workplace. This may be because the education system in the UK has increased the awareness of dyslexia and therefore the association is made between dyslexia and education. It may also be the case that it is within the education system that individuals are required to engage in the kinds of tasks that dyslexic children and adults find most difficult, and so the limitations of the dyslexic person are more likely to be exposed in this setting. The umbrella term for the group of difficulties within which dyslexia is located, the specific *learning* difficulties, reinforces the association with learning and thereby, in the minds of many, with education. It was clear that the Buckingham sample had a diverse range of career choices and that some will have found a better fit between their skills and their employment role than others. However, the consistent response of some that they saw dyslexia as a problem associated with education, and by implication one that no longer applies after formal education is completed, is something that should be pursued in future research. It may be more useful to think of SpLD as referring to specific *life* difficulties rather than specific learning difficulties so that awareness of the broader impact of these problems is raised.

Conclusion

Gerber and Price (2008) point out that the hidden nature of dyslexia means that dyslexic people have greater choice over whether or not to disclose; we found that the majority of our sample was choosing not to disclose. They also point out that part of the process of disclosure involves educating the person one is disclosing to. The small number of participants who had disclosed gave some indication that they had a duty to disclose and educate their employers. However, they did not always do this prior to employment.

If dyslexic people wish to access resources and secure adjustments when applying for, and during the course of, a job, they do need to consider the matter of disclosure very carefully. There are three key issues they need to address: (i) when to say something; (ii) whom to tell; and (iii) what to say.

(i) When to say something

To some extent addressing this has been resolved by the greater awareness that has resulted from disability legislation. Application forms often contain questions asking about issues such as disability. In the main, dyslexic people should not be afraid to 'tick the dyslexia box' as its existence suggests that the organization might already be dyslexia friendly. If a dyslexic person makes it past the first stage – submitting an application that secures an interview – they might raise the issue when interviewed; a second interview is a particularly good time for this.

(ii) Whom to tell

The work that organizations such as the British Dyslexia Association do to promote understanding has helped to reduce the stigma sometimes associated with specific learning difficulties. Many organizations will have within their human resources department individuals who have knowledge of disability provision; they will also have occupational health teams. It is within the human resources department that one is most likely to find someone who can treat the matter confidentially and advocate for a dyslexic person by accessing resources and assisting them with career development. At a less formal level one might advise a supportive line manager or colleague.

(iii) What to say

Whilst there is likely to be some expertise within an organization, this does not mean that the syndrome is properly understood. The common understanding of dyslexia is a misunderstanding. It is evident, for example, from the research referred to above that many dyslexic people themselves still think of it as a reading and spelling problem or at least an educational matter. They have never been told that the processing problem that creates difficulties with literacy persists into the adult years, often undermining performance as demands increase.

The greatest expert on an individual's dyslexia should be the dyslexic person themselves. They know how it affects them daily, and they usually have a good idea of how they work best. It is unreasonable to expect businesses to be experts in dyslexia. Disclosure is an exercise in self-advocacy, so people need to develop their understanding of themselves and how dyslexia affects them in the workplace. Saying 'I am dyslexic' is not enough. They need to explain what it means to them and offer solutions. For example:

- 'I read thoroughly so I need more time' is better than 'I read slowly'.
- 'I prefer dictating so I use voice recognition software' is better than 'I am poor at typing'.
- 'I am a bit of a perfectionist so I like to have others check over my work' is better than 'I am not good at proofreading'.
- 'I like instructions in writing' is better than 'I can't remember instructions'.
- 'I never forget a face' is better than 'I can't remember names'.

In other words, dyslexic people need to be positive, able to explain how they work best, and suggest adjustments that will facilitate this. In our experience, dyslexic people rarely seek to advantage themselves by requesting adjustments. All they are asking for is to be valued for their abilities, persistence and determination, and to be treated equally. Adjustments do not give extra knowledge, talent or abilities. They just allow dyslexic people to show that they can do the job. Having said that, it is essential that dyslexic people are realistic about what they can achieve. They do need to have most of the competencies required, otherwise no amount of adjustment can make up the difference. The underlying philosophy of disability legislation is integration. Too many adjustments can lead to isolation as well as a great deal of frustration and stress. Research has suggested that 'goodness of fit' is essential to success (Gerber *et al.* 1992). Disclosure, although a complex issue and process, is fundamental to achieving this. When done positively it should ensure that employers are able to meet a dyslexic person's needs and enable him or her to become increasingly successful. Nevertheless, more work needs to be done in the area of disclosure so that we can know exactly what will facilitate the process.

Future Research

The online survey research will continue as part of the Research in Adult Dyslexia (ReAD) group at the University of Buckingham. The questionnaire used for the research listed here has now been refined and will be distributed to a wider range of adults with SpLD to assess their experiences in the workplace. This can most effectively be done through university student welfare departments because they will have records of students who have received services for assessment, guidance, counselling or accommodations. It is also in the interests of universities to do so as part of the Quality Assurance Agency's requirements for monitoring the progress of students with disabilities. However, it is also important that the research not be limited only to graduates, as the problems specific to dyslexia mean that many people with dyslexia will not have wished to go to university or have satisfied the entry requirements for doing so.

Finally, one of the problems facing researchers interested in dyslexia as it affects adults is accessing those who have left formal education. The methodology described here suggests a way forward. It will always be difficult to find truly representative samples of people but internet-based research does allow for an economical way of reaching large numbers.

References

Gerber, P.J., Ginsberg, R. and Reiff, H.B. (1992) Identifying alterable patterns in employment success for highly successful adults with learning disabilities. *Journal of Learning Disabilities*, 25, 475–487.

Gerber, P. and Price, L. (2003) Persons with learning disabilities in the workplace: What we know so far in the American with Disabilities Act era. *Learning Disabilities Research and Practice*, 18, 132–136.

Gerber, P.J. and Price, L.A. (2008) Self-disclosure and adults with learning disabilities: Practical ideas about a complex process. *Learning Disabilities*, 15, 21–23.

Gerber, P., Price, L., Mulligan, R. and Shessel, I. (2004) Beyond transition: A comparison of the employment experiences of American and Canadian adults with LD. *Journal of Learning Disabilities*, 37, 283–291.

Madaus, J.W., Ruban, L.M., Foley, T.E. *et al.* (2002) Employment self-disclosure of postsecondary graduates with learning disabilities: Rates and rationales. *Journal of Learning Disabilities*, 5, 364–369.

McLoughlin, D., Leather, C.A. and Stringer, P.E. (2002) *The Adult Dyslexic: Interventions and outcomes*, Whurr, London.

14

Self-Disclosure in Adults with Learning Disabilities and Dyslexia

Complexities and Considerations

Paul J. Gerber, Virginia Commonwealth University, USA
and Lynda A. Price, Temple University, USA

Introduction

The year 1973 was a watershed year in the United States for people with disabilities, with the passage of the Rehabilitation Act and its signature provision Section 504. Often called the 'civil rights law' for people with disabilities, this enabled individuals to take increased responsibility for their own lives. Two decades later, the Americans with Disabilities Act (ADA) was passed in 1990 and fully implemented in 1992. When President George H.W. Bush signed it into law, a new era began for people with disabilities that moved them away from paternalism and towards empowerment.

Underpinning these two significant pieces of legislation, as well as the ADA Amendments of 2008, was the necessity for people with disabilities to be able to advocate for themselves. Such is also the case in the United Kingdom, where many of the same protections are guaranteed by law.

The Importance of Self-Advocacy

Empowerment and self-determination, the hallmarks of a new philosophy for human service delivery, cannot be fully achieved if self-advocacy is not well understood or used effectively. The essential elements of self-advocacy are self-awareness, self-knowledge and self-disclosure, the latter being the catalyst that sets the whole process in motion. Self-disclosure has been described by Lynch and Gussel (1996, p. 354) as:

> an intended release of personal information by individuals regarding their tastes, interests, work, money, education, attitudes, opinions, body, and personality. Moreover, the content and timing of self-disclosure are important and potentially have an impact on outcomes (e.g. [they] determine how an individual is perceived and how corresponding requests are treated).

Disclosure needs to be done in a strategic and successful manner if it is to be effective. Moreover, when the issue of disability enters the mix, it becomes more complicated. In the case of adults with learning disabilities (LD) and dyslexia[1] there are disability-specific and

[1] Hereafter, both LD and dyslexia will, for the most part, be referred to as dyslexia.

Supporting Dyslexic Adults in Higher Education and the Workplace, First Edition. Edited by Nicola Brunswick.

stage-specific issues. When considering the general prognosis of adults with dyslexia, the outcomes of the after-school years are competitive employment, independent living, community and civic involvement, participating in familial roles, leisure pursuits and general social interaction (Gerber, Ginsberg and Reiff 1992). Each domain has its challenges as well as its traps. More important when transitioning from school-to-work or school-to-school-to-work is that dyslexic adults carry on their lives consistent with their chosen values, goals and unique circumstances.

The experience of a dyslexic adult is very different from that of a dyslexic child/adolescent. During the school years when dyslexia is identified, students receive legally-mandated special education services (under the Individuals with Disabilities Education Act (IDEA) in the US, and the Special Educational Needs and Disability Act (SENDA) in the UK). However, upon leaving school and entering adulthood, dyslexic individuals move into a world where there is often little understanding of dyslexia's ramifications, and the invisibility of dyslexia is confusing to many (Gerber 1993; Price and Gerber 2001).

Invisibility as the 'Wild Card'

The decision 'to be or not to be' dyslexic in adulthood has many layers of complexity (Price, Gerber and Mulligan 2005). Invisibility is viewed as a 'wild card' with short-term and long-term consequences driven by dynamics that are both contextual and situational. The contexts are many – employment, education, community, family, leisure and social – and the possible situations endless, depending on the nuances of adult functioning. Consequently, the ultimate question arises for adults with dyslexia: what contexts and circumstances trigger them to disclose their dyslexia?

There are two contexts in which dyslexic adults disclose that are protected by law. These are education and employment. In post-secondary education, adults must disclose to receive special consideration in admissions, learning, testing, and examinations for professional licensing. Reasonable accommodations in employment such as pre-employment testing, accommodations at job entry or any time thereafter are also accessed via disclosure.

The majority of adult contexts, however, are not directly covered by law. They are driven by personal choice. How one conveys dyslexia in community, familial, recreational or other social settings is up to individuals as determined by their own assessment of disclosure risk and reward. Personal choice is not to be underestimated, as the invisibility of dyslexia truly allows for a person 'to be or not to be' dyslexic.

Studies in Self-Disclosure and Learning Disabilities

A few studies have investigated self-disclosure since the beginning of the ADA era in 1990. Studies that have been excluded from this review subsume LD or dyslexia into a rather imprecise generic category such as 'high incidence disabilities' or 'mild disabilities'.

Roffman, Herzog and Wershba-Gershon (1994) measured the effects of a college course on specific LD awareness; they found that it promoted greater self-understanding and willingness to disclose in social and employment settings. A couple of years later, Greenbaum, Graham and Scales (1996) found that most adults with LD were happy in terms of their occupational and social status, although 80% did not disclose their LD in their employment settings, fearing job and personal discrimination. In a post-secondary setting, Lynch and Gussel (1996) found that former students with LD 'feared stereotyping and attribution of unfounded characteristics associated with LD' and were subsequently reluctant to disclose their disability. Witte, Philips, and Kakela (1998) investigated college students after they had obtained employment and found that they rarely disclosed their LD in the workplace. Vogel and Adelman (2000) studied former college students 8 to 15 years after graduation and found that only 41% disclosed in employment, specifically for the purpose of receiving job accommodations. More recently, Price, Gerber and Shessel (2002) and Price, Gerber and Mulligan (2005) found a reluctance to disclose LD in work settings across North America. The primary reason given for non-disclosure was lack of confidence in discussing one's LD, and lack of knowledge of the disability legislation's viability in the workplace.

The overall trend in these studies shows that disclosure is rare. When it is done, it is for the expressed purpose of obtaining accommodations in employment settings. The Roffman, Herzog and Wershba-Gershon (1994) study does show that effective preparation increases the likelihood of individuals with LD using disclosure effectively. None of the other studies indicated that there was an effort to develop disclosure strategies prior to leaving school. Lack of preparation, including not knowing an individual's LD profile, and the protections of the disability laws, have been pointed out as chief reasons for non-disclosure in the workplace.

Stigma and Self-Disclosure

Self-disclosure for dyslexic adults is clearly a multi-faceted, complicated process (Price and Gerber 2008). It has been over four decades since the term 'learning disabilities' was first coined in the United States. Currently, approximately half of all special education students in American public education are still diagnosed with LD (Raymond 2004; Smith *et al.* 1997). One would think this high prevalence would foster familiarity about LD in the US but, instead, there still seems to be confusion and ignorance about these difficulties (Roper Stanch Worldwide 1995). This also makes it more difficult for adults to disclose, as few people seem to understand what they are talking about.

American children and their families have a built-in legislative safety net through the IDEA, as it covers all education from age 5 to 21 (this is also true for the UK through SENDA and the Equality Act). Legislative compliance implies that there are people in public schools who have a working knowledge of LD and how to address individual student need. In its absence, adults with dyslexia often find an inconsistent reception when they talk about what they need and why. This seems especially true in the workplace.

Some American adults find encouragement and support after disclosure (Price, Gerber and Mulligan 2005). Many others report being stigmatized in their daily lives specifically because of their dyslexia (Price and Gerber 2010). This frequently translates into fear of being judged by others. Also, because adults juggle many roles (parent, friend, employee, neighbour, church member, sports coach, etc.), this fear is situation-specific. Moreover, it seems to be an especially critical factor for employment success (Price and Gerber 2010). For instance, dyslexic adults know how 'invisible' disabilities such as auditory memory problems or visual–spatial difficulties will impact their workplace performance. But, when they explain that to co-workers or managers, they run the risk of dealing with unintended ignorance or negative reactions such as rejection, frustration, anger or denial. This can lead to feelings of isolation, loneliness and a sense of disconnectedness from others. Clearly, such discouraging experiences could lead many to conclude that it is better to keep quiet than to self-disclose and face the consequences.

The self-disclosure experiences discussed in the American literature are not unique to individuals with learning disabilities in the US. A study is currently under way in the UK to examine the phenomenon of self-disclosure for adults with dyslexia as well. Research details are given below. They reflect many of the issues and challenges previously described by adults in the US who also have learning disabilities and dyslexia.

Self-Disclosure and Dyslexia in the UK

A pilot study was designed and carried out in the London area during 2008–2009 to explore the ramifications of dyslexia for adults in the UK. Local researchers interviewed a selected sample of adults with documented dyslexia, using questions based on American interviews of adults with learning disabilities previously conducted by Gerber and Price (Price and Gerber 2001; Price, Gerber and Mulligan 2005) as well as the current literature on dyslexia and LD. The focus of the face-to-face interviews was an in-depth examination of individual perceptions about dyslexia in various adult-oriented environments (i.e., the workplace, the home, the community, and post-secondary education). Self-disclosure and self-advocacy were also investigated when these themes were revealed after using qualitative data analysis.

Sample description

Fifteen individuals with documented dyslexia took part in the pilot study. All were clients at a London-based, private agency that focused on the diverse needs of adults with dyslexia in the UK. The mean age of the interviewees was 31, with participants ranging in age from 23 to 50 years. Sex was evenly split between males and females as there were seven males and eight females who were interviewed. In terms of race and ethnicity, thirteen individuals were white, one was Bengali, and one was Afro-Caribbean. A strength of the pilot study was the diverse background in terms of education and employment that the participants brought to the research. Their education ranged from passing their A-level exams to obtaining a PhD. Current occupations were equally diverse: interviewees had job experience including being a rugby teacher, a handbag designer, a security officer and a policy researcher (details are provided in Table 14.1).

Table 14.1 Pilot sample demographics.

ID[a]	*Education*	*Occupation*
1	Master of Arts	Trainee psychologist
2	Bachelor of Arts	Law student
3	PhD	College teacher
4	Master of Arts	Policy researcher
5	A-levels	Police officer
6	National Vocational Qualification	Multiple (TV, circus, etc.)
7	Bachelor of Arts	Information technology (IT)
8	A-levels	Supply teacher
9	Master of Arts	Rugby teacher
10	Bachelor of Arts	Lighting technician
11	General National Vocational Qualification	Handbag designer
12	? Unclear from interview	Security officer
13	Engineering degree	Broadcast librarian
14	University degree	Supervisor of a drama education program
15	University degree	Marketing

[a]NB These are random ID codes given to our participants. They do not relate in any systematic way to the quotes provided in the text.

Research questions

The pilot study centred on three primary research questions:

1 How has self-disclosure affected you personally?
2 How have others reacted/supported you once you self-disclosed?
3 What has been the impact of the Disability Discrimination Act (DDA)?[2]

Subpatterns that emerged from the data analysis are described below. The questions are also illustrated with quotations from the interviews.

The first question that guided the pilot was: How has self-disclosure affected you personally? After data analysis, four findings were uncovered that were directly related to this question. The first finding showed that the responses dyslexic adults received after self-disclosure were clearly based on the environment in which the self-disclosure took place.

For instance, most of the sample said that disclosing in educational settings had been positive for them. As one person said:

> I went through all of the needs assessments which took for ever. But this is the first time I actually got this support.

Another explained:

> They [the postsecondary counsellors] immediately put into action the things I needed, the extra time for my exams.

However, the second finding showed that discussing one's dyslexia was negative for many at work who were treated differently after self-disclosure. One of the interviewees talked about his own experience by saying:

> It was time consuming trying to explain; it makes me feel low. It really wasn't a good work situation for me for the next six months.

Other adults also had this experience. In fact, of the total pilot study participants, only a few found self-disclosure beneficial to them as employees.

Since environment seemed to be such an important factor when talking about their dyslexia, a fourth finding also emerged from the interviews. Because the adults had to be careful to choose which environment was receptive for self-disclosure, many in the sample found a new self-awareness and deeper understanding of themselves as part of the process. As one explained:

> I am confident that it won't be a problem in the workplace and there will be a way to work around it. I know I do take a long time to do things which means I will be in the office longer than others. There are other things I do quite quickly.

[2] The Disability Discrimination Act (HMSO 1995), which was in force at the time that this pilot study was carried out, was mostly replaced in October 2010 by the Equality Act (Office for Disability Issues 2010).

Another echoed many in the study when she said:

> [As] a teenager, I hated the fact that it took me twice as long to do anything. I hated the fact that my mates were down having fun and I was sitting down two hours later still trying to write an essay. It gets to a stage where you realize that there are things you want to do but to do those things you just have to accept the way your brain works.

Research Question number 2 asked: How have others reacted/supported you once you self-disclosed? This question addressed another critical factor in self-disclosure – the persons who heard the message. The adults in the pilot study found a plethora of responses from people with whom they interacted every day but who may or may not have been aware that they had an invisible disability. Some individuals were very responsive and helpful. Other reactions were complicated and much less supportive. Nonetheless, the environment once more played a crucial factor in self-disclosure. For instance, when the interviews were analysed, the data patterns again fell naturally into four related settings with different audiences: employers, supervisors and co-workers on the job; family and friends at home; acquaintances, neighbours and professionals in the local community; and educators in post-secondary education.

As the findings showed in Research Question number 1, the dyslexic adults told the researchers that in general, educational settings provided a supportive environment. Since the students in the pilot study were already aware of the help they could receive in college, they often took advantage of those benefits. One student spoke for many when he said, 'In terms of extra time for exams, which is massive help.'

Employment, on the other hand, presented a different set of challenges and attitudes for the dyslexic adults. Many of the interviewees clearly felt that employers need to be better educated about the DDA, which could lead to more supportive work environments. As one study participant explained:

> I know it, but you can't police [discrimination]. There is no way. Employers can find their way around it.

Disclosing to family and friends often created a different kind of experience, as these reactions were often complicated by ongoing family dynamics. For example, when one person told his mother, she said, 'Don't be ridiculous.' He found her response to be 'a bit off-putting', but he persevered and also mentioned it to his brother 'because [he was] close to him and he was quite interested'. Other study participants reported a similar curiosity about dyslexia from their family and friends. When they explained about their own challenges and strengths, they found that they sometimes found a very strong support network. As one adult explained:

> Most of my friends are dyslexics so we all have a good laugh – a lot of jokes [about] being dyslexic. I think being with them has helped us all a lot.

While adults told the researchers that they had talked about their dyslexia at work, at school or at home, another trend was found in the data – most of the adults did not self-disclose *at all* in their local community. It appeared that they saw no reason to share information about their dyslexia with the general public or acquaintances in their neighbourhood. One adult stressed:

> If it arises in conversations, I will talk about it. If I'm asked to reverse park or something I might have an issue with that, because I'm dyslexic and I have left–right coordination issues.

The third research question was: What has been the impact of the DDA? This query moved beyond one's personal space to address the legislative safety net available to dyslexic individuals in the UK through the DDA. The adults stated repeatedly that they themselves needed a better understanding of the DDA, especially in the workplace. This trend was seen when the majority of the pilot study sample gave no response at all to Question 3 as it applied to their own lives. Nonetheless, one adamantly said:

> My understanding is that dyslexia is covered by this Act. I guess I'm not even 100% sure of what it says . . . and how successful I would be in terms of reasonable accommodations.

Connections between Two Models: Acceptable Loss/Potential Gain and Reframing

The pilot interviews with the dyslexic adults in the UK routinely underscored the advantages and stigmas of self-advocacy and self-disclosure for adults. But a new pattern also emerged from the data – the risk-management of private, often sensitive, personal information. The idea of balancing the benefits and risks of dyslexia can be best summarized in a model called 'acceptable loss-potential gain'.

Acceptable Loss-Potential Gain

An American Business Strategies coach stressed the advantages of 'calculated risk', which she defined as: 'A risk that has been given thoughtful consideration and for which the potential costs and potential benefits have been weighted and considered' (Tuminello 2010, p. 2). This calculated risk becomes a personalized decision that dyslexic adults face constantly in everyday life. Such unpredictability also describes the crux of acceptable loss-potential gain, self-disclosure and self-advocacy. It is important to understand that this concept – while used in business circles for many years – is relatively unknown in education and has never been applied to students with disabilities. But this idea gives the concept of self-advocacy for students with disabilities, especially those with invisible disabilities, a wealth of new, previously unexamined, possibilities.

For instance, an advocacy group of people with disabilities emphasized that:

> Self-advocacy is a powerful term. It tells people that we have equal rights, that we deserve dignity and respect, and that we can make decisions about our lives. (*Advocating Change Together, 2009, p. 1*)

They were referring specifically to individuals with moderate or severe physical, cognitive, and sensory disabilities. Nevertheless, one can speculate if this quote is applicable to people with invisible disabilities as well. For instance, do people with invisible disabilities deserve dignity and respect? Can they make decisions about their lives? If so, then dyslexic individuals must carefully weigh the risks and benefits of their actions before revealing such personal information to others. The process of self-advocacy clearly becomes more complex than seen at first glance.

Adults with learning disabilities and dyslexia have told the authors repeatedly during over 12 years of research that self-advocacy – and its companion component self-disclosure – are unique for each individual (Price and Gerber 2010; Price, Gerber and Mulligan 2005; Price, Gerber and Shessel 2002). In fact, interviews with adults with dyslexia in previous studies have underscored that this population is made up of individuals who share a common goal for a satisfying quality of life as adults but who pursue that 'satisfaction' in multiple, unique ways. This quickly becomes the heart of self-advocacy – the way people with learning disabilities and dyslexia 'make decisions about their lives' as they cope daily with an invisible disability. This critical factor moves beyond self-advocacy into much more complex, adult-oriented, questions. Examples are:

- Will this help me?
- Will this hurt me?
- If I talk to this person, what changes for me?
- If I talk in this situation, what stays the same or becomes worse?
- Why is it worth it to self-advocate at all?

One simple scenario that adults with invisible disabilities face illustrates this complexity well. Adults in the pilot interviews from the UK have said that it is acceptable to talk about the challenges and strengths of their dyslexia at home with family and friends. However, they stressed to the researchers that it was a risky business, at best, to have the same discussion at work. This same sample felt that both they and their employers needed much more information about the DDA. They were concerned that they might not know enough about their own disability, so revealing personal information about their dyslexia could easily lead to misinterpretation or misunderstanding. They were also not sure how well such new information would be received. This paradox makes self-disclosure, self-advocacy and self-awareness an even more complicated, confusing process.

It is clear from the UK interviews that these individuals often found self-disclosure and self-advocacy to be daunting hurdles in their lives. They learned through hard lessons that self-disclosure does not always follow firm, well-defined rules. Instead, for most adults, it is a set of constantly-changing factors and expectations. One size clearly does not fit all. Both the American and British interviewees repeatedly stressed that having an invisible disability such as dyslexia is a daily exercise in self-awareness where personal judgement and ownership are important components of self-disclosure and self-advocacy. This moves beyond a lesson in 'self-advocacy' from a curriculum taught in secondary school or a way to fulfil a transition objective on an Individualized Education Program (IEP).[3] It is like playing three-dimensional chess in that self-disclosure in adult life (outside the protected world of academia or public schools) becomes a set of continually shifting puzzle pieces.

Because there is a choice regarding whether to reveal one's dyslexia in adulthood, the individual needs to weigh up the acceptable loss and potential gain that may follow self-disclosure. At the heart of this is a risk assessment in which the individual considers:

1 *The context.* In the US, are there legal protections embedded in the context such as Section 504 or the ADA that pertain to domains such as education and employment? Does the context reside in a personal/social realm where relationships foster an understanding of individual differences, strengths and weaknesses?
2 *The situation.* Is it short term or will the situation necessitate disclosure for greater understanding of performance and responsibility? These considerations can be familial or

[3] This is a written statement including information about a dyslexic child's current academic performance in addition to his or her future educational needs and goals.

they can emerge as individuals participate in community events and a variety of adult activities.

3 *Audience knowledge.* Another important component is the degree to which dyslexia is understood, and how receptive others are to hearing what kinds of challenges exist for those with dyslexia. People who are likely to be sympathetic and understanding are the best people to disclose to. Such understanding also breaks the cycle of fear and stigmatization previously generated by self-disclosure.
4 *Self-knowledge.* Individuals need to understand their own dyslexia before they can speak about it with others. Self-understanding includes awareness of personal strengths and weakness as well as any accommodations needed to bypass barriers to performance.
5 *Legislation.* When disclosure is used to access rights contained within laws, it is imperative to understand the laws and how they can be used to secure fair practices and accommodations. It must be remembered that those who disclose have the onus of making the laws work for them, tailored to their unique circumstances.

Individuals who choose not to disclose must be willing to carry on their lives as they are with the 'acceptable loss' of not confronting a situation related to disability to make their quality of life better. That may be the best choice for some to avoid the possible consequences of stigma and ostracism. On the other hand, when the risk is viewed as being worth it, the 'potential gain' of disclosure can facilitate better performance and quality relationships based on deeper understanding.

A Fresh Look at Reframing

The previous material underscores the need to look at the complexities of self-advocacy and self-disclosure in greater depth, not as professionals see it, but from the perspective of dyslexic adults themselves. One way to do this is to examine the concept of loss and gain through the eyes of adults with dyslexia and learning disabilities who are already living successful lives. Gerber and Reiff (1991) did just this when they conducted an American study on common factors in the lives of 71 successful adults with learning disabilities. These factors fell into two categories: (i) Internal Decisions (for example, a powerful desire to succeed, a clear sense of goal orientation, and the reframing of the LD experience), and (ii) External Manifestations (for example, persistence, goodness of fit, learned creativity, and a social network that provides support rather than encouraging dependence).

Both the Internal Decisions and External Manifestations found in successful adults echo the risk-taking analysis inherent in self-disclosure. But one factor seems to fit especially well into the complexities of the acceptable loss-potential gain model for dyslexia. That factor is reframing, which is defined by Gerber, Ginsberg and Reiff (1992. p. 481) as:

> a set of decisions relating to reinterpreting the learning disability experience in a more productive and positive manner.

Gerber, Reiff and Ginsberg (1996, p. 98) later added that:

> [Reframing] clearly allows for one to identify strengths and parlay them into success experiences, while still being aware of weaknesses that have to be mitigated or bypassed.

It is this constant, internal weighing of personal knowledge, skills and emotions that underlies the choice of whether to self-disclose or self-advocate. The struggle can often take on a life of its own when one feels deeply the stigma of an invisible disability in different environments or with different groups of people. Dyslexic adults in the pilot study talked about this over and over in many different contexts. For instance, a teacher in the pilot study initially found it intimidating to teach students in years five and six due to her word decoding and auditory memory skill deficits. She was very hesitant to self-disclose, because she:

> . . . just desperately wanted to say: 'Look I just feel this way (I can't teach year five and six) because I'm dyslexic' but then I didn't want to tell them in case they did think I was not worthy of doing something [the job] that I think I am quite capable of doing.

However, she later used reframing in a totally different context, as she explained:

> I have mentioned it [my dyslexia] to my friends. Some of my friends think I am not listening to them correctly, not concentrating on what they are saying and that is not true, I do always obviously try but someone can tell me something (e.g. I meant a flat mate) and he has told me about four times where he was working. I still could not tell you. Someone asked me last night and it is not that I have not listened; it's not that I have not spoken to him about it because I have. It's literally if I get told something a few times I won't remember it. They laugh and it's OK.

Risk-taking through acceptable loss-potential gain is not an end in itself. As the previous quotation illustrates, the power of reframing can move acceptable loss-potential gain one step further into much deeper levels of self-awareness and, ultimately, self acceptance (Reiff 2004). Gerber, Reiff and Ginsberg (1996) call this the four stages of reframing, which are: (i) recognition, (ii) understanding, (iii) acceptance and (iv) developing a plan of action.

Do successful adults with learning disabilities and dyslexia know a hard-won secret that is not a part of any IEP goal or self-advocacy curriculum? Is the new concept of acceptable loss-potential gain a critical pre-step to potential reframing for dyslexic adults? Is it another set of skills that can be taught to adolescents and adults with LD or dyslexia? All these questions, and many more, must be answered as the millions of dyslexic adults in the UK and US search for a satisfying quality of life at home, in the workplace and in their local communities. While only future research will adequately address these issues, the story of one individual from the UK pilot study highlights the connections between acceptable loss-potential gain and reframing. Her name is Mickie.

Mickie

Mickie is an Afro-Caribbean female in her mid-thirties who has an NVQ[4] in Audio-Visual Design and a university degree in Homeopathy. She has held multiple jobs, including being a freelance trampoline coach, an acrobat gymnastics coach, a circus trainer, a homeopathic medical teacher, a children's youth worker, and had an extensive career in television. She was diagnosed with dyslexia at the age of 29 after years of difficulties reading, writing, and spelling. Mickie often compensated for problems at work or school by teaching herself independently or being extremely well

(*Continued*)

[4] National Vocational Qualification.

organized. These skills helped her to rise quickly to a well-paid, high pressure, supervisory position coordinating seven television channels.

While Mickie was very successful in the workplace, she was still curious about why reading and writing were so hard for her, so she took a test in a magazine. The results showed that she might be dyslexic but she wasn't convinced. As she said:

> 'Dyslexia is when you write things backwards. I don't write things backwards – what a load of rubbish, but it stayed in my head.'

She was later tested properly and the diagnosis was confirmed. She explained:

> 'When the psychologist said I was severely dyslexic I was just like confused, how could I do the job I did and be severely dyslexic? It makes no sense, but in hindsight, I can see how parts of me could be very dyslexic because it's just I learn differently that's all.'

Mickie was told to go to her employer and disclose this new information to obtain assistance in the workplace. She did this – against her better judgement – and found out straightaway that it was a mistake, as she continued:

> 'Then shortly after that, things started to change. They started to stop giving me work to do or started to pass through notices or jobs to some other people. Since I used to do it all, I knew when things were not coming my way. I was copied in on lots of things as it had been my job so I knew exactly what they were doing. Their attitude changed . . . because I got the label dyslexia and they have to spend a tiny bit of extra money. They thought suddenly I was dumb and they did treat me as if I was dumb.'

Eventually, Mickie was let go and went to a solicitor to sue her former employer. After receiving a settlement from them she went on to do other things in her life, but told the researchers that she had learned a valuable lesson:

> 'I think I never want to be in that kind of job again . . . I don't have that any more and I don't really want that barrier, I do miss the part of me that can get so motivated.. So I think what I would recommend is find out and then realize that you have got a learning difference and it's hard to wear it as a label. There are certain things that I can do amazingly well that other people can't do, because I am dyslexic and I think differently but it means that, when people force me to think like, they do like in a sausage factory, and university I have to churn it out in a particular way and I find it incredibly difficult. So knowing and talking about it has helped me and made things really hard too.'

Clearly, Mickie's story shows the risks inherent in self-disclosure. In her case, the acceptable loss may not have outweighed the potential gain. However, the last quotation underscores how she moved beyond the risks to reframe her perceptions and take control of her own life. Mickie did this when she accepted her dyslexia, understood her strengths and weaknesses and took action towards the new goals of taking care of her aging mother and going back to school to expand her medical skills.

Is Mickie a successful adult? That is an important question because Mickie is a survivor in a tough world of adults with or without dyslexia. Her story can teach us a great deal about how dyslexic adults use acceptable loss-potential gain and reframing to facilitate a personally satisfying quality of life for themselves. These are valuable lessons indeed.

Discussion

During the latter part of the school-age years it is typical for part of the self-determination curriculum for dyslexic students to include self-advocacy. Part of the process of self-advocacy is the all-important process of self-disclosure. As has been discussed here, there are numerous traps when it comes to self-disclosure, but it can also be fruitful.

Those who teach the skills of self-determination as part of transition preparation must come to realize that it is not a generic skill but one that includes a complex set of challenging processes. Specifically, the dynamic nature of disclosure includes risk that does not allow for 'do-overs'. Therefore, disclosure is unforgiving if it is not done correctly, not done with the proper timing and not done in the right social milieu.

Much work still needs to be done in this area for self-disclosure to have a 'positive' effect on one's quality of life. The wanton approach of disclosing dyslexia without first assessing the risks is perilous, and very few do it. It is no wonder that, even with legal protections, dyslexic adults are often reluctant to disclose. Ironically, laws that have been put in place over the years are underused as the invisible difficulties of dyslexia allow for the choice of being dyslexic or letting the issue slide by altogether. Sadly, when empirical work is done to measure the realities of adulthood vis-à-vis the disclosure of dyslexia, there is little evidence of the value that it affords when this is weighed against its potential risks.

References

Advocating Change Together (2009) *The Self-Advocacy Quick Guide*, Advocating Change Together, St Paul, MN.

Gerber, P.J. (1993) Researching adults with learning disabilities from an adult development perspective. *Journal of Learning Disabilities*, 27, 62–64.

Gerber, P.J. and Reiff, H.B. (1991) *Speaking for Themselves: Ethnographic interviews with adults with learning disabilities*, University of Michigan Press, Ann Arbor, MI.

Gerber, P.J., Ginsberg, R. and Reiff, H.B. (1992) Identifying alterable patterns in employment success for highly successful adults with learning disabilities. *Journal of Learning Disabilities*, 25, 475–487.

Gerber, P.J., Reiff, H.B. and Ginsberg, R. (1996) Reframing the learning disabilities experience. *Journal of Learning Disabilities*, 29, 98–101.

Greenbaum, B., Graham, S. and Scales, W. (1996) Adults with learning disabilities: Occupational and social status after college. *Journal of Learning Disabilities*, 29, 167–175.

HMSO (1995) *The Disability Discrimination Act 1995*, Her Majesty's Stationery Office, London.

Lynch, R.T. and Gussel, L. (1996) Disclosure and self-advocacy regarding disability-related needs: Strategies to maximize integration in postsecondary education. *Journal of Counseling and Development*, 74, 352–358.

Office for Disability Issues (2010) *Equality Act 2010*, Office for Disability Issues, London.

Price, L.A. and Gerber, P.J. (2001) At second glance: How adults with learning disabilities are faring in the Americans with disabilities act era. *Journal of Learning Disabilities*, 34, 202–210.

Price, L.A. and Gerber, P.J. (2008) Adults with learning disabilities and self-disclosure in higher education and beyond, in *The SAGE Handbook of Dyslexia* (eds G. Reid, A. Fawcett, F. Manis and L. Siegel), Sage Publications, London, pp. 457–474.

Price, A. and Gerber, P. (2010) Self-disclosure and dyslexic adults: Workplace implications, in *British Dyslexia Association Employment Handbook* (eds C. Leather and D. McLoughlin), Sage Publications, London, pp. 56–63.
Price, L.A., Gerber, P.J. and Mulligan, R. (2005) To be or not to be learning disabled: A preliminary report on self-disclosure in adults with learning disabilities. *Thalamus*, 23, 18–27.
Price, L.A., Gerber, P.J. and Shessel, I. (2002) Adults with learning disabilities and employment: A Canadian perspective. *Thalamus*, 4, 1–32.
Raymond, E.B. (2004) *Learners with Mild Disabilities: A characteristics approach*, Allyn & Bacon. Boston, MA.
Reiff, H. (2004) Reframing the learning disabilities experience redux. *Learning Disabilities Research and Practice*, 19, 185–198.
Roffman, A.J., Herzog, J.E. and Wershba-Gershon, P.M. (1994) Helping young adults understand their learning disabilities. *Journal of Learning Disabilities*, 27, 413–419.
Roper Stanch Worldwide (1995) *Learning Disabilities and the American Public: A look at America's awareness and knowledge*, Roper Stanch Worldwide, Washington, D.C.
Smith, T.E.C., Dowdy, C.A., Polloway, E.A. and Blalock, G. (1997) *Children and Adults with Learning Disabilities*, Allyn & Bacon, Boston, MA.
Tuminello, C. (2010) Business perspective: Taking calculated risks to succeed. *The Greater Lafayette Business Journal*, 3, 3.
Vogel, S.A. and Adelman, P.B. (2000) Adults with learning disabilities 8–15 years after college. *Learning Disabilities: A Multi-Disciplinary Journal*, 10, 165–182.
Witte, R.H., Philips, M. and Kakela, M. (1998) Job satisfaction of college graduates with learning disabilities. *Journal of Learning Disabilities*, 31, 259–265.

Further reading

Americans with Disabilities Act (1990) *Public Law* 101–336. 42 USC.
Amendments of the Americans with Disabilities Act (2008) *Public Law* 110–325, September 25.
Rehabilitation Act. (1973). *Public Law* 93–112, Title V, Section 504.

15

Dyslexia on the Defensive

Sylvia Moody, Dyslexia Assessment Service, London, UK

Introduction

Nowadays dyslexia is much less 'on the defensive' than it was a few decades ago. It is more likely to be recognized early and to be regarded not as a shameful weakness but simply as a manageable set of difficulties – at worst a nuisance and at best a challenge, an opportunity to develop skills and abilities that may be less well-developed in non-dyslexic people.

However, many people, particularly those now in middle age or older, may feel less positive about their difficulties. They may not even know that their difficulties are dyslexic in nature; or even if they do know, they may feel reluctant to speak about them publicly.

No doubt there are also some young people who have unidentified dyslexic difficulties. And if such young people go straight from school into the workplace, their difficulties could easily remain unrecognized, as dyslexia awareness is still far less general among employers than among education professionals.

Again, a young person, even if he[1] has realized he is dyslexic, may have reasons for not talking openly about this – for example, he may fear it would upset his family to hear he had such difficulties. In some cases, reluctance to acknowledge a dyslexic problem 'in their midst' can be so strong that families will refuse to accept the clear findings of a dyslexia assessment, and continue to insist that the family member in question has no significant problems.

Thus, even today, there are still many and varied reasons why dyslexia might be on the defensive. In this chapter I will discuss this issue in a workplace context and look at three different scenarios:

1 An employee is aware that he is having difficulties at work, but does not recognize his difficulties as dyslexia.
2 An employee knows or suspects that he is dyslexic, but fears to disclose this to his employer in case it costs him, if not his job, at least prospects of promotion.
3 A dyslexic employee has disclosed his difficulties to his employer but finds that the employer, and possibly also his colleagues, are unsympathetic.

[1] In this chapter *he* is used for *he/she* except in the case studies.

Supporting Dyslexic Adults in Higher Education and the Workplace, First Edition. Edited by Nicola Brunswick.

Scenario 1: Dyslexia not recognized

In general, human beings find uncertainty to be threatening. Although we are aware that we develop over time, and probably welcome this, at any given moment we like to feel that we have a stable and coherent self-image and that we have a good understanding of ourselves, of both our strengths and our weaknesses.

A feeling commonly experienced by an 'undiagnosed' dyslexic person is that he doesn't really know who he is: he seems to be a puzzling muddle of strengths and weaknesses. At some moments he may feel himself to be an intelligent person: he can catch on quickly to another person's meaning and has an intellectual curiosity and a general desire to learn. At other moments, perhaps whenever he attempts higher-level study or takes on a challenging job, he feels more like a fool, constantly making errors, forgetting things and failing to get himself properly organized.

To a dyslexia assessor, this collection of inefficiencies is immediately recognizable as a common syndrome of difficulties, all of which relate to each other in meaningful ways. However, to the person who experiences them, they often feel bewildering, even shaming. Inevitably the emotional consequences are lack of confidence, low self-esteem, frustration, even depression. And what may follow on from this is a sort of social nervousness, a reluctance to take part in conversations or discussions, perhaps a tendency to avoid other people – often with the result of being seen as a loner, an outsider, an unfriendly or difficult person.

This situation will also present genuine difficulties to the managers and colleagues of such an 'undiagnosed' dyslexic person: they may feel baffled and annoyed at his inefficiency, resentful that they have constantly to recheck or redo his work, and be offended by his social manner. All this is likely to make them less helpful to him, if he is finding difficulties with his job, and this will increase his difficulties still further.

The story of Muriel, a 40-year-old woman, who worked as a care assistant, illustrates this:

Muriel

Muriel had always found difficulty with work that required writing skills, but she had excellent social and practical skills; she had good relationships with her clients and felt confident that she could make sensible judgements about their needs. She did have some difficulty with the paperwork attached to the job but, fortunately, this was quite a small element in her work and she had help with it both from a sympathetic colleague and from her son, who was now in his final year at school. In general Muriel was regarded as a hard-working and valuable employee, and she enjoyed her work.

Then in the space of a single year everything changed. The agency that Muriel worked for introduced a more efficient management style and changes were made to Muriel's job specifications. She was now obliged to keep careful written records of her meetings with clients, to take a more prominent role in meetings and to do some informal supervision of a trainee. At the same time the sympathetic colleague who had always helped her moved on to another job, and her son entered a university in another town and so was rarely at home to give her any assistance.

Muriel suddenly found herself, to use her own expression, 'totally at sea'. She tried to cope with the situation by working longer hours but this simply caused her to feel tired and stressed and led to her being even more inefficient at work. She felt frightened to speak about her difficulties to her colleagues or to her line manager, because she felt she would be seen as a failure.

It was not long before Muriel began to dread going into the office at all. She felt that the people around her were starting to become impatient with her and, whereas before she had been regarded as an asset, she was now being seen as something of a liability. As so it was that Muriel, who previously enjoyed her job and the companionship of her colleagues, now began to take days off because of stress. Eventually the situation became so bad that she had to take an extended period of sick leave because of anxiety and depression. All her attempts to return to work failed and in the end it was more with relief than sorrow that Muriel heard she had been dismissed from her post.

But even worse for Muriel than losing her job was the way she had now come to feel about herself: useless, despairing, bewildered. She described herself as 'a waste of space' and felt that she could not succeed in anything. It had reached the stage where even simple household tasks seemed overwhelming.

But then, suddenly, life took an unexpected turn. Muriel happened to hear a radio programme on the subject of dyslexia. In the programme, a woman who described herself as dyslexic explained to the listeners about all the problems she had and the way they had affected her performance at work. As the woman talked on, she mentioned problems not just with literacy but also with memory and general organization, and Muriel had the odd experience of hearing *herself* described: the same problems, the same workplace difficulties and, most of all, the same debilitating emotions.

At the end of the programme a helpline number was given and, after a few days of hesitation, Muriel telephoned the helpline. That was the moment when her life turned around, 'the moment of revelation', as Muriel herself called it. As a result of her talk with the helpline adviser, she found a local adult dyslexia group and also started to take some classes in literacy, communication skills and work organization.

There was no instant transformation in Muriel but she had suddenly found an explanation for her difficulties; she had found a way forward, a focus and a purpose. The negative emotions she had been experiencing gradually faded away; she became calmer, more confident and more appreciative of her good qualities. She was able to get her difficulties into perspective, realizing that they were not something to be ashamed of or embarrassed about. Within a year she became confident enough to think about looking for a new job and, with the advice of a dyslexia careers adviser, she found a niche that suited her: she became a counsellor in a school for children with learning difficulties.

Scenario 2: Dyslexia recognized, but not disclosed

A common question that dyslexic people ask is: when I apply for a job, should I tell my potential employer that I'm dyslexic? Usually there is no simple 'yes or no' answer; various factors need to be taken into account.

There are a number of reasons why a person may not disclose his dyslexia:

- He may feel embarrassed about it.
- He may not feel embarrassed, but simply feel that it is a private matter.
- He may have developed compensatory strategies and so feel that his dyslexia will not affect his ability to do the job he has applied for.
- He may feel that, even though he himself is confident he could do the job, a potential employer might doubt his abilities.

On the other hand, disclosure has a number of benefits. It allows the applicant to request reasonable adjustments during the recruitment process, and these could enhance his chances of gaining employment. It will also enable him to request reasonable adjustments as soon as he is in post, giving him the support he needs to perform effectively. It will also offer him legal protection, as an employee who has disclosed his dyslexia cannot be placed on a capability order or be dismissed until reasonable adjustments have been properly trialled. It also has the advantage that the dyslexic employee will not have the stress of having to conceal his difficulties and perhaps have them misinterpreted as being the result of laziness or incompetence.

If a job applicant has disclosed his dyslexic difficulties to his potential employer, the likelihood of his being given the job will depend very much on his performance in the interview. If the applicant seems defensive or awkward about his difficulties, this is not likely to impress an employer. If, on the other hand, he is able to talk confidently about his dyslexia, to explain that he has strategies for dealing with his difficulties, and that with reasonable support he will be able to perform in the job effectively, then all this could be very much in his favour – the employer could well see him as being assertive, enterprising, honest, ambitious and determined to work hard to achieve his goals.

There are a number of reasonable adjustments that a dyslexic applicant could request at the application stage. He could request that he be allowed to have some brief notes with him during the interview, explaining that this will allow him to express himself more clearly; and he could ask for the interviewers to be sympathetic if he needs a little extra time to formulate his answers, or if he needs to have a question repeated.

Everything that has been said in this chapter so far about dyslexic people also applies to people who have dyspraxic difficulties, and many people are both dyslexic and dyspraxic. For an illustration of a skilful way to manage an interview, I will present the case of Maureen, a severely dyspraxic person, who was preparing for her first interview with her new line manager.

Maureen

Maureen felt anxious that she would not be able to explain to the line manager the nature of her difficulties and how they might affect her work. She took control of the situation by writing down clearly on one side of an A4 sheet her main difficulties, stating in each case what strategies she had for dealing with them and how the employer could be helpful.

At the interview, when the line manager began to ask about her dyspraxia, Maureen spoke out in a confident – not anxious or demanding – way. She explained she had felt worried that she might fail to explain her problems clearly, and so she had made a written note of them. She then handed this note to the manager.

This had several beneficial effects: Maureen felt less anxious in the interview because she knew that, come what may, she would be able to get her message across. The manager was very impressed with Maureen's efficiency and proactive attitude and was grateful for the fact that he could now easily pass Maureen's information on to relevant colleagues. In this way Maureen used the interview process itself to demonstrate how she could turn her weaknesses into strengths and act in a way that would be helpful both to her managers and to her colleagues.

Scenario 3: Dyslexia disclosed, but with bad results

People who have disclosed their dyslexic difficulties to an employer will probably expect their managers and colleagues to be more understanding of, and sympathetic to, their situation.

Alas, this is not always the case. Sometimes, when reasonable adjustments are put in place to support an employee, these are seen by others in a negative light. There can be a perception that the employee is 'skiving', or covering up fundamental inefficiencies, or getting some kind of unfair advantage. Below, I will give some examples of how such negative feelings on the part of colleagues or managers can escalate from resentment to hostility and even to cruelty.

Resentment

Leila

Leila worked as a customer adviser in a call centre. When a customer telephoned with a query, Leila either dealt with this herself or, if appropriate, referred it on to another department. Simultaneously she had to make notes on the computer of how she had dealt with the call. The advisers were given targets for the number of seconds they should take on each call but Leila rarely managed to meet the target time. Further, the notes she made on the computer were often incomplete or garbled.

She was referred for a cognitive assessment, which showed that she had some dyslexic difficulties and also significant visual stress problems. The latter made looking at a computer screen very tiring for her and so, during the course of her working day, she became more and more fatigued, stressed and inefficient.

Reasonable adjustments were put in place: Leila was supplied with a screen-reading ruler to reduce her visual stress problems; she was allowed a slightly longer time than her colleagues for dealing with calls, and she was also permitted regular short rest breaks. Leila herself was content with these arrangements but her colleagues were not. They continually made jokes about her special privileges and started referring to her as 'Your Highness'. Leila felt very upset and anxious about this, and this led to her becoming ever more inefficient, and so needing even more breaks. This in turn led to an increase in the resentment felt against her. Although her manager was prepared to support her, the unsympathetic attitude of her colleagues eventually led to her leaving this job.

Jonathan

A similar situation arose with Jonathan, an administrative assistant in a government department. Jonathan had difficulty with any task that required him to follow the alphabetic sequence, for example, filing or putting letters in pigeonholes. He had himself developed strategies for dealing with this problem – in particular, he made good use of an alphabet arc[2] – but he was still relatively slow in doing these alphabetic tasks. Here again, the line manager concerned was sympathetic and dealt with the situation by re-allocating some of Jonathan's work to other people. However, this caused resentment because some colleagues felt that they were being required to work harder because of Jonathan's inefficiency.

[2] That is, the letters of the alphabet are printed out on a piece of paper or card in an arc.

Hostility

In some situations resentment can intensify and eventually become outright hostility, for example, when the slowness or inefficiency of one employee is felt to 'let down' other people in the organization.

Ahmed

Ahmed worked for a telecommunications company and was assigned to a team that was responsible for selling the company's products by telephone. The team was split up into smaller groups, called *cadres*, and the cadres were encouraged to compete against each other in reaching ever higher sales targets. Bonuses were awarded each month to the winning cadre.

Ahmed, who was dyslexic, took longer to deal with calls than his colleagues, with the result that his cadre never won bonuses. Here again, as in the previous examples, managers showed themselves more sympathetic than workmates. It was agreed that Ahmed could personally have lower targets than the rest of his cadre but, of course, this meant that there was virtually no hope that his cadre would ever be successful in the competitions. His colleagues became increasingly hostile towards him and the situation deteriorated to such an extent that he was removed from his cadre and allowed to operate independently. This reduced the hostility towards him to some degree but at the same time it left him isolated, as both the professional and social life of the office centred around the cadres.

There are also cases in which managers come to feel hostility towards dyslexic employees who, they feel, have 'let them down'. An example of this is Simon, a line manager who had responsibility for a dyslexic employee, Jane.

Jane

Jane was a slow worker and made careless mistakes in her written work. Initially Simon was sympathetic to her and readily agreed to give her extra supervision and provide ongoing mentoring. Unfortunately, despite all this help, Jane's performance did not improve significantly, and this in turn meant that Simon did not meet his efficiency targets. Consequently he became increasingly hostile to Jane, accusing her of not really trying to improve her performance despite all the help he was giving her. Jane in turn complained that Simon was putting too much pressure on her and eventually the relationship between them broke down completely in mutual recriminations.

Cruelty

Hostility can sometimes rise to such a pitch that it turns into actual cruelty, usually in the form of bullying. Examples of this are provided by the cases of Joanna and Carlo.

Joanna

Joanna, a young dyspraxic woman who worked as a teacher in a secondary school, was very committed to her work, but she was ill-organized and had poor social skills, often appearing abrupt or abrasive in conversation.

Interestingly, this did not affect her teaching abilities. Her pupils were not in the least 'put out' by her rather offhand ways and they appeared to regard her as a likeable eccentric. However, her colleagues were less forgiving and, after a series of unpleasant 'scenes' in the staffroom, Joanna was virtually 'sent to Coventry' (i.e. shunned) by the rest of the staff. Although Joanna was aware that it was largely because of her own behaviour that conflict had arisen, she was unable to find any way to change the situation and eventually left her post.

Carlo

Another example is that of Carlo, a clerical officer in a large hotel. His work mainly involved routine paperwork but, occasionally, he had to take telephone messages. He would then email these on to the appropriate member of staff. However, because of his dyslexic difficulties (which he had not disclosed to his employer) he found it difficult to compose these emails in a logical way and he made mistakes particularly with names and numbers.

Sometimes these errors had a comic effect, for example, when he wrote *dinner* as *sinner*, or *booking* as *cooking*. One of his colleagues, to whom he regularly sent emails, found it amusing to read the more comical ones out to the whole office, and then one or two people started sending joke emails back to Carlo.

Feeling humiliated, and having no way to deal with the situation (which his manager regarded as normal office 'high jinks'), Carlo eventually 'snapped' and threatened to punch his tormentor. The latter then made a complaint. In the ensuing investigation, Carlo was forced to be more open about his difficulties, which resulted in his being given appropriate support. As a result, his confidence improved and he became more able to shrug off jokes made at his expense. This in turn soon resulted in his colleagues refraining from making such jokes and treating him with more respect. And so this story, at least, had a happy ending.

All the above examples show how easily a dyslexic person can become victimized, even demonized. One reason for this may be that, while somebody who is obviously disabled, for example a blind person, is readily accepted as having genuine difficulties, a person with 'hidden' difficulties such as dyslexia, dyspraxia or visual stress, can be regarded as being, at best, work-shy and, at worst, a fraud.

These difficult situations resolve themselves in many different ways: sometimes the dyslexic person decides the situation is intolerable and leaves the job; in other cases the person concerned may receive help and support that enables him to become more confident and assertive and so to stand up to hostility or bullying; sometimes extra help can be provided in the form of a support worker, thereby obviating the need for work to be reallocated to others; sometimes dyslexic employees can, with appropriate training, improve their skills sufficiently to be efficient in their job, even at the cost of sometimes having to work longer hours than their colleagues.

However, for a successful outcome, it is usually not enough for a single employee to be made more efficient, or a single manager to become more sympathetic: there needs to be a whole-organization culture of understanding of, and support for, people who have 'hidden' difficulties. Only then can people with such difficulties be enabled to work to their full potential and be protected from resentment, hostility and bullying from managers or colleagues.

A common theme in all the case studies I have reported in this chapter is that many problems arise out of a lack of understanding of dyslexia and, in particular, its effects in the workplace. This lack of understanding can be in the dyslexic employee himself in that he may not recognize his difficulties as dyslexia. Even if he does understand the nature of his difficulties, he may not know how to present these in a way that allows other people to help him. Or there may be a lack of understanding of dyslexia in a dyslexic person's immediate family or social circle, and in his workplace.

As regards the workplace, there is an obligation on employers not only to give appropriate support to dyslexic employees, but also to have sufficient awareness of dyslexic difficulties to be on the lookout for these – even in cases where an employee himself has not realized that he is dyslexic, or has not disclosed his difficulties.

As regards the dyslexic person himself, an understanding of his difficulties usually brings a sense of relief, as he is now enabled to assemble all his puzzling inefficiencies into a coherent picture, which helps him to explain his problems in a clear and confident way to other people. However, for many dyslexic people who have been unaware of their dyslexic difficulties, or who have kept them secret for many years, confidence does not come overnight. It may take time for individuals to come to terms with the fact that they have been in a muddle about themselves for many years, that they have consequently lost opportunities for study or work, and that they have perhaps been let down by other people who should have recognized their difficulties or been more sympathetic to them.

It can, therefore, sometimes be helpful for a dyslexic person to complement skills training with some psychological intervention to help build his confidence and self-esteem and to give him ways of dealing with difficult emotions. For some people the help of a behavioural/cognitive psychologist could be useful in teaching strategies for dealing with anxiety attacks, for controlling feelings of anger or violence, and developing practices such as deep breathing or meditation in order to promote long-term anxiety reduction.

In other people, the emotions they feel specifically about their dyslexic difficulties may be entwined with similar emotions stemming from general life experiences, for example, from having had a childhood in which parents had constantly been undermining and dismissive of their child. In this case, counselling or psychotherapy ('talking cures') can be helpful in bringing greater understanding of past life events and experiences, and in disentangling dyslexia-related anxieties from more general ones.

Thus, if dyslexic difficulties are fully recognized and confidently disclosed to other people, if appropriate support in the way of skills training and counselling is provided, then it is more likely that a dyslexic person will get off the defensive. Without moving to the opposite pole of aggressiveness, he may then become able, in both his professional and social life, to confront the world in an assertive and confident way. And it is the way of the world that, the more a person respects himself, the more respect he tends to be given by the people around him.

Resources

For a detailed discussion of these issues, see:

Bartlett, D. and Moody, S. (2010) *Dyslexia in the Workplace: an introductory guide*, 2nd edn, Wiley-Blackwell. See Chapter 1, Dyslexia in the workplace; Chapter 18, Working with dyslexia; Chapter 19, Reasonable adjustments.

Moody, S. (2009) *Dyslexia and Employment: A guide for assessors, trainers and managers*, Wiley-Blackwell. In particular, see, Chapter 7, Disputes around dyslexia; Chapter 10, Dyslexia: attitudes and emotions; Information point A: Disclosure guidelines.

16

Achieving Success in the Workplace

Carol Leather and Bernadette Kirwan, both with Independent Dyslexia Consultants, London, UK

Introduction

Many dyslexic people have achieved success in the workplace. Some of them – those who are highly successful in terms of reaching the top of their profession, running their own business and/or being very well financially rewarded – are easily identifiable. There are other dyslexic people who are just as successful, finding their niche in a job that best suits their skills and interests, and there are those who experience high levels of job satisfaction and self-efficacy. This suggests that dyslexia should not be a barrier to success. Indeed, self-employed dyslexic people often attribute their success to their ability to think differently, to get on well with people, to be good at negotiating and at delegating tasks, having learned at an a early age to avoid doing tasks they were not good at (Logan 2009).

It is becoming more widely acknowledged that the impact of dyslexia is different for every person, and that it varies for individuals depending on the environment they are in and the support and understanding they receive from others. Some dyslexic people just get on with their job and others manage with minimal input in terms of workplace adjustments. Some need quite a lot of help and some go unnoticed. Dyslexia is a hidden disability and the understanding of its nature in adulthood is still under-researched. This lack of research, particularly as to how it manifests itself in the workplace, means that much of the information concerning dyslexia is still focused largely on educational issues. As a result, recommendations for adjustments and support tend to be primarily literacy-based. There is no doubt that literacy plays a large part but the difficulties that dyslexic people experience in the workplace can be much broader than that; problems with organization, communication and lack of confidence are also important areas for consideration. It is the combination of all these factors that leads to dyslexia being much misunderstood by employers and the individuals themselves (McLoughlin, Leather and Stringer 2002). Furthermore, the abilities of dyslexic people are also often hidden both from themselves and their employers, yet dyslexic people can bring many skills to the workplace; better understanding of dyslexia by the individual and the employer will access these skills and potential.

The impact of dyslexia is perhaps even more pronounced in the communication culture of the twenty-first-century workplace where the product is most likely to be information. The tools used to facilitate that communication are the telephone, meetings, teamwork, written and electronic text and images. Since dyslexia is in essence a difference in the way verbal, visual and auditory

Supporting Dyslexic Adults in Higher Education and the Workplace, First Edition. Edited by Nicola Brunswick.

information is processed, it is not surprising that the skills and tools of communication can pose a challenge to the dyslexic person at work. Sometimes the difficulties people present can be quite obvious, for example, weak literacy skills. They can also be more subtle, for instance, always missing deadlines, and this can be easily misunderstood. The need for paper qualifications to demonstrate competency in all occupations also places dyslexic people at a disadvantage. Furthermore, people are now required to be generalists, this being made possible by technology, in that they are responsible for their own administrative tasks and there is an increasing emphasis on written documentation. There is some irony in the fact that, whilst information technology (IT) was, and still is in some ways, hailed as the answer to a dyslexic person's literacy difficulties, it has also potentially increased their problems. The sheer volume and speed at which written information must be delivered nowadays is a challenge for everyone, but can be a nightmare for people with dyslexia. So what is it that enables people to achieve success?

Dyslexia and Success

Research with dyslexic people suggests that there are four factors that enable them to be successful: (i) self-understanding; (ii) being in a job that taps their strengths; (iii) making use of technological and creative solutions; and (iv) the understanding and support of the people around them (Gerber, Ginsberg and Reiff 1992). This places the onus on both the individual and the organization: dyslexic individuals need to be able to understand their dyslexia, be aware of their abilities and advocate for themselves; the organization needs to understand the individual nature of dyslexia and that its impact can change at certain times, particularly those of transition, for example, a change in job role, change of personnel, or a promotion (McLoughlin and Leather 2009). It is then that adjustments may need to be made to enable the dyslexic person to perform effectively.

The Role of the Organization

Greater awareness of dyslexia in adulthood and the responsibility on the organization to support the dyslexic person was promoted by the introduction of the Disability Discrimination Act (HMSO 1995).[1] There are many ways in which this can be done. The Act requires employers to make reasonable adjustments to compensate for the individual's specific difficulties. These adjustments should be evidence-based and usually include:

- extra time in selection and promotion examinations, in training, and when learning new procedures
- adjusting the job role, for example exempting the individual from taking minutes in meetings
- making changes to the workplace – moving the desk, being exempt from 'hot desking' and therefore being assigned a personal work desk
- providing technological aids to support dyslexic individuals in their work, and
- providing skills and strategy coaching to explore personalized solutions.

For adjustments to be put in place dyslexic people must disclose their dyslexia. However, research has revealed that many are reluctant to do so for fear of being misunderstood (see Chapter 13 for a discussion of this issue). It is important that the organization develops an environment of trust by having an accessible policy and raising awareness through the dissemination of information via the intranet, telephone help lines and support groups.

[1] This was replaced in October 2010 by the Equality Act.

Providing awareness training throughout the organization can make a big difference, particularly for departments such as:

- HR, recruitment and promotion boards
- occupational health, health and safety, and
- departments that provide training such as IT and communication skills.

Awareness training promotes general good practice and can also be cost effective; often the adjustments or changes in procedure and practice are quite simple and inexpensive. Furthermore, they can benefit the whole organization or team, for example, asking people to sum up the points raised at a meeting or to send out brief minutes can remind everyone of the important facts. It can also mean that general information is presented in a variety of ways that benefits everyone.

It has been written that employers cannot be expected to be experts in disability (Gerber 2002) and, given the complex nature of dyslexia, it is sensible to seek specialist advice. It is, however, essential that the awareness training is delivered by someone who has some experience of the culture of that organization. The impact and solutions for dyslexic people in desk-bound jobs are likely to be very different from those for dyslexic people in risk-critical occupations such as the police, the fire service or the medical profession. Understanding the nature of dyslexia within the context of the job is essential in enabling the dyslexic person to perform more effectively.

The Workplace Assessment

One of the ways in which an organization can develop understanding, provide a positive working environment in which individuals feel more supported, and make some adjustments to their job role, is through the workplace assessment. This is sometimes confused with the diagnostic assessment. The latter is usually carried out by a psychologist or a dyslexia specialist assessor. It provides the formal evidence for dyslexia or other specific learning difficulty such as dyspraxia, by investigating cognitive processes and literacy attainments. The purpose of a workplace assessment is to provide the employee and employer with evidence-based recommendations for reasonable adjustments within the context of a job.

The workplace assessment should look at the whole person, including his or her skills and abilities. It should be flexible, individualized and provide a wide variety of solutions and suggestions for skill development. The resulting recommendations should facilitate progression and independence. There should be monitoring and evaluation to consider the effectiveness of the recommendations and, if the job role changes, then the adjustments may need to be reviewed.

Office-based jobs are likely to tap the dyslexic literacy and numeracy problems that are relatively well understood, and technological aids are frequently the solution. But even then the different task demands should be considered: for example, writing a policy document is very different from preparing a project management report. Text-to-speech and speech-to-text software do help people produce more accurate written work. For some dyslexic people this software changes their lives by addressing their literacy difficulties and they go on to become confident, successful people. This is not always the case, however. Some people's spelling may be too weak to take advantage of the spellchecker, and they may feel overwhelmed by computers.

Some job roles do not require large amounts of writing and, when much of it can be done using templates, specific technical literacy training might be more effective than using specialist software packages that demand considerable IT skills and new learning. In fact, the recommendation of IT can undermine a person's performance and confidence, the 'solution' becoming a barrier to success. However, in spite of this, technological aids are important for dyslexic people. They are most effective when they are tailored to the individual's IT competency and job role. Standardized solutions are not the answer to very specific difficulties.

Table 16.1 Aspects of the workplace assessment.

The job	**The person**
• main duties of the job • the context of the job role • competencies and skills required • outline of concerns • indicators of performance levels	• skills and abilities • personal strengths/attributes • transferable skills • personality characteristics – levels of self-understanding • external constraints concerns – travelling time, childcare arrangements
The environment	**The impact of dyslexia – difficulties with**
• structure of the department/team • features of the workplace • social aspect – teamwork, colleagues • physical aspects/office ergonomics – size, open plan	• literacy • memory • organization • confidence • specific work skills

Aspects of the Workplace Assessment

The workplace assessment should be carried out in the individual's place of work and it should address the areas shown in Table 16.1.

The report should be a summary of the information gathered. It can encourage good communication and understanding between the dyslexic person and his or her managers

The role of the manager is crucial to the dyslexic person's success. Understanding the demands that the job might make on the dyslexic person will help managers to provide appropriate advice. They need to appreciate that there are certain situations in which a dyslexic person may lack confidence. Listening to the dyslexic person and discussing any concerns can often lead to simple solutions such as:

- providing checklists or more detailed and prioritized task lists
- being flexible on deadlines when possible and offering to proofread documents
- being happy to clarify or reiterate instructions or give them in a visual format.

Taking on board all the complexities of dyslexia can be demanding, so it is essential that the manager can seek advice and support from human resources (HR) and from dyslexia specialists where possible.

Good Practice

Examples of good practice can be found in an increasing number of organizations. Many government departments and most large employers provide awareness training and individual support. Some organizations have very visible policies in place; others take a lighter, but often no less effective, approach as it tends to be more individualized. Two organizations, the Metropolitan Police Service and the London Fire Brigade, have developed an integrated policy from recruitment through all the transition and promotion stages.

In 2003 the Metropolitan Police developed a three-pronged strategic approach involving:

- awareness training days throughout the whole organization
- training for the trainers at Hendon Police Training College, and
- assessment of, and one-to-one skills training for, trainee police officers by external specialists.

This approach was successfully implemented and over 200 dyslexic trainee police officers benefited from it. However, in 2006 it was felt that there was such a demand for the provision that it would be better to train police staff to become dyslexia advisers. This was promoted for two reasons: it would be more cost effective but, more importantly, it was thought that police officers involved in training had a much better idea of how dyslexia might impact on an individual's performance. The work of a police officer is complex, requiring multitasking such as taking notes at the scene of an incident, following procedures correctly in custody suites after making an arrest, and dealing with paperwork generally. As they are aware of these requirements, police officers involved in training would be better able to give targeted and appropriate support.

Trainers in the Skills to Achieve Results Team (START) received dyslexia specialist training. They were able to make recommendations about reasonable adjustments such as allowing extra time to complete training and during examinations, and they were able to provide specialist skills training. The advisers were also trained to carry out workplace assessments to support dyslexic officers already working in the field. Understanding the job enabled trainers to make very specific and realistic recommendations. There were also other benefits: the awareness and understanding of dyslexia has improved throughout the organization. Disclosure is not mandatory in the Metropolitan Police Service, but dyslexic trainees at Hendon and serving police officers are increasingly willing to seek advice.

The London Fire Brigade adopted an equally proactive and specialist approach. There are regular dyslexia awareness training events throughout the whole organization. Individuals who are underperforming or who feel they might be dyslexic are offered an interview and screening by the learning support department; if there are sufficient indicators, they are referred for a formal assessment. Following an assessment, the dyslexic officers are automatically offered dyslexia skills coaching sessions to develop their understanding of the impact dyslexia might have on them in their job role, and to explore solutions to specific difficulties they might be experiencing. Managers and trainers can seek advice and support from either the dyslexia consultant or the learning support advisers. This integrated policy within the London Fire Brigade is resulting in dyslexic people feeling comfortable about disclosing, and also receiving very specific, realistic advice that addresses the difficulties that are hindering their performance.

The Individual

Although organizational change is essential, the adjustments put in place will not be effective unless the dyslexic person can become proactive. The understanding of the employer and being in the right environment is only part of the picture (Goldberg *et al.* 2003). The success of people with SpLD will not be contingent upon the law and businesses. It will be linked to the capabilities and the performance of the individuals themselves (Gerber 2002). Two of the factors identified that facilitate success for people with specific learning difficulties are the development of self-understanding and the development of strategies and skills. Promoting these can be achieved through coaching.

Coaching is now a familiar activity in the workplace and it is an obvious choice for an effective recommendation/intervention. The term coaching is sometimes used quite colloquially; an enduring definition explains its purpose as unlocking individuals' potential to *maximize* their own *performance*. It is helping them to *learn* rather than teaching them. There has been controversy about the distinctions between mentoring, defined as an activity that develops individuals by focusing on their career progression, and coaching, defined as personal development activity that focuses on performance (Hawkins and Smith 2006). Coaching is now more widely recognized as sitting along the continuum of helping relationships and can overlap with consulting, mentoring and counselling (Witherspoon and White 1996).

Coaching is clearly 'a relationship-based intervention' (Passmore 2007, p. 10). In order for coaching to be effective, the person being coached (the coachee) needs to be involved in defining the overall aims of the coaching and setting the specific goals to attain them. In a collaborative working relationship the coach and the coachee focus on individual strengths as a way of increasing self-efficacy; they create specific action plans, monitor and evaluate the coachee's progress and, following implementation and feedback, modify the action plan (Grant *et al.* 2010; Hawkins and Smith 2006). This 'cycle of self-regulated behaviour' (Grant *et al.* 2010, p. 127), to which Grant and colleagues draw attention, comprises the activities of executive functioning. Executive functioning, which is controlled by one of the components of the working memory system, refers to the mental processes that allow us to plan, organize tasks, monitor progress, manage distractions, manage our time and respond to change. Most of us benefit at times from the assistance of an external interlocutor in monitoring and directing these activities. For the dyslexic person who has an inefficient working memory that will impact negatively on their executive functioning, coaching would seem to be the ideal model for addressing their difficulties (McLoughlin and Kirwan 2007).

Research and practice in business coaching tends to focus on executive coaching, and the implication is that coaching is for the exceptionally talented or senior management personnel only (Toscano 2006). Dyslexia coaching with our clients in work shows that well-organized and well-delivered specialist coaching can be a good economic choice for employees at all levels within an organization because its focus is the professional and performance development of the individual in his or her job role. We achieve this by recognizing that individuals have the expertise in their job while the coach provides the specialist knowledge to address the impact of dyslexia on individuals in their job role and in their relationships with colleagues and clients/customers. We draw on available coaching models, which include cognitive behavioural coaching, solution-focused coaching and person-centred coaching, and provide a dyslexic coaching model to our clients. This is dependent on the individual. Its particularities are that it often takes place at times of transition (e.g. when someone is promoted), and it generally has a reframing element to it, that is, providing positive explanation and analysis. It leads people to become more aware of their skills and their abilities, developing their self-understanding, and it is goal-orientated and collaborative in practice. Evaluation is included at the end of the coaching and the individual is also required to conduct self-evaluation.

The process of learning in coaching involves discussion and practice. The change and development process usually requires that individuals learn through self-reflection and analysis and practice in different ways of working. The coaching partnership proceeds ideally with the coach and coachee establishing mutual trust. The coach asks questions and the coachee reflects on these questions; the coach responds to these reflections and both then agree on what needs to be learned. The coachee then acts on this and takes responsibility for maintaining the new knowledge. Our work with dyslexic individuals and those with other hidden disabilities such as dyspraxia engages this type of learning.

Coaching is on a one-to-one basis and the initial session includes discussion to clarify the meaning of the diagnosis of dyslexia or specific learning difficulty for the individual. Strengths and weaknesses are outlined, specific goals are set and strategies to achieve them are explored. The coaching is usually non-directive but sometimes it needs to be instructive and explicit in order to overcome the processing difficulty that prevents the dyslexic person finding the right solutions. It is usual to set a short-term time frame that allows for review and extension according to individual need. The focus of the coaching is both to improve performance and develop the individual's skills. It is assumed that the dyslexic individual is generally psychologically healthy but the emotional issues and negative thought processes that derive from the inefficiency in working memory are always addressed. So too are any personal issues that might arise in discussion in so far as they impede the person's ability to focus and attend to work-related personal and performance development (McLoughlin and Kirwan 2007). At different times the coach could be:

- offering instruction in a tutoring role, for instance by advising on more efficient strategies for reading and assimilating written information
- facilitating learning by exploring with individuals how their participation in meetings could be made more productive through planning and more preparation in advance, and
- discussing the emotional factors that might prevent someone exploring different ways of working.

Coaching offers dyslexic employees the chance to raise awareness about their strengths and weaknesses. This self-knowledge will contribute to their ability to make decisions about what they can do, and where they need more training; it will also help them to focus their attention, in an encouraging environment, on improving their weakest skills. The goal is to help individuals to advocate better for themselves by taking more responsibility for their personal development and their job performance. Coaching for dyslexic employees can be offered by a helpful colleague or manager who is doing a formal or informal type of mentoring, or it could be delivered by a business or performance coach. If these interventions are not working successfully, it would be advisable to seek dyslexia specialist coaching, perhaps for just a small number of sessions, to allow the employee to work with someone who has an understanding of the impact of dyslexia. The most important factor is that the type of coaching is right for the individual dyslexic person. Equally, the pace and intensity of delivery has to take account of individual capacity for learning, retention and consolidation. As with most coaching practice, the individual gains the most benefit from hourly or two-hourly input over a period, with scheduled reviews.

A case study

John was in his late twenties and was working as a programme researcher in television when he sought coaching. He had recently been diagnosed with dyslexia and dyspraxia and he was studying part-time for a higher degree. He had done well in his A-level examinations and had attained a first class degree in Classics from a prestigious university. He had proficient literacy skills but still experienced difficulties with speed of reading and writing.

John started experiencing problems in his job following a period of restructuring and redundancies, and everyone had to meet much tighter deadlines. In particular he:

- was overwhelmed by the volume of information he had to absorb and was frequently working overtime
- was making many mistakes and forgetting to do things
- frequently lost his temper with colleagues, and
- was often late for work through oversleeping.

John had begun to doubt his ability to do the job that he had been doing for the past five years. He felt anxious and unhappy, he was ignoring colleagues and avoiding conversations so that he would be less distracted and more focused on his work, and he avoided work social activities too. He was missing deadlines on his MA degree course and had hardly any time to spend with friends or his family.

John evaluated the strengths and weaknesses in his performance at work as shown in Table 16.2.

Table 16.2 John's self-perceived strengths and weaknesses.

Strengths	*Weaknesses*
Good problem-solving and creative skills	Finds it hard to maintain good organization all the time
Very good people skills; good listener and quick to respond to other people's needs	Finds it hard sometimes to communicate quickly and clearly in meetings
Hard-working and committed and has always done a good job, until recently	Does not regularly meet deadlines on written work
Very organised, likes to be thorough and detailed	Finds it hard to concentrate in a busy office with lots of talk and activity taking place

Setting goals

Setting goals gives a focus and framework to the content of the sessions, and John's goals were identified as being to:

- develop his understanding of his specific difficulties
- improve management of his workload
- identify ways of improving memory and recall
- develop confidence in dealing with change.

Promoting self-understanding formed a significant part of the earlier coaching sessions and discussion focused on the meaning and implications of the diagnosis of dyslexia and dyspraxia. John was able to understand that his behaviour and his relationships with others were a consequence of the way he perceives ideas and events and what he hears and sees in the world around him, rather than concluding that they were indicative of difficulties in his past. Over the course of the seven sessions John became relaxed about accepting that his thinking is not always clear and logical, accepting his need for strict organization and accepting that at times he is slower than he would like to be in completing tasks. He commented on how he had become more tolerant of himself since gaining understanding of how his brain absorbed information and worked things out. The consequence of that was to reduce his anxiety about getting things right and thereby reduce self-criticism. That in turn benefited his self-belief and inspired more courage regarding trying things out, and risking error and less than perfection.

John came to the conclusion that he was more effective in managing and prioritizing his work when he was in tune with the progress of other people he worked with. He recalled that regular discussion in the past with colleagues gave boundaries and deadlines to his work and he needed that in the present to help him identify what was important and what had to be abandoned. More communication with colleagues gave him more time because he deliberated less and got things done.

John was able to identify the times when he felt memory and recall posed a problem for him; this was usually in meetings when having to respond to multiple demands and interact with many people. He resolved to plan his participation in meetings more precisely, to use visual notes and to use them frequently. These small changes allowed him to explain his ideas better to colleagues. The changes were made possible because John was willing to accept that, in a situation where work was greater in volume and more demanding, he had to work in a different way in order to thrive. Understanding dyspraxia provided the rationale for having to make adjustments to his way of working. And, with that, accepting change was possible because he accepted a new understanding of himself.

Self-Advocacy

Developing self-advocacy skills was a key part to John's coaching. These skills are very important. Employers and managers will have a variable amount of knowledge and interest in specific learning difficulties, so dyslexic people will often be asked what can be done to help them. They need to be able to:

- explain dyslexia and how it affects them
- say what their skills are
- explain what they need to work well.

They also need to be able to outline their difficulties and provide solutions. For example, saying:

- 'The quickest way for me to get my ideas on paper is to use voice recognition software.'
- 'I like to clarify information before I spend hours doing a report.'
- 'My memory is not great so I always note things down.'

Being able to advocate for themselves enables people to feel in control and builds their confidence.

Providing a personal interpretation of dyslexia can also help. It can be best explained simply as an information-processing difference that means that dyslexic people can take longer to process certain types of information. Some find it helpful to use an analogy to describe it. For example, likening their difficulties with working memory to a computer with insufficient RAM,[2] that is, they can do the work but it just takes them longer, or too much information will slow them down. Others liken it to a table top without enough space to hold all the items, so they have to be much more organized and deal with all the information in small bits.

The difficulties surrounding disclosure are discussed in other chapters of this book. It is a personal choice and, clearly, many people do not disclose. This is understandable in the current economic climate, as people fear discrimination. The latter is, however, minimized if through effective coaching individuals are able to present to others in a positive and constructive way. It is through this that they will be able to receive appropriate support and suitable adjustments can be made for them.

Conclusion

The skills dyslexic people can bring to the workplace include original problem-solving, strategic thinking, good people skills, and big-picture thinking. As indicated in the case study outlined here, the solutions can often be simple and cost effective. Certainly good communication can avoid much misunderstanding, heartache and lost productivity. In the case of the Metropolitan Police and the London Fire Brigade, described above, the proactive policies adopted have led to many people commenting on how the training of all the new recruits has improved because the methods employed to help the dyslexic people have benefited everyone.

The keys to individual success are self-understanding, determination and confidence, in addition to being in a job that allows the demonstration of skills and abilities. Creating the

[2] Random Access Memory.

right environment where individual differences are valued, and making appropriate adjustments, leads to organizational success.

References

Gerber, P.J., Ginsberg, R. and Reiff, H.B. (1992) Identifying alterable patterns in employment success for highly successful adults with learning disabilities. *Journal of Learning Disabilities*, 25, 475–487.

Gerber, P.J. (2002) Navigating the beyond school years: Employment and success for adults with learning difficulties. *Career Planning and Adult Development Journal*, 18, 136–144.

Goldberg, R., Higgins, E., Raskind, M. and Herman, K. (2003) Predictors of success in individuals with learning disabilities: A qualitative analysis of a 20-year longitudinal study. *Learning Disabilities Research & Practice*, 18(4), 222–236.

Grant, A.M., Cavanagh, M.J., Parker, H.M. and Passmore, J. (2010) The state of play in coaching today: A comprehensive review of the field, in *International Review of Industrial and Organizational Psychology* (eds G.P.
Hodgkinson and J.K. Ford), Volume 25, John Wiley & Sons, Ltd, Chichester, pp. 125–167.

Hawkins, P. and Smith, N. (2006) *Coaching, Mentoring and Organizational Consultancy*, Open University Press, Maidenhead, Berkshire.

HMSO (1995) *The Disability Discrimination Act 1995*, Her Majesty's Stationery Office, London.

Logan, J. (2009) Dyslexic entrepreneurs: The incidence, their coping strategies and their business skills. *Dyslexia*, 15, 328–346.

McLoughlin, D. and Kirwan, B.M. (2007) Coaching and dyslexia in the workplace. *Selection and Development Review*, 23, 3–7.

McLoughlin, D. and Leather, C.A. (2009) Dyslexia: Meeting the needs of employers and employees in the workplace, in *The Routledge Companion to Dyslexia* (ed. G. Reid), Routledge Oxon., pp. 286–294.

McLoughlin, D., Leather, C.A. and Stringer, P.E. (2002) *The Adult Dyslexic: Interventions and Outcomes*, Whurr, London.

Passmore, J. (2007) Coaching and mentoring – The role of experience and sector knowledge. *International Journal of Evidence Based Coaching and Mentoring*. Special Issue, Summer.

Toscano, J. (2006) The case for coaching. *Selection and Development Review*, 22, 12–13.

Witherspoon, R. and White, R.P. (1996) Executive coaching: A continuum of roles. *Consulting Psychology Journal: Practice and Research*, 48, 124–133.

17

The Knowledge and Skills Required by a Specialist Tutor within the Field of Adult Support

Margaret Malpas, the British Dyslexia Association, UK

Whilst the teaching and support of children and students is a well trodden and researched path, there has been relatively little work done with adults either within or outside the workplace beyond a few projects on screening and literacy support for those in the prison population (e.g. Baker and Ireland 2007; Elbeheri, Everatt and Al Malki 2009). The traditional view that adults with Specific Learning Difficulty (SpLD) would find employment in manual work is being challenged within the UK Government and think tanks as opportunities for manual work are reducing considerably. There has been for the first time, therefore, a concern at Government level about the effects of lack of literacy in the adult population on the UK's economy.

I have assisted the British Dyslexia Association (BDA) to take centre stage in developing workplace assessors and support mechanisms at this opportune time. We have now trained over 200 individuals skilled in providing both this form of assessment and appropriate support mechanisms. There is a strongly held belief amongst those responsible for the provision of educational support to children with SpLD that this work with adults should also be part of their preserve. It is, therefore, a very good time to look at the skills and knowledge required by specialist tutors who may wish to work in the field of adult support. This is the aim of this chapter.

Knowledge Required

In addition to detailed knowledge of dyslexia, the specialist SpLD tutor who wishes to work in the area of adult support must possess knowledge in three key areas:

1 A sound understanding of the principles and psychology of adult learning.
2 An appreciation of the context in which they will be working; this could be the workplace or with those who are not currently in employment.
3 Specific literacy and numeracy programmes that work with adults and a range of coping strategies to deal with problems of personal organization, information processing and memory issues.

Each of these will be discussed. However, before doing so it may be interesting to note that diagnostic testing has not been included in this list, and this is not an oversight. The development of assessment skills in specialist tutors in education arose specifically to meet the need for these tests before access arrangements could be implemented. This has not

Supporting Dyslexic Adults in Higher Education and the Workplace, First Edition. Edited by Nicola Brunswick.

happened within employment, or unemployment, of adults where Government financial support is provided without the need for a full assessment. This shifts the priority of what needs to be learned, and done, from assessment to support.

The lack of a diagnostic assessment has not proved to be the impediment that one might at first expect. During 2009, the BDA had a contract with the West Midlands Police Force to provide services including screening, training and coaching for officers who thought they might be dyslexic. Very few of these officers sought to have a full diagnostic assessment but many sought our help with screening, and many did show a high risk of dyslexia. These officers were then offered individual support with coping strategies designed around elements of their job that they believed to be affected by their likely dyslexia. The feedback from these officers was that they had found the process extremely helpful. Frequently they reported that just knowing that they were probably dyslexic, and that this was the source of some of their challenges, made a huge difference to how they felt about themselves. It also created the desire to do something about these challenges that they had previously, largely, tried to ignore. Many officers found concept mapping to be extremely useful, and some of the memory techniques were invaluable where officers needed to be able to record points within the evidence chain.

It was also an interesting experience from the point of view of cost effectiveness for the Force. In six months, the BDA provided a conference for senior officers, workplace assessments, individual coaching strategies, training courses on awareness, and expert opinion in case conferences. It was estimated that this saved the Force over £100,000.

The Principles of Adult Learning

Generally, the research into effective teaching of children does not overlap with the research into adult learning. However, given that maturation of learning is a continuum where the style of learning of adolescents is likely to morph into their adult approach, many teachers of teenagers will be familiar with the basic features of adult learning. However, there are key differences in teaching adults that specialist tutors need to understand. These are that they will:

- evaluate new information on the basis of its relevance and use to them
- have motivations for learning that are complex and related to their past and current emotional states
- be problem-centred; for example, individuals may have been motivated to ask for an assessment because their managers are giving them feedback about a particular area where their performance is reduced. This differs from our approach in education, which is more content-centred and usually around the setting of a syllabus to teach, such as a phonics programme
- learn more effectively if they are actively involved in the design of their learning.

Much of the recent research in the area of disability support has come from health education, particularly relating to managing chronic illness and disability. There is much of relevance in this work for teaching adult dyslexic readers who need to manage their disability. In practice, this means that the tutor needs to:

- be aware of individuals' levels of motivation for this learning and what is driving their motivation
- recognize the individuals' particular needs so that they can present what is to be learned in a way that makes clear its relevance to them
- involve them in the planning of lessons to some extent. This will mean agreeing midterm objectives with the individual and explaining how the teaching method and content will enable these objectives to be met

- gather information subtly about the individuals' self concept as learners and also their levels of self-esteem. The tutor may have to provide considerable amounts of praise for progress to begin to build the individual's self-esteem and develop their concept of themselves as effective learners.

One difficulty with adult learners is that they are prone to lose their motivation for learning. Adults require an end goal that they continue to value, and they need to receive frequent feedback that they are en route to achieving this goal. For example, the father whose motivation to tackle his lack of literacy is driven by the desire to read bedtime stories to his child may well lose his motivation if there is a divorce and his access to the child is severely reduced. Similarly, if his progress in reading is considerably slower than he expected so that he begins to feel that he will never learn to read before the child has lost interest in bedtime stories, then he may well also lose his motivation to learn.

As dyslexia is a genetic inheritance, there is currently no cure for the difficulties it may impose and so the solutions are largely pragmatic. For learning, this means making use of strong channels of communication and teaching using multisensory approaches so that areas of difficulty are supported. For example, if individuals have a specific problem with phonological awareness (with detecting and producing the sounds of the spoken language), it may be necessary for them to learn primarily via visual and kinaesthetic (physical, hands-on) methods. The specialist tutor therefore needs to have knowledge of different visual, auditory and kinaesthetic modes of learning. The tutor should also be aware that adult learners may have a preferred learning style as an activist (someone who learns by doing), reflector (someone who learns by watching and thinking), theorist (someone who learns by thinking through concepts), or a pragmatist (someone who learns by trying things out to see if they work) (Honey and Mumford 1982). This may be driven by their personality or their difficulties but, in either case, if people's learning style can be expanded, they will have greater opportunities for learning from their experiences.

Everything we experience presents opportunities for learning and, if individuals can be encouraged to see this and to act upon it, then their learning styles will naturally expand into the areas defined by Honey and Mumford. To explain this, we can take the example of building flat-pack furniture. Some individuals will take all the pieces out of the box and experiment to see how they go together; this is typical of someone with an activist or pragmatist learning style. Others will carefully study the instructions; this would be expected of someone with a reflective or theoretically-biased learning style. In fact, the most efficient method is to do all these things: to study the diagrams, lay out the materials and work out how they fit together. By doing this, individuals will almost certainly also learn a thing or two about tackling flat-pack furniture in future. They are using the experience and the full range of learning opportunities this affords. This is a very simple example but the effect of broadening individuals' ability to learn from experience can have quite a profound effect on their future ability.

Finally, the tutor should know how to increase individual's knowledge of themselves and their methods of learning effectively. In teaching terms this would be described as metacognition and, in adult learning circles, developing their self-concept as effective learners. As long as the specialist tutor is aware of the need to do this, no specific planning may be required as opportunities to explain and confirm effective personal learning occur spontaneously and these learning moments are the best time for the adult to make the leap to self knowledge.

Knowledge of the Context Surrounding the Learner

There are two relevant issues here. The first is the acceptance of the tutor to the learner. If the tutor is ignorant of normal managerial practices or common working practices (e.g. 'hot desking' or working from home) outside education, then he or she will immediately be seen by the adult learner as lacking face validity and will be rejected. In addition, the typical experience of dyslexic adults in education may lead them to be highly suspicious of any tutor, and so establishing rapport is more difficult. Thus the specialist tutor must have knowledge of normal working practices to make the bridge with the learner.

Second, it is important to take into account the setting, culture and constraints directly on the learners as this will affect how much and how well they are able to change their behaviour through learning. This is likely to be the most difficult area of knowledge for most tutors to gain, as much of it is likely to sit outside their personal experience. There will be radically different contexts here as to whether the learner is in employment or not, so these will be considered separately.

Working with People in Employment

With people who are employed, tutors will need to have a good appreciation of the context of standard employment practices; they could learn the basics through reading books such as Gennard and Judge's (2010) *Managing Employee Relations*. This would enable them to relate to the concept of master and servant that underpins all employment law and which gives an indication of the power balances at work. From this, the specialist tutor would gain an appreciation of the way performance management systems are generally operated outside the teaching profession through the use of personal objectives and pay systems. Unlike teachers, employees often do not have dedicated workspaces that are their domain, and they also often work with others in close teams where their performance is mutually affected by that of others. This is often an area of contention for employees with SpLD and, consequently, an understanding of team dynamics and power shifts within groups of adults is also very useful (of course, the teacher may have encountered this previously through being part of the senior management team at school). It would be impossible to empathize with the problems dyslexic individuals may be facing, or to relate to their emotional state, without this understanding but both are essential for effective teaching of adults in the workplace.

Frequently, individuals with SpLD are working directly and continuously with customers, and this can cause particular frustrations on both sides where the conditions are ill understood. The specialist tutor may need to appraise themselves of the usual methods of customer service and what happens when these are breached by the individual. They should also gain an understanding of workplaces where there are recognized trade unions where employee relations activities are more regularized and formal.

Following on from this general background, the specialist tutor would need some very specific and detailed knowledge, for example about grievance, disciplinary and capability procedures. It is quite common for an employee to disclose their SpLD only upon threat of dismissal. Thus, fairly typically, the employee has already reached the second of three stages of the disciplinary procedure which, at this juncture, may be turned into a capability procedure. Therefore, the specialist tutor is faced with trying to support the individual, who is under considerable stress with the likelihood of losing his or her job. There are also usually strict time frames on the operation of these procedures and it is essential that the tutor is familiar with all this. Most commonly, an improvement in performance is required within weeks and this is usually impossible given the type of teaching intervention required. This knowledge can be imparted to the employer and may make the difference between the person being dismissed or not.

It would be advisable if the specialist tutor also learned at least a minimum amount about the Disability Discrimination Act (DDA 1995, revised 2001, now subsumed into the Equality

Act (EA) 2010), and the findings of recent case law. This has established that it is unfair to dismiss someone through reason of his or her disability without first attempting to provide reasonable adjustments. For example, case law has established through the *Paterson vs. Metropolitan Police Force* case that all forms and levels of SpLD are covered by the DDA and now, consequently, by the EA. Furthermore, through the *Brooking vs. Essex Police Force* case it has established that training of colleagues in awareness is a normal, reasonable adjustment and that harassment of disabled staff will carry serious penalties. Knowledge of these legal requirements will ensure that specialist tutors know that organizations have to provide reasonable adjustments to the individual with SpLD and what some of those adjustments might be. This will enable them to plan and provide appropriate support to the individual.

Finally, the tutor will need to know about Access to Work. This is the UK government agency that provides funding for reasonable adjustments to be made in the workplace. Access to Work operates via call centres across the UK and has prime contracts with organizations that provide workplace assessments and recommend coping strategies for employees. The provision of support for the majority of dyslexic people through this system has been in place for only the last two years. The UK Government is currently re-tendering on the provision of workplace assessments, with new contracts coming into place in November 2011. The Government has declared that people with dyslexia and those with mental health issues are a priority within the new contracts. It is anticipated, therefore, that the provision of support for dyslexic people will be even better in future than it is now.

The BDA has been providing many coaching sessions for individuals with dyslexia under the Access to Work programme. The process we have used includes a detailed analysis with individuals on the areas of their work that they find difficult. These individuals are included in the planning of their coaching sessions, and feedback is sought at the end of every session so that adjustments can be made if they are not satisfied with any aspects of the activity. There have been common themes to the feedback we receive; for example, individuals saying that this is the first time anyone has really explained what dyslexia is and that it is a genetically inherited condition. They also report that this is the first time anyone has taken their issues seriously and really listened to them. Finally, we find that they often report finding renewed energy for tackling their challenges and learning coping strategies.

However, organizing and delivering coaching sessions is not always plain sailing. Some individuals are very anxious about facing up to their difficulties in performing their jobs effectively. This can sometimes manifest itself as an emotional outburst, and at other times the person simply does not turn up to the meeting that has been arranged. Part of the process for us is that individuals have to take ownership of their situation, as adults; their dyslexia is part of them and they need to feel this. We provide a very encouraging climate to those who seek help. However, if we are being paid by the Government to provide a coaching service, we contract with individuals and their organization so they know that, if they fail to arrive for the session, then that is a session lost. It cannot be freely provided again. This may sound harsh, particularly when one of the typical themes we encounter is that of individuals having difficulties with organizing their time, but we will already have deployed a number of coping strategies such as confirming the time of the appointment with them in writing in advance, and then re-confirming the session the night before.

A particular issue we have also encountered really exists outside the individual, with the employer or manager. Often the reason we have been asked to coach the person is because their underperformance has reached a stage where their manager has invoked the disciplinary procedure. Providing support is not well understood generally, neither is dyslexia. Consequently, there is often little anticipation by their manager that the coaching will result in a considerable improvement in performance. It is often merely seen as part of the legal requirement in the dismissal process. This is clearly not a helpful backdrop to the coaching sessions, and it can mean that the manager does not engage fully in enabling the person to deploy the coping strategies we have recommended. It is also the case that, to be truly effective, it will take the people up to six months to integrate their coping strategies fully into their performance, but we rarely see this amount of tolerance to the condition.

We have also encountered several requests by managers to be present at the coaching sessions, but this presents a difficulty. The employer is contributing to the cost of the sessions and therefore naturally feels some involvement in the process, but this is rarely successful. The coach's time is taken up contracting with employees about whether they are comfortable for their manager to be present. Furthermore, if the reason we have been invited in is that of underperforming, then there is often at least a partial breakdown in the relationship between manager and employee. It is genuinely difficult to manage someone's performance through official processes while maintaining a reasonable working relationship, so this is no surprise. However, we have also experienced managers operating a blame culture within the coaching session and this just destroys all hope of anything being achieved. The fundamental reason for these difficulties is a lack of understanding about dyslexia in the workplace, how it manifests itself and a lack of appreciation that it is genuinely a disability. This will be addressed only over time as more awareness-raising is achieved by charities such as the BDA and other interested parties.

Under the Access to Work scheme, employers are required to contribute to the costs of providing reasonable adjustments – the larger the organization, the bigger the contribution it is expected to make. This is particularly helpful to small organizations that employ people with disabilities. It has also been shown by research carried out by the Department of Work and Pensions that small organizations are generally more effective at coping with the flexibility required to employ disabled staff and at profiting from their talents.

Working with People Not in Employment

For people not in employment, the specialist tutor would need to know more about opportunities for unemployed people. In practice, in the UK, there is little specific, funded support. The government retraining programme 'Train to Gain' can be used for short-term interventions but there is little available formally for SpLD literacy or numeracy coaching. Many centres of adult education have teaching staff who have been encouraged to learn about SpLD and relevant teaching strategies, and many staff in further education colleges are familiar with the needs of adults with SpLD as they meet them so frequently in their student population. However, neither of these is funded to provide appropriate learner support. If the specialist tutor is going to work with adults who are embarking on a first degree, then there is considerable support available through the Disabled Students' Allowance, and so this also should be investigated in this scenario.

The dynamic of communication between the specialist tutor and the adult learner is a tricky area. In the teaching context, there is an immediate danger that the tutor will inevitably step into the role of the 'nurturing parent'. The problem with this is that the natural response from learners is to allow the tutor to take over the resolution of problems and the responsibility for their learning. This is not going to be effective. Worse still is when tutors step into a 'controlling parent' style of communication where they are setting rather than agreeing and contracting objectives. This is likely to promote childlike responses from learners that are both ineffective in learning and likely to produce feelings associated with being patronized. Understanding how to generate an 'adult to adult' relationship will be very helpful in guiding behaviours for both parties.

This whole area of the specialist tutor and the workplace raises issues relating to the difficulty of acquiring the appropriate understanding, attitude and application. It is possible to acquire the knowledge through reading but this is not the same as having the appropriate understanding through assimilating this knowledge and constructing meaning through personal experience of it. There is also the issue of jargon, that is, the specific vocabulary encountered in different business sectors. Whilst it is not reasonable to expect the specialist tutor to understand immediately technical jargon in industrial or commercial settings, there is vocabulary that simply would not be used in a school setting but which would be prevalent in other workplaces. One way to tackle this is to use work shadowing as an appropriate way to develop this knowledge and skill. It would also obviate the very real moral issues that are present for specialist tutors in entering a world they do not fully understand and be able to support individuals at risk in that environment with appropriate and workable advice and support.

Literacy and Coping Strategies for Adults

The majority of adults with SpLD who have very weak literacy skills are not likely to be found in the workplace (depending on the nature of the work, of course) but those who are in the workplace may need support to help them cope with the extent of reading and writing required to do their job. In this situation the specialist tutor would need to know about study skills-type coping strategies in order to teach the person to skim and scan, to produce concept maps and so on.

Tutors would need to know how to teach employees with poor reading ability how to read. They would need to know how to use an integrated multisensory approach to learning (combining information from the visual, auditory and kinaesthetic modalities), how to generate effective mnemonics, and the use of effective reinforcement strategies. They would also need to know about resources that are relevant to adult learners. These might include *Toe by Toe*, a multisensory reading scheme that is used extensively and successfully within the offender projects on literacy but is reported by many tutors to be rather monotonous;[1] *Alpha to Omega*, a phonics-based reading, writing and spelling scheme (Hornsby, Shear and Pool 2006), or one of the recent computerized learning programmes built on Alpha to Omega, such as *dyslexikit*.[2]

It will almost certainly be necessary to top up this work with personalized learning activities that tackle areas of relevance to the individual. For example, reading and spelling specific job-related vocabulary, aspects of the Highway Code, or menus and wine lists. In each of these cases, high-frequency words and important technical terms may be written out in a reference list for the individual to consult as needed.

Sadly, there is very little external funding for literacy teaching with adults and so the concentration on supporting adults is generally within a very short timescale and focused upon coping strategies. Either way it is essential that the specialist tutor has a sound understanding of a wide range of coping strategies that the adult with SpLD can use. These coping strategies largely subdivide into two types. There are organizational tips such as using a mobile phone alarm and message systems to ensure that the individual remembers to attend meetings with the correct papers. There are also assistive technology solutions. These include the use of computerized concept mapping, text-to-speech software, voice-activated software and specific programs for particular use such as literacy development and touch typing. The specialist tutor needs to have a good awareness of common organizational coping strategies and the general functions of key software programs. However, this is a rapidly developing field and it is impossible for individual tutors to keep fully current with all developments in it. They need to ensure that they are connected to communities that are able to keep up to date, such as the BDA with its technology committee and national telephone helpline whose volunteers receive regular training from software providers and others. This will enable them to signpost to learners ways forward to tackle individual needs.

[1] www.toe-by-toe.co.uk/index.html.
[2] www.dyslexikit.co.uk.

Skills for the Specialist Teacher of Adults

To be able to support the adult learner effectively, a range of skills is required. These skills, which relate to management and assist learning to take place, will be discussed individually.

- **Establishing empathy and rapport**
  Adult learners will not take the teacher's support uncritically. Teachers have to be able to command respect and learners have to be willing to give up power and authority so that teachers can manage their learning. Important skills to assist the specialist teacher in this include the ability to monitor the emotional state of individuals, to analyse and mirror their language, and to use a spectrum of strategies gleaned from psychological research on managing emotional states. For example, it is not uncommon for adults with dyslexia to have considerable unresolved anger that their education was not tailored to their needs, and their recognition that this has held them back from achieving more in life. Understanding anger management techniques can be part of the tutor's toolkit to enable the person to move on effectively. Using empathy and discussion can also be helpful if the individual is embarrassed by his or her lack of literacy skills. This needs to be addressed before the person can really develop holistically.
- **Listening skills**
  These need to be finely honed to pick up nuances and the emotional state of the learner. Adults may well have developed strategies to avoid being seen as stupid or to enable them to cope with life generally. This may mean that they have hidden their difficulties deeply to protect their self-esteem, although clues to their presence may still be identified by the perceptive listener. For example, one individual we coached recently was actually deeply anxious about the sessions and what they would reveal about him. He reported that he had no time management issues and was extremely organized. He clearly believed this and could not understand why his workmates complained about his lack of prioritizing and rather disorganized approach to his work. We were able to work through this with him and he now successfully uses a colour-coded diary system to organize his time.
- **Analysis**
  The specialist tutor will need to be able to analyse learners' motivations, self-concept and self-esteem, and also where their individual difficulties lie within the spectrum of SpLDs. Whilst diagnostic tools are very helpful in providing levels of attainment against standard scores, observation of learners and analysis of their strengths and difficulties is very helpful when planning an intervention to support them. Within the workplace, fast analysis of the culture (i.e. the norms, prevailing attitudes and what is valued) is essential so that appropriate solutions can be proffered.

  Sometimes this means recognizing that some coping strategies will not work in this setting. I can recall two examples of this from recent experience. The first is that there are some jobs that simply cannot be changed easily to accommodate a 'reasonable adjustment'. The BDA has done a lot of work with various police forces, including extensive work with the West Mercia Force. The team there is extremely keen to do all it can to assist dyslexic officers and civilian staff. However, clearly we cannot proffer coping strategies to officers on the beat requiring them to carry a portable computer complete with the full range of assistive technology. We were able to investigate with them whether head-mounted cameras might be useful, although not if the police officer is entering someone's home to conduct an interview, as the legal protection of that householder takes precedence.

  The second example involved someone working in a call centre. Dyslexia rarely comes as a single condition and this woman also had aspects of other co-occurring difficulties. In particular, she was easily distracted. The usual solution to this would be for her to work in a cellular office where distractions could be minimized. However, this office did not have any cellular spaces as it was large and open plan. The best we could implement in this situation was to provide her with screens around her desk, and this proved to be partially effective.

- **Synthesis**
The ability to make constructs of one's observations and analyses is vital. This will provide the theoretical analysis that will inform the teaching and support plan. It is also a vital skill when working with the individual and being able to make best use of learning moments when the plan may need to be flexed and something done quickly to reinforce learning.
The best example of this is when people have just had a revelatory 'light bulb moment' about their dyslexia and how it affects them. This can be a time of considerable energy and motivation to move forward through making change. However, the coach has to recognize that moment when it occurs and think quickly about how best to make use of it. It is not predictable.
- **Planning and contracting**
Absolute requirements for an effective intervention include the skill of identifying what needs to be done; creating SMART objectives[3] that will deliver the overall goal; taking account of factors that will act as barriers or enhancements to learning; recognizing critical incidents; and being able to fit all this into a practical time frame. In addition, in an adult context this all has to be done with the explicit agreement of the learner. Therefore, the skills of contracting – being able to define succinctly what is required, being able to seek agreement on the way forward, including milestones, and gaining agreement from the learner – are also useful.
This is intrinsic to the BDA method of contracting to undertake work. A specific contract document is used that is simple but which does record the agreed goals, how many sessions will take place, and when. We are currently working on incorporating wording into the contract document about the nature of dyslexia and the responsibilities of employers as a means to address some of the difficulties described earlier in this chapter.
- **Coaching**
Adult learners must take responsibility for their own learning, and this learning has to be active rather than passive. Therefore the skills of coaching – providing stretching objectives, enabling individuals to tackle things for themselves, challenging behaviour, supporting and rewarding where necessary – are all critical skills.
One of the constraints we encounter in this is the rapidity of the timescale. Support in the workplace is generally seen as a quick fix. We may have anything between three to six sessions with someone to make a difference. Occasionally the recommendation is for ten sessions but this is not the norm. Therefore, the coaching process has to begin quickly and make rapid progress through these stages. There is considerable skill in engaging learners to taking responsibility for their own progress in such a short time. However, this is possible, and we have only to look at the feedback from our learners to see how much can be achieved in a short time, and how worthwhile coping strategies are to them.
- **Monitoring**
Reviewing what the learner is achieving against expected progress, and then being flexible in adapting the learning programme, are essential to effective learning.
In fact, we have found that we need to be *very* flexible and it is common to need to adjust what we are doing after the second session. Much of the reason for this is that by then people have really begun to understand the challenges associated with their dyslexia, and so the agenda of what they need help with grows.

[3] That is, ones that are Specific, Measurable, Achievable, Relevant and Time-bound.

- **Evaluation**
  Being able to evaluate what learners are achieving, how their motivation affects their learning, and what strategies are working most effectively are all necessary. Evaluation of one's own practice is also a critical component of continuous professional development (CPD) and this is key to performing in this arena.
  We have built in CPD as a mandatory element of our programme to develop workplace assessors and coaches. All trainees with the BDA on these programmes automatically become members of the BDA, which entitles them to reduced prices on all our other training courses and conferences. We run a specific event for the workplace coaches each year to maintain their knowledge and skills, and their membership also gives them access to all the BDA networks, so there are many naturally occurring learning opportunities. This presents a huge difference from even two years ago when there was very little for people with an interest in this field.

Conclusion

Research into how best to support adult learners with SpLD is a rapidly expanding field, and the body of available knowledge is extensive. Whilst there are aspects of this knowledge that all specialist tutors should have, it is impossible for a single individual to keep up with all advances in the field. Therefore, it is recommended that specialist tutors of adults with SpLD develop a basic level of knowledge in the areas discussed above. They also need to develop a wide range of managerial skills to supplement their teaching skills. Their approach to supporting adults needs to take into account differences in the way adults learn as compared to children. As the field of knowledge is rapidly expanding, continuous professional development is essential. Furthermore, it is likely that a multidisciplinary team response to the adult's needs in the workplace will be necessary where specialist tutors play their part alongside those with detailed knowledge of assistive technology, and others with specialist skills in conflict resolution and counselling.

The BDA's work in this area continues, and one of its key successes has been the ability to draw people with an interest in this area into its networks. We now have a number of communities and an online forum where specialist tutors can gather updates and discuss difficult cases with each other as well as being connected continuously to the experts and to sources of new research findings. We hope that the level of information, support and training opportunities that we can offer will continue to increase in the years to come.

References

Baker, S.F. and Ireland, J.L. (2007) The link between dyslexic traits, executive functioning, impulsivity and social self-esteem among an offender and non-offender sample. *International Journal of Law and Psychiatry*, 30, 492–503.

Elbeheri, G., Everatt, J. and Al Malki, M. (2009) The incidence of dyslexia among young offenders in Kuwait. *Dyslexia*, 15, 86–104.

Equality Act (2010) Office for Disability Issues, London.

Gennard, J. and Judge, G. (2010) *Managing Employment Relations*, 5th edn, Chartered Institute of Personnel and Development, London.

Honey, P. and Mumford, A. (1982) *The Manuals of Learning Styles*, Honey Press, Maidenhead.

Hornsby, B., Shear, F. and Pool, J. (2006) *Alpha to Omega: The A-Z of teaching reading, writing and spelling* (6th edn), Heinemann Educational, Oxford.

The Disability Discrimination Act (1995) Her Majesty's Stationery Office, London.

18

Dyslexia and Disability Discrimination
The Legal Requirements

John Mackenzie, Discrimination Law and Employment Law Consultant, Henley-on-Thames, UK

Dyslexia and related specific learning difficulties (SpLDs) are disabilities covered by the UK Equality Act (EA) 2010, formerly the Disability Discrimination Act (DDA: 1995 onwards). All organizations, except the Armed Forces, are required to ensure that people with disabilities are not treated unfavourably and are offered reasonable adjustments. Originally intended to combat discrimination in the workplace, the EA now covers education, suppliers of goods and services, public bodies and local authorities.

Since 2005, The Disability Equality Duty has highlighted anti-discriminatory practices, requiring all public bodies to adopt a proactive approach to incorporating disability equality into all decisions and activities, encapsulated in a Disability Equality Scheme and reviewed under regular Equality Impact Assessments. To date this process has focused on physical disabilities and mental illness, and has tended to neglect the needs of the large population with specific learning difficulties.

A disabled person is defined by the EA as one who has a long-standing condition that has an adverse effect on his or her ability to perform day-to-day tasks. As dyslexia is a lifelong condition, provided it is sufficiently significant, an employee with dyslexic difficulties is considered under the Act to be disabled. The condition needs only to be 'more than trivial' to be disabling. In practice, where a dyslexic candidate is considered to be in need of 25% extra time in tests and exams (an almost standard recommendation in assessment reports that diagnose dyslexia) the individual will be classed as disabled under the Act.

Reasonable adjustments are styled 'reasonable' rather than mandatory to take into account particular circumstances. For instance, a small newsagent in a listed building with a doorstep would not be expected to install a wheelchair ramp but may be expected to serve someone in a wheelchair from the door. Smaller organizations may not be in a financial position to offer the accommodations that are expected of larger ones.

Many organizations have a long way to go to make their services dyslexia friendly, from accessible web sites through to offering information in electronic format, to helping with form filling. Many service providers, including Jobcentres, banks and the retail sector, still have some work to do here in relation to specific learning difficulties.

In employment, an employer can receive help from the government's Access to Work scheme, which is essentially a grant to the employee to help with the cost of implementing appropriate reasonable adjustments. A workplace Needs Assessment identifies and recommends the appropriate adjustments, but it is down to the employer to implement these if

Supporting Dyslexic Adults in Higher Education and the Workplace, First Edition. Edited by Nicola Brunswick.

they are 'reasonable'. In the case of dyslexia, employers can sometimes be slow to implement the recommended adjustments, and failure to make reasonable adjustments is a common finding in dyslexia Employment Tribunal cases.

Legislation Overview

In 2001, the DDA (1995) was amended to cover education providers in the Special Educational Needs and Disability Act (SENDA), incorporated as Part 4 of the DDA. This makes unlawful unjustified discrimination against disabled pupils and students, including adult learners. In summary it states that learners should not be treated unfavourably because of a disability, and should be offered reasonable support or adjustments to ensure that disabled learners do not suffer a substantial disadvantage in comparison to non-disabled learners.

A Special Educational Needs (SEN) Code of Practice was drawn up based on Part 4 of the DDA, and a summary version entitled *Special Educational Needs (SEN): A guide for parents and carers* is available to parents.[1]

The Disability Discrimination Act was further amended in 2005 to give public authorities a positive duty to promote disability equality. Part 5a imposes a specific duty on key public bodies, such as higher education institutions, to produce a Disability Equality Scheme. Statutory guidance in the form of a code of practice was published by the Equality and Human Rights Commission.

Schools

The Local Government Ombudsman now has greater powers to intervene in SEN matters: if an individual child is being damaged by a blanket policy of the local authority, for example, by not giving Statements, not assessing for dyslexia, unreasonable Statement criteria for dyslexia, or unreasonable criteria for the provision of equipment, parents can now appeal to the Local Government Ombudsman.

For pupils with severe specific learning difficulties, obtaining effective support is often becoming harder to achieve, and budgets are limited. Local authorities are reluctant to offer Statements for dyslexia and related conditions, and they have stringent criteria that some parents may feel to be unreasonable. Some have stopped offering Statements altogether and expect the schools to be able to offer all the appropriate support. The problem is that many schools are not equipped to do this, lacking both the expertise and financial resources.

Applying for a Statement of Special Educational Needs

Whatever the local authority policy on Statements, a parent and/or the school still has a right to apply for appropriate support. The first step in the process is to apply for a Statutory Assessment. If this application is turned down by the local authority, the parent can appeal through the SEN and Disability tribunal, or SEND. If, following a Statutory Assessment a child is then refused a Statement by the local authority, the parent can further appeal to SEND.

Parents can appeal on a number of issues, including:

- if they are refused a Statutory Assessment
- if, following a Statutory Assessment, they are refused a Statement of Special Educational Needs

[1] This guide may be downloaded from: https://www.education.gov.uk/publications/standard/publicationDetail/Page1/DfES%200800%202001.

- if they wish to amend the proposed Statement
- if they wish to change an existing Statement, for instance if circumstances change or it transpires that all the difficulties have not been addressed in the original Statement and the Local Authority refuses to reassess within six months (NB a Statement should always be updated at transfer stage, e.g. when the child moves from primary school to secondary school)
- where they are refused a change to the Statement after reassessment
- if the local authority decides to cease to maintain a Statement.

In all cases, parents have two months to appeal to the SEND tribunal from the date of the decision letter from the local authority (not from the date they receive the letter). Parents are advised to keep the envelope, if it is postmarked, as proof of when the letter was sent. Details can be found on the SEND tribunal web site.[2] Parents should request a copy of the SEND Guide for Parents, or download a copy directly from the web site.

The SEND tribunals now come under the Ministry of Justice and they have been revamped to make the process more streamlined. The tribunal panels have a legally qualified chair and two advisers who are specialists in the field of SEN and disabilities.

SEND is a first-tier tribunal that deals with the main process. There is also the second tier, which now replaces the need for a claimant to go to court. If it is felt that a tribunal decision is wrong on a point of law, an appeal can be made to the second-tier tribunal, which replaces the old High Court appeal system. Parents have 28 days to appeal to the second tier following the decision of the first tier. They will need a solicitor for this.

One of the major improvements in the new system is the introduction of a case management stage. This is a meeting with the judge, attended by both parties, at which the issues can be identified as early as possible and the judge gives instructions, known as directions, for both parties. These would ensure that clear evidence is seen by both parties at an early stage, and that there is sufficient and clear evidence for the hearing in front of the tribunal panel.

All information has to be supplied to the tribunal by week 16 and the full hearing takes place in week 20. In some instances a parent can request an expedited hearing in order for a decision to be in place for, say, the start of the autumn school term.

Parents now have the right for outside experts to assess a child in school. If the school refuses, the parents can request the tribunal to order the school to allow this. Similarly the local authority can apply to assess a child in reasonable circumstances.

The views of the child on particular issues within the appeal are also taken into account. Care needs to be taken with this: some local authorities have contracts with organizations such as the NCH[3] and the Children's Society; others use their own educational psychologists. It is generally a good idea for parents also to have their own impartial person to record their child's views on the specified issues.

Agreeing a Local Authority Statement

It is important to ensure that the Statement specifies the most appropriate support. For instance, a Statement for severe dyslexia should include a specified number of sessions per week with a specialist dyslexia teacher, followed by support from a dyslexia-trained support assistant. Some Statements will say that a child should receive 20 hours of support, but not say what type of support. This can translate in practice to a bit of help from an overworked learning assistant who has received no training in supporting dyslexia. Parents need to ensure that expert advice is sought before agreeing to a proposed Statement. If necessary, they

[2] http://www.justice.gov.uk/guidance/courts-and-tribunals/tribunals/send/index.htm.
[3] Formerly known as National Children's Home.

should appeal to SEND straightaway and before negotiating with the local authority, both to save time and to put the local authority on notice of intent.

Implementation of a Statement

If the local authority or school fails to implement the agreed Statement in any way, the parent can now complain to the Local Government Ombudsman to investigate the situation.

Disability Discrimination in Schools

Under SENDA (2001) schools must not treat disabled pupils less favourably because of their disability, without justification. An example of unfavourable treatment would be not allowing a pupil with Attention Deficit/Hyperactivity Disorder to go on a school trip. Keeping a pupil with dyslexia in over break times to finish work, insisting on large amounts of homework, or using demeaning language towards a child with dyslexia would be examples of discrimination at a lower level.

More serious discrimination could surround failure to implement appropriate accommodations in exams or not allowing a child to enter Standard Assessment Tests (SATs) so that the school's position in the league table will not be compromised. Alternatively, not disallowing SATs where a child has severe difficulties that would make the exercise inappropriate and cause significant distress to the child.

Selective exams such as the 11+ are often areas where parents seek advice on disability discrimination, both in regard to the style of the test and failure to implement appropriate accommodations.

The SEND web site has a section on disability discrimination in the 'parent' section. The problem with the process of instituting proceedings for disability discrimination against a school or local authority is the time the whole business takes and, before the situation has been resolved, the child may have moved on. Also, some parents are reluctant to take proceedings for fear of alienating the school. Perhaps for these reasons, SEND reports that there are very few cases of parents taking proceedings for disability discrimination.

Parents seeking to take further legal action would be looking at an action in the County Court. Apart from the very few cases where parents qualify for legal aid, this is a risky procedure, as losing would entail paying the other side's costs, and the total legal bill could be substantial.

Admissions Arrangements and Exclusions

Schools must not discriminate in relation to admissions arrangements and exclusions from school. Where parents feel that their children have been discriminated against, they can appeal to the local education appeals panels.

Further Education

Since April 2010, local authorities have had responsibility for the education of 16- to 19-year-olds in sixth forms, colleges and other private or voluntary sector providers, including Young Apprenticeship schemes. The Apprenticeships, Skills, Children and Learning Act (2009) created a new non-departmental public body, the Young People's Learning Agency (YPLA),[4]

[4] See www.ypla.gov.uk.

with a statutory responsibility for the funding of education and training provision for young people aged 16 to 19 years, and to help local authorities in their new responsibilities for this age group. This new body replaces the former Learning and Skills Council. The Act also seeks to address discrimination issues in the area of appropriate testing for apprenticeships. At present many of these can be highly discriminatory for many dyslexic apprentices. Alternative methods of assessment came into force in 2011.

Higher Education

Cases of disability discrimination at university level can be referred to the Office of the Independent Adjudicator for Higher Education (OIAHE),[5] but only after having exhausted the university's own appeals process. Again this is not a fast procedure, with rulings taking from two to six months. Further legal action could be taken in the County Court, although, once again, with the difficulty in obtaining legal aid, this could be a risky and costly procedure.

Areas of discrimination at this level could include a failure to make appropriate adjustments in examinations, including the format of the examination; failure to provide appropriate support or accommodations; or direct discrimination because of disability, harassment and victimization.

A recent OIAHE ruling in favour of a dyslexic medical student found that the university had failed to offer reasonable adjustments in its reluctance to provide an alternative format to onscreen, multiple-choice format examinations (a style of examination that can be very discriminatory for many dyslexic students), resulting in the student having to repeat a year, at considerable expense.

Employment

The Equality Act (2010) makes an employer liable to pay compensation for discrimination to a disabled person, whether an employee, a contract worker or a job applicant (all referred to as 'employee' in this chapter).

Actions on the part of the employer that can give rise to liability are:

- failure to appoint to a position
- failure to promote
- dismissing or causing 'any other detriment'.

Discrimination can be caused by:

- direct discrimination
- indirect discrimination (or disability-related discrimination)
- harassment
- victimization
- a failure to make reasonable adjustments.

These can be characterized in the following examples:

- 'You are sacked because you are dyslexic' = direct discrimination.
- 'You are sacked because you are slow in reacting to instructions (due to dyslexia)' = indirect or disability-related discrimination.

[5] See www.oiahe.org.uk.

- 'Because you are slow in reacting to instructions, I am going to reduce your pay' = harassment.
- 'Because you are taking me to the employment tribunal for reducing your pay, you are sacked' = victimization.

The Malcolm Case

The area of disability discrimination was thrown into confusion by the House of Lords' decision in the case of *Malcolm vs. the London Borough of Lewisham* in 2008.[6] This case effectively removed the claim of disability-related discrimination, leaving harassment and the failure to implement reasonable adjustments. In many cases it is possible to articulate a claim in these two remaining areas, but not in all cases. However, this situation has now been resolved since the Equality Act came into effect in October 2010. The Equality Act puts the various forms of discrimination on an equal footing.

Reasonable Adjustments

Dyslexia may not be recognized either by the employee with dyslexic difficulties or by the employer, as dyslexic adults often develop coping strategies that may conceal the underlying disability from others. Many dyslexic adults are unaware that they are dyslexic.

It is not a legal requirement to disclose dyslexic difficulties, and it is not always necessary for the employer to know that the employee is disabled. However, where there are disability-related problems relating to performance, failure to implement reasonable adjustments becomes a discrimination issue.

The obligation to implement reasonable adjustments for an employee arises when an employer's system, categorized in the EA as a 'provision, criterion or practice', places the dyslexic employee at a substantial disadvantage in comparison with persons who are not dyslexic. It is then the duty of the employer to institute reasonable adjustments to prevent the system having that effect.

To establish discrimination through failure to implement reasonable adjustments, it is necessary to prove that the employer knew or ought to have known that the person was disabled and in need of the adjustments. An employer, particularly a large and sophisticated organization, will increasingly be expected to pick up the signs that an employee may be dyslexic, even if the employee is not aware of the condition. If a tribunal finds that, objectively, a particular adjustment should have been implemented, it will not matter that the employer was unaware of the adjustment: there will have been a breach of the EA.

Identifying Reasonable Adjustments

What steps should an employer take to ensure that it complies with the EA in respect of reasonable adjustments? The first and essential step is to ensure that all key staff, including in particular line managers, Occupational Health (OH) and Human Resources (HR) staff are trained in the effects of dyslexia and how it may be identified in an employee. In an individual case, where an employee has declared himself/herself to be dyslexic, or it is suspected that the employee may be dyslexic, the employer must ensure that he or she has

[6] Mr Malcolm, a tenant of the London Borough of Lewisham, breached the terms of his tenancy by subletting his council flat without permission. When the council tried to repossess the flat, Mr Malcolm argued that he was being discriminated against because of his disability (schizophrenia), which was to blame for his irrational thinking. The House of Lords rejected this argument.

prompt access to a full professional assessment of the employee's condition. If no historic assessment is available from the employee, an assessment will have to be commissioned. There are many expert chartered psychologists across the country, and organizations such as the British Dyslexia Association, that will assist in identifying a suitable expert. It should take no longer than a month for the assessment to be carried out and the report provided to the employer and the employee.

Once the employee is identified as dyslexic and the assessment has identified the areas of strengths and weaknesses, line managers, OH and HR need to be fully briefed so that accommodation of the employee's dyslexia can begin without delay.

The next essential stage is to commission a Workplace Needs Assessment to determine what adjustments are required to compensate for the employee's dyslexia. An employee in the UK can be encouraged to make an application to Access to Work, the JobCentre Plus department that looks after the interests of disabled workers. Access to Work will conduct a workplace assessment, advise on the adjustments required and provide a substantial proportion of the cost of the adjustments from government funds. Access to Work makes a charge for this service, but it is free to small organizations with fewer than 10 employees, to new employees in their first six weeks of employment, and to the self-employed.

The workplace assessment report will constitute compelling evidence for an employment tribunal of the adjustments that the employer should implement or should have implemented, so it is essential that the employer moves swiftly to implement the adjustments that are recommended.

These adjustments may include:

- dyslexia awareness training for the employer's staff
- specific dyslexia-related coaching or training for the employee
- technological aids such as voice-to-text and text-to-voice computer software, a digital recorder to record information and instructions, headphones for the software, mind-mapping software, special spell checks and other equipment
- adjustments to working practices and the working environment.

It may be necessary to change the employee's responsibilities or to provide additional training, and it may in some cases be necessary to offer the employee a transfer to other duties. The EA sets out a list of areas of adjustment that may be appropriate.

Legal Implications

In employment tribunal claims brought by dyslexic employees, the failure to implement reasonable adjustments can be a significant aspect. Often failures arise because no one seems to have had the responsibility to implement the adjustments once they were identified.

There are two further features of cases brought under the EA that are particularly significant:

- The first is the shifting burden of proof: if the employee establishes that there have been circumstances that might, if unexplained, amount to actionable discrimination, the onus falls on the employer to prove that the circumstances were not actionable discrimination.
- The second consideration, and an important one, is that there is no cap on the compensation that an employment tribunal may award a claimant under the EA. If, for example, a dyslexic apprentice is dismissed because he failed an exam that, with reasonable adjustments, he would have passed, the employer may have to compensate the ex-apprentice for the loss of an entire career in that field.

Time Limits

The application of the time limit for bringing claims can be a particular difficulty in disability discrimination claims. The basic time limit is three months from the act complained of, or the end of a sequence of acts of similar character. A tribunal has the discretion to extend this limit if it considers it 'just and equitable' to do so. This is a discretion, not an entitlement. In the case of *Matuszowicz vs. Kingston upon Hull Council*[7] the Court of Appeal held that a failure to make reasonable adjustments was a continuing omission that ended when the employer did some unequivocal act showing that it was not going to implement the adjustments. The Court implicitly conceded that a claimant might not be aware that such an act had been carried out and that time was running. The Court urged that tribunals should be generous in extending time under the 'just and equitable' concession. The question must be whether there is a sufficient compliance with the European Equal Treatment Directive where a claimant has to rely upon a tribunal's discretion to bring a claim.

References

Equality Act (2010) Office for Disability Issues, London.

Malcolm *vs*. the London Borough of Lewisham (2008) UKHL 43 (2008) IRLR 700. See: http://www.bailii.org/ew/cases/EWCA/Civ/2007/763.html (accessed August 1, 2011).

Matuszowicz *vs*. Kingston upon Hull Council (2009) EWCA Civ 22 (2009) ICR 1170 (also at [2009] IRLR 288). See: www.bailii.org/ew/cases/EWCA/Civ/2009/22.html (accessed August 1, 2011).

The Disability Discrimination Act (1995) Her Majesty's Stationery Office, London

John Mackenzie may be contacted at: www.johnmackenzielawyer.co.uk.
Acknowledgements: BDA Befriender and Helpline staff.

[7] Mr Matuszowicz was employed by Hull City Council in September 2003 as a teacher in Hull prison. However, as his arm had been amputated above the elbow, he had difficulty opening the heavy prison doors. In July 2005 he was transferred to another prison where it was hoped that he would have less difficulty, but he did not. Mr Matuszowicz claimed that it was clear by August 2005 that working in prisons was difficult for him, because of his disability, so his employer was duty-bound to transfer him to more suitable work. On August 1, 2006 his employment was transferred to a city college. Mr Matuszowicz's claim, filed in October 2006, related to the council's continuing failure to make reasonable adjustments to his employment up to August 1, 2006. The council argued, however, that the need for more suitable work was clear from August 2005. If the three-month time limit for the claim ran from this time, then it was out of time. The Court of Appeal agreed that the window of opportunity for filing a claim begins from the end of the period during which the employer might have been expected to make a reasonable adjustment.

19

The Design and Development of the Sylexiad Typeface

Robert Hillier, Norwich University College of the Arts, UK

The Sylexiad family of fonts has been designed and tested to cater specifically to the needs of dyslexic people. The characteristics of the typeface have been developed to help the dyslexic reader to distinguish more easily between letters, words, sentences and paragraphs. The evolution of the Sylexiad fonts involved a series of studies designed to measure the legibility and readability of various texts. These studies had two clear stages that accommodated two established word recognition models – word shape and parallel letter recognition. I refer to these studies as developmental typeface testing. Data were gathered from dyslexic and non-dyslexic reader groups and the findings identified which typographic characteristics the readers preferred and why. The outcomes and issues that have been identified as a result of developmental typeface testing have raised issues that confirm and contradict current typographic principles of legibility.

Origins and Early Recommendations

The origins of Sylexiad were at Norwich University College of the Arts in 2001. At that time there was great interest in the art and design higher education sector concerning dyslexia. Central St Martin's College of Art and Design put forward the proposition that there would be 'more dyslexia among art and design students than non-art students' (Padgett and Steffert 1999). The Surrey Institute of Art and Design (now named the University for the Creative Arts) estimated that the prevalence of dyslexia among art and design students could be as high as 15% (Surrey Institute of Art and Design, 1999) whereas Miles (2004) estimated that only 3% of the general population display severe characteristics of dyslexia, while a further 6% display mild characteristics. These figures clearly indicated a higher than expected incidence of dyslexia within art and design institutions. I became more interested in my own students' reading difficulties and I also began to question my own difficulties, particularly my frequent misreading of texts. I was assessed by an educational psychologist who confirmed specific learning difficulties, specifically dyslexia due to 'slow speed of visual processing, and a slight weakness with working memory' (Smallwood 2000, p. 3).

In 2001, the typographic recommendations by the dyslexia organizations were limited and tended to be for sans-serif fonts.[1] For example, The British Dyslexia Association recommended,

[1] That is, those without the little 'ticks' that are often found at the end of letter strokes in printed text.

Supporting Dyslexic Adults in Higher Education and the Workplace, First Edition. Edited by Nicola Brunswick.

supporting dyslexic adults
SUPPORTING DYSLEXIC ADULTS

supporting dyslexic adults
SUPPORTING DYSLEXIC ADULTS

supporting dyslexic adults
SUPPORTING DYSLEXIC ADULTS

Figure 19.1 From top to bottom: Lowercase and uppercase examples of Arial, Sassoon Primary and Times New Roman.

and still recommends, the Arial font (British Dyslexia Association, no date) which was designed by Robin Nicholas and Patricia Saunders in 1992 as a Microsoft version of the classic Helvetica font (see Figure 19.1). The web site Dyslexic.com recommended Sassoon Primary, a children's text font based on handwriting, which was designed by Rosemary Sassoon in 1984 (Dyslexic.com 2006). The only serif font recommendation was by Bevé Hornsby of the International Dyslexia Centre, who favoured Times New Roman (Hornsby 1996, p. 84), a newspaper font designed by Stanley Morison and Victor Lardent in 1932 (see Figure 19.1).

It is worth emphasizing that none of these typefaces was designed specifically for the dyslexic reader. They are fonts developed by non-dyslexic designers for a non-dyslexic audience. Indeed, at that time, this was the situation with all text typeface designs. Although a number of dyslexic fonts have emerged since my own research, widespread interest in dyslexia and typography can be viewed as only a relatively recent phenomenon. As such, I would argue that typographic rules and principles have consequently been framed from a literate, non-dyslexic, viewpoint.

Two Models of Legibility

A key typographic principle relating to legibility concerns the idea of *word shape*. It was the psychologist James Cattell (1886) who first proposed the word shape model. This model states that words are recognized as whole units according to the outlines made by their shape. Therefore, according to the word shape model, lowercase letters are more legible than uppercase letters because ascenders and descenders (the letter strokes that protrude above the x-height[2] and below the baseline[3] in lowercase letters) provide a more distinctive word shape for the reader: compare, for example, 'WORD SHAPE' and 'word shape' (see Figure 19.2). This is the earliest recognition model in the psychological literature and it is still widely accepted within the contemporary field of typographic legibility.

The influential typographer and author Ruari McLean suggested (in a manner typical of mainstream typographic thinking) that in order to provide good word shape, the following aesthetic principles should be observed:

[2] An x-height is the height of a lowercase 'x' letter form.

[3] This is the imaginary line that defines the visual base of a lowercase letter.

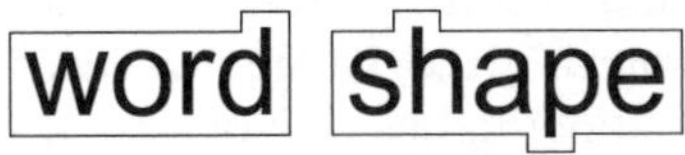

Figure 19.2 Lowercase and uppercase examples of Arial illustrating Cattell's word shape model of legibility.

1 'Sans-serif type is intrinsically less legible than seriffed type.'
2 'Well-designed roman upper and lower case is easier to read than any of its variants, e.g. italic, bold, caps, expanded or condensed versions.'
3 'Words should be set close to each other (about as far apart as the width of the letter 'i'); and there should be more space between the lines than the words.' (*McLean 1980, pp. 44–45*)

These recommendations tend to contradict the use of sans serif fonts such as Arial, favoured by the dyslexia organizations, and they do not accommodate newer theories of word recognition from other fields. For example, the word shape model is no longer part of the dominant thinking within the practice of cognitive psychology. The model currently accepted as the most accurate within this field is called 'parallel letter recognition'. This model states that the reader identifies all the letters within a word simultaneously. The letter information is then processed to enable the reader to recognize the word (Larson 2004). Therefore, to put it another way, the word is identified by the actual letters within that word and *not* by its intrinsic shape.

As a designer myself, with a particular interest in typography, and as a dyslexic reader, I began to question the typographic recommendations of the various dyslexia organizations. In doing so, I also started to question the established rules of typographic legibility and, eventually, the notion of word shape. I found the recommendations by both the typographic establishment and the dyslexia organizations to be too prescriptive and contradictory. My research was therefore prompted by the need to bridge the gap between the fields of typographic design and cognitive psychology in order to identify the most appropriate recognition model for the adult dyslexic reader, and also to allow for the possibility of developing new design models.

Developmental Typeface Testing

The aim of my research was therefore to test the dyslexia typeface recommendations against my own evolving typeface designs in order to establish which typographic characteristics dyslexic readers actually preferred and why.

To do this I originated a testing model that involved a series of evaluative studies that measured the legibility and readability of different typefaces. I call this model 'developmental typeface testing'. The model is grounded within the cognitive aspects of dyslexia and, in particular, the visual aspects of the condition. It incorporated features from existing legibility research, including ideas such as comparative typeface testing and the primacy of uniform letters (Spencer 1968), the primacy of the upper half of a word (Huot-Marchand 2004), the testing of serif and sans-serif forms (Zachrisson 1965), aesthetic preference (Burt 1959) and reading rates (Wilkins *et al.* 1996). It also combined elements of a literacy developmental stage reading model (Frith 1985). Additionally, developmental typeface testing accommodated a comparative approach to measuring legibility (Tinker 1963 and 1965) that allowed for the testing of text formations concerning individual characters, individual words, individual sentences and individual paragraphs. The model is linear and flexible in structure and has two distinctive stages. The formative stage, responsible for the testing and development of my Dine typefaces *Dine 1*, *Dine 2*, *Dine 3*, and the summative stage for the Sylexiad typefaces *Sylexiad Serif* and *Sylexiad Sans*.

It is interesting to note that it is psychologists rather than typographic designers who have conducted the majority of studies that have impacted on ideas concerning legibility. For that reason, tests on many typefaces can be seen to be retrospective in that testing is conducted *after* the design process, never during or before that process. What makes my research unique is that, rather than being an exclusively retrospective activity, it has stages that allow typefaces to be designed and developed in tandem with the testing process. Developmental typeface testing is therefore distinctive within the field of legibility research in that it accommodates a formative and summative aspect to the design, development and testing of fonts. It also exclusively incorporates both of the word recognition models I have described. Initially the focus was on word shape but latterly that focus shifted to include parallel letter recognition as the design and development of the fonts progressed.

Developmental typeface testing comprised seven discrete studies involving both dyslexic and control (non-dyslexic) reader groups. The formative stage accommodated three of those studies and was exclusively dyslexic in terms of readership. The structure and content of the studies at this stage was fluid and organic. As each study evolved, the outcomes generated by the readers informed subsequent studies. In many ways the experimental testing process used during the formative stage acted as a dry run for the summative stage. A raft of tests was trialled throughout the formative stage, with the most successful in returning meaningful data (both quantitative and qualitative) being incorporated into the summative stage. The summative stage can therefore be viewed as being more fixed in terms of its structure and content. It was also more comparative in that it comprised four studies that included both dyslexic *and* control groups. The novel aspects of the formative and summative stages allowed the design process to be developed in tandem with the testing process rather than being independent of it.

Arial, Sassoon Primary and Times New Roman were chosen as the test fonts and were used throughout the developmental typeface testing procedure for two reasons. First, they were considered to be dyslexia-friendly fonts. Second, due to their distinct and differing forms, they enabled me to categorize them into archetypal or, what I refer to as, 'standard' font types. Therefore, Arial (recommended by the British Dyslexia Association) was used as a 'standard sans-serif' font. As the design of Sassoon Primary (recommended by Dyslexic.com) was based on handwriting, it became a 'standard handwritten-style' font. Finally, Times New Roman (recommended by the International Dyslexia Centre) was used as a 'standard serif' font. This simple classification of three key typographic styles seemed appropriate in providing a focus and continuity throughout the research. The use of more historical styles such as old style, transitional and modern serifs, and grotesque, geometric and humanist sans serifs within the testing process was rejected. Such inclusions would have over-complicated and unnecessarily broadened the investigation.

The Dine Fonts and the Formative Stage of Research

The formative stage of the research was conducted at Norwich University College of the Arts. This stage, as well as facilitating reader group feedback, also included an analysis of my own reading difficulties. I started to compile a personal diary of misread words that included examples such as 'Special Events' misread as 'Special Effects', 'CLASS WAR' as 'GLASS WAR' and 'deaf signers' as 'deaf singers'. The outcomes from both the diary and the reader feedback resulted in the design, development and testing of a number of radical and experimental fonts called *Dine* (this name was given when I misread what I thought was an exhibition of the work of the artist Jim Dine with what was, in fact, a Jive Dance demonstration!). Each version of the Dine font was tested against lowercase and uppercase forms of Arial, Sassoon Primary and Times New Roman set as individual characters, words, sentences and paragraphs. During each study, test comparisons were made concerning the design, readability and legibility of each font.

Dine 1 is a 'monocase' font that consists of a combination of uppercase and lowercase letters. It was designed that way to provide each letter character with a distinct shape without compromising any meaning associated with that shape. This initial concept would, in theory, maximize word shape and overcome typical dyslexic difficulties concerning letter reversals in characters such as the lowercase c, n and u; b, d, p and q and uppercase N and Z. The design of Dine 1 was also based on a diagnostic dyslexia handwriting checklist produced by Linda Silverman from The Gifted Development Centre that identified possible dyslexic indicators in handwriting. These indicators included characteristics such as unusual letter spacing, strange letter formations, a combination of upper- and lowercase letters and an overall lack of letter fluidity (Silverman 2003). In many respects, the form of Dine 1 can be viewed as being illegible. This was, however, an appropriate starting point for the investigation as the Dine 1 testing outcomes informed subsequent (and more moderate) font development. Consequently, Dine 2 was designed as a 'duocase' font that contains a discrete set of uppercase and lowercase letters. Although the typeface still contains radical design elements, its form is more conventional and legible than that of its predecessor. The outcomes from the testing of Dine 2 in turn led to further modifications resulting in the design of Dine 3, with its comparatively shorter and more refined ascenders and descenders (see Figure 19.3).

It is important to stress that the Dine fonts are *not* typefaces for the adult dyslexic reader. They are experimental and theoretical fonts based exclusively on a radical form of word shape. In analysing the formative data, an appraisal was made of the reader feedback about matters such as dyslexia and reading, the reading of different text formations, and general typographic design issues as well as issues specifically relating to the Dine fonts. I attempted to highlight the differences experienced by the readers when reading different typefaces and texts. An attempt was also made to identify the particular design, style, reading, legibility and font preferences of the groups in order to develop a preferred typeface for the adult dyslexic reader. It is interesting to note that, of all the typefaces tested during the initial stage (including Arial, Sassoon Primary and Times New Roman), the readers found Dine 1 (the font with most shape) to be their least favoured font while Dine 3 (the font with the least lowercase shape) was their most favoured font. The analysis also informed the design of a series of typefaces I call *Sylexiad*, specifically developed for the adult dyslexic reader (Hillier 2008).

SupportiNG dySLeXic AduLtS

supportiNg dysLexic AdULts
SUPPORTING DYSLEXIC ADULTS

supporting dyslexic adults
SUPPORTING DYSLEXIC ADULTS

Figure 19.3 From top to bottom: An example of the monocase Dine 1 and lowercase and uppercase examples of Dine 2 and Dine 3.

supporting dyslexic adults
SUPPORTING DYSLEXIC ADULTS

supporting dyslexic adults
SUPPORTING DYSLEXIC ADULTS

Figure 19.4 From top to bottom: Lowercase and uppercase examples of Sylexiad Serif and Sylexiad Sans.

The Sylexiad Fonts and the Summative Stage of Research

As a result of my analysis of the formative data I began to question the appropriateness of the word shape model. The data indicated that word shape was not as critical a factor as I initially thought. It did not explain the preference by the reader groups for Dine 3, the typeface with the least lowercase shape. It also did not explain the preference by some readers for uppercase font forms that have no real word shape when compared to lowercase forms with more pronounced shape. The design of Sylexiad therefore attempted to include the two models of legibility I have identified.

The word shape model was still employed in the design of the lowercase Sylexiad forms, with a distinct emphasis on the ascenders and descenders. Conversely, the parallel letter recognition model influenced the design of the uppercase forms. Contrary to McLean's (1980) aesthetic principles concerning lowercase letters being easier to read than uppercase letters, I made an attempt to design the uppercase forms of Sylexiad to enable extended paragraph texts to be read more easily in all uppercase letters. The inclusion of both models is also evident (but to a much lesser extent) in the two versions of the font – the serif version Sylexiad Serif having slightly more shape than the sans-serif Sylexiad Sans (see Figure 19.4).

As well as accommodating both recognition models, other key outcomes from the formative data that informed the design of Sylexiad included the use of duocase (rather than monocase) alphabets, relatively light letter strokes and relatively long ascenders and descenders. There was also an attempt to make each character as clear and distinct as possible without compromising the meaning of the character. Finally, and again contrary to McLean's aesthetic principles, the design included a generous inter-word spatial quality. The design of Sylexiad did not include the use of oblique or italic letter forms, compact letter forms, relatively bold letter forms or any radically shaped letter forms.

The summative phase of research involved the comparative testing of both Sylexiad Sans and Sylexiad Serif against the other test fonts of Arial, Sassoon Primary and Times New Roman. The subject of typographic legibility is inherently visual. Therefore, in order to overcome any potential bias to the outcomes in regard to the visual aspects of the typefaces tested, I considered it important to conduct some of the tests outside the art college environment. It also seemed appropriate to develop both internal *and* external trials to compare and contrast data. Consequently, the internal trial continued to be based at Norwich University College of the Arts whilst the external trial was conducted at The University of East Anglia. Both trials comprised a dyslexic group and a non-dyslexic (control) group. As with the formative stage, the summative stage involved tests with uppercase and lowercase texts set as individual characters, words, sentences and paragraphs. Comparisons were made between the readability and legibility of each font.

Findings and Analysis

An evaluation of the summative data was produced from both the internal and external trials. As with the formative evaluation of outcomes, the appraisal focused on reader feedback concerning matters such as dyslexia and reading, and the reading of different text formations as well as typographic design issues. It also identified specific issues concerning the Sylexiad fonts. The evidence gathered also resulted in a comparative analysis between the dyslexic and non-dyslexic reader groups. The findings and analysis of outcomes highlighted distinct differences in typographic preferences (as well as similarities) between the two groups.

For the majority of non-dyslexic readers, their typographic preferences were for serif-style fonts, lowercase forms, large x-heights, medium letter weights, variable strokes, normal inter-word spacing and familiarity of form. They also preferred Times New Roman as a family.

The majority of dyslexic readers, however, preferred handwritten-style fonts, uppercase (Sylexiad) forms rather than lowercase forms, long ascenders and descenders, light letter weights, uniform strokes, perpendicular design, generous inter-word spacing and, as with the non-dyslexic readers, familiarity of form. Unlike the non-dyslexic readers, they preferred Sylexiad Serif as a family.

For the non-dyslexic readers the typographic preferences tend to confirm the accepted aesthetic typographic maxims concerning legibility that McLean suggested. The evidence also indicates that, for *most* readers, the familiarity of a font facilitated effective reading. My findings, however, indicate that for the majority of dyslexic readers tested, it was the typographic characteristics of generous inter-word spacing allied to the light letter weight and slightly perpendicular form of the Sylexiad fonts that were important. The investigation also indicates that, for individuals with reading difficulties such as dyslexia, it is the combination of spacing, weight and form that is often more important than individual letter form design. More controversially, my research questions the importance of word shape as a useful recognition model for dyslexic readers.

During the formative stage of testing, Dine 1 (the font with maximum word shape) was the least favoured font whereas Dine 3 (the font with the minimum lowercase shape) was the most favoured by the dyslexic readers. The formative stage also highlighted a preference expressed by some dyslexic readers for uppercase rather than lowercase forms. This preference became more pronounced during the summative stage, particularly for paragraph texts set in uppercase rather than lowercase forms. These findings, coupled with the fact that more letter-reversal difficulties occur in lowercase rather than uppercase forms, would tend to support the parallel recognition model favoured by cognitive psychologists rather than the word shape model favoured by typographers.

For some dyslexic readers it seems clear that certain current typographic legibility principles may not be appropriate. These principles were established by non-dyslexic typographers for a non-dyslexic audience. The current typographic advice for dyslexic readers given by many dyslexia organizations is often confused as it both supports and contradicts these principles. The British Dyslexia Association, for example, offers advice supporting one current typographic maxim by recommending that documents for dyslexic readers are written in lowercase rather than capital letters as capitals are much harder to read (British Dyslexia Association, no date). As my research has shown, this is not necessarily the case.

Many dyslexia organizations (e.g. the British Dyslexia Association 2011; Dyslexia Action, no date; Dyslexic.com, 2006) also advocate the use of sans-serif fonts such as Arial rather than serif fonts. This advice, I would argue, is because of a practice effect associated with easily available and familiar fonts such as Arial rather than any intrinsic design qualities concerning the legibility of those fonts. Although other fonts are recommended, I feel that they

Supporting Dyslexic Adults
Supporting Dyslexic Adults
Supporting Dyslexic Adults
Supporting Dyslexic Adults

Supporting Dyslexic Adults
Supporting Dyslexic Adults
Supporting Dyslexic Adults
Supporting Dyslexic Adults

Figure 19.5 From top to bottom: Examples of the various styles and weights of Sylexiad Serif Medium and Sylexiad Sans Medium.

are too limiting. My research indicates that there are fonts that are more legible than Arial. With this in mind, I would like to see new typographic rules and guidelines concerning legibility for dyslexic readers to be considered by the dyslexia organizations.

Applications and Uses

In 2007, Sylexiad was expanded to include a full range of weights including italic, bold and italic bold.[4] There are also medium and thin styles of the font as well as versions containing extra word spacing (see Figure 19.5). The first independent application of the typeface was for the Dyslexia Action/Serpentine Gallery art and research project Neveroddoreven, which explored the relationship between dyslexia and creativity.[5] As part of the project, Sylexiad Sans Medium was used exclusively for a pack of playing cards developed to investigate a dyslexic person's ability to think divergently.

Since then, Sylexiad has been used by academic institutions and learning centres across the United Kingdom, including Norwich University College of the Arts. Here the font has been used for texts on the BA Graphic Design and MA Design courses for documentation including project briefs, course handbooks, timetables, registers, tutorial feedback sheets, notices, student letters and project support materials (see Figures 19.6 and 19.7). The font has also been the subject of articles in numerous international design magazines including *Novum*, *Ultrabold* and *étapes*.

I am currently using the font as part of my own practice that investigates the different ways in which we read texts. My *List Landscapes* (see Figure 19.8) uses Sylexiad Serif Medium to create a systematic series of lists whilst, for my *Garden Bird Portraits* (see Figure 19.9), Sylexiad Sans Medium is used in a more decorative and pictorial manner. All these applications of the font are designed to show the range, versatility and beauty of a typeface for the adult dyslexic reader.

Although Dine was not specifically designed for the dyslexic reader, it was a key element in the development of Sylexiad. A basic version of the Dine font is available and a full range of weights is planned for release in 2012.

[4] Sylexiad in all its forms is available online at www.robsfonts.com.

[5] www.serpentinegallery.org/neveroddoreven.

BA (HONS) COURSES 2009/2010
LEVEL ONE: UNIT 3 and UNIT 4 ASSESSMENT NOTICE

For this assessment you are required to present *all* project work undertaken and completed during Units 3 and 4. This will include all finished projects up to the end of week 12 of Teaching Block 2. All roughs /scamps /note books /sketch books, research information and ideas sheets must be included in the form of workbooks *with* the relevant completed piece of work for each project.

All finished work should be *neatly* presented in plastic sleeves housed in A2 portfolios **clearly labeled with your name.** Please also provide in full a complete contents list of all work presented. This list should be located at the front of your portfolio. It is always helpful in these assessments to present each subject area project and related workbooks into categories clearly labeled Design for Publishing, Illustration, Graphic Design, Photography and Personal Work. All workbooks must be contained inside your portfolio. Any 3D work produced during Units 3 and 4 should be photographed and presented in sleeves in your portfolio.

This assessment will take place in Room 128 in the first year studio on 17th, 18th and 19th May 2010 (week 6 of this term). Your portfolio of work must be left in that room by *0930 on Monday 17th May. The assessment will commence at 10.00.* Any portfolio presented late after *10a.m. will incur a technical fail* – **do not let this happen** as this can affect your progress and future on this Course.

All work can be reclaimed by you on Monday 24th May.

Each assessor will be evaluating all your work independently. Your results, feedback and tutorials will be available during the following week.

The following subject projects should be completed and in evidence for this assessment:

Either:
All Graphic Design Projects or
All Design for Publishing Projects or
All Photography Projects or
All Illustration Projects
Plus:
New York or Norwich Postcards
PDP File (containing a 300 word statement outlining your progress during the unit)
Personal Work (if you have any)

Do your best, don't panic, do **not** include work from Unit 1 and don't lose this information sheet! Let me know if you have any concerns or problems.

Rob

Figure 19.6 A Norwich University College of the Arts unit assessment notice set in Sylexiad Sans Medium.

Norwich University College of the Arts
BA (Hons) Graphic Design programme

Assessment Submission List : Semester One 2009–10

Level 1 **Unit** 4: Introduction to Design /Design for Publishing / Illustration / Photography Practice 2	Student (PRINT NAME)

Projects Please list all work submitted under each of your three subject headings.

Illustration

Graphic Design

Design for Publishing

Photography

Project workbooks/sketchbooks

PDP File

I agree that this is a complete record of the work submitted for assessment.

Student signature Date

Staff signature Date

Figure 19.7 A Norwich University College of the Arts unit assessment submission list set in Sylexiad Sans Medium.

A systematic list of birds seen on a walk from Cantley to Buckenham (Norfolk).
Sunday 11th April 2010
Cloudy, cool, sunny

GREAT CRESTED GREBE
(Podiceps cristatus)

GREY HERON
(Ardea cinerea)

MUTE SWAN
(Cygnus olor)

GREYLAG GOOSE
(Anser anser)

CANADA GOOSE
(Branta canadensis)

EGYPTIAN GOOSE
(Alopochen aegyptiacus)

SHELDUCK
(Tadorna tadorna)

WIGEON
(Anas penelope)

TEAL
(Anas crecca)

MALLARD
(Anas platyrhynchos)

TUFTED DUCK
(Aythya fuligula)

SCAUP
(Aythya marila)

KESTREL
(Falco tinnunculus)

GREY PARTRIDGE
(Perdix perdix)

COOT
(Fulica atra)

OYSTERCATCHER
(Haematopus ostralegus)

LAPWING
(Vanellus vanellus)

REDSHANK
(Tringa totanus)

BLACK-HEADED GULL
(Larus ridibundus)

HERRING GULL
(Larus argentatus)

GREAT BLACK-BACKED GULL
(Larus marinus)

FERAL PIGEON
(Columba livia) domest.

STOCK DOVE
(Columba oenas)

WOOD PIGEON
(Columba palumbus)

COLLARED DOVE
(Streptopelia decaocto)

MEADOW PIPIT
(Anthus pratensis)

BLACKBIRD
(Turdus merula)

DUNNOCK
(Prunella modularis)

BLUE TIT
(Parus caeruleus)

GREAT TIT
(Parus major)

JACKDAW
(Corvus monedula)

ROOK
(Corvus frugilegus)

CARRION CROW
(Corvus corone corone)

STARLING
(Sturnus vulgaris)

HOUSE SPARROW
(Passer domesticus)

CHAFFINCH
(Fringilla coelebs)

REED BUNTING
(Emberiza schoeniclus)

R. A. HILLIER 12.04.10

Figure 19.8 An artwork that forms part of the List Landscapes series (594 mm x 841 mm) set in Sylexiad Serif Medium.

Figure 19.9 An artwork that forms part of the *Garden Bird Portraits* series (594 mm × 841 mm) set in Sylexiad Sans Medium.

References

British Dyslexia Association (no date). *Dyslexia Style Guide*, available from http://www.bdadyslexia.org.uk/files/BDA%20Dyslexia%20Style%20Guide.pdf, accessed September 28, 2011.

British Dyslexia Association (2011) *Typefaces for dyslexia*, available from http://bdanewtechnologies.files.wordpress.com/2011/03typefaces1.pdf, accessed September 28, 2011.

Burt, C. (1959) *A Psychological Study of Typography*, Cambridge University Press, Cambridge.

Cattell, J.M. (1886) The time taken up by cerebral operations. *Mind*, 11, 220–242, available from http://psychclassics.yorku.ca/Cattell/Time/part3.htm, accessed September 27, 2011.

Dyslexia Action (no date) *Dyslexia friendly criteria*, available from http://www.dyslexiaaction.org.uk/Pages/Display.aspx?IDPost=7e8a2161-2f99-48d3-b8f9-6d093f3372bc, accessed June 28, 2010.

Dyslexic.com (2006) *Typefaces for dyslexia*, available from: http://www.dyslexic.com/articlecontent.asp?CAT=dys_Accessibility&slug=67, accessed June 28, 2010.

Frith, U. (1985) Beneath the surface of developmental dyslexia, in *Surface Dyslexia: Neuropsychological and cognitive studies of phonological reading* (eds K.E. Patterson, J.C. Marshall and M. Coltheart), Lawrence Erlbaum Associates, London and Hillsdale, New Jersey, pp. 301–330.

Hornsby, B. (1996) *Overcoming Dyslexia*, 3rd revised edn, Vermilion (Ebury Press), London.

Hillier, R.A. (2008) Sylexiad: A typeface for the adult dyslexic reader. *The Journal of Writing in Creative Practice*, 1, 275– 291.

Huot-Marchand, T. (2004) Minuscule. *Typografische Monatsblätter*, 2, 45–60.

Larson K. (2004) *The Science of Word Recognition: Or how I learned to stop worrying and love the bouma*, Advanced Reading technology, Microsoft Corporation, available from www.microsoft.com/typography/ctfonts/WordRecognition.aspx, accessed June 28, 2010.

McLean, R. (1980) *The Thames and Hudson Manual of Typography*. Thames and Hudson, London.

Miles, T.R. (2004) Some problems in determining the prevalence of dyslexia. *Electronic Journal of Research in Educational Psychology*, 2, 5–12.

Padgett, I. and Steffert, B. (eds) (1999) *Visual spatial ability and dyslexia: A research project*, Central St Martin's College of Art and Design, London.

Silverman, L.K. (2003) The power of images: Visual-spatial learners. *Gifted Education Communicator*, 34, 14–17.

Smallwood, R. (2000) Unpublished psychological assessment for Robert Hillier, Norfolk Psychological Service, Norwich, August 12.

Spencer, H. (1968) *The Visible Word*, Lund Humphries and Royal College of Art, London.

Surrey Institute of Art and Design (1999) Dyslexia in HE Art and Design, *The HEFCE SPLD (Dyslexia) Special Initiative 1996–9*, Surrey Institute of Art and Design, Farnham.

Tinker, M.A. (1963) *Legibility of Print*, Iowa State University Press Ames, Iowa.

Tinker, M.A. (1965) *Bases for Effective Reading*. University of Minnesota Press, Minneapolis.

Wilkins, A.J., Jeanes, R.J., Pumfrey, P.D. and Laskier, M. (1996) Rate of Reading Test: its reliability, and its validity in the assessment of the effects of coloured overlays. *Ophthalmic and Physiological Optics*, 16, 491–497.

Zachrisson, B. (1965) *Studies in the Legibility of Printed Text*, Almqvist & Wiksell, Stockholm, Goteborg and Uppsala.

20

Dyslexia and Creativity

Tapping the Creative Strengths of Dyslexic People

Morag Kiziewicz, retired from the University of Bath, UK

A former student of mine came to see me recently, many years after I had taught her, and said 'You are the only person I have ever met who is positive about dyslexia'. In the twenty-first century I found this a shocking statement. However, given the 2009 claim by a British member of parliament that dyslexia is a myth (a claim that was immediately and roundly dismissed) I realize that we are only one generation away from where it was the norm for school teachers to deny dyslexia's very existence. It is still possible for dyslexic people not to know that they are dyslexic and to suffer terribly as a result. It is certainly the case that many non-dyslexic people find dyslexic people difficult to understand and support, and often frustrating to teach and to work with.

Over the last ten years our education disability policies have become focused on the social model of disability, and these identify dyslexic people as being disabled by their academic and workplace environments. However, acknowledging dyslexic strengths such as social and strategic skills tends to encourage us to regard dyslexic people as not 'truly' disabled. Meanwhile, the number of dyslexic students entering higher education has soared as dyslexic students in schools experience more inclusion. Additionally, the numbers of students first identified with dyslexia in university has continued to increase, and inclusive education policies attempt to address the exclusion these students have experienced.

However, at the same time, support costs have increased due to this surge, and the true value of inclusion is often not identified in institutional and company budgets. As a result, rather than become inclusive environments as a more cost-effective option, some organizations are concealing exclusion through reduction in the identification and support of people with dyslexia, with some professionals mistakenly claiming that dyslexia is simply the inability to read. I recently met a dyslexic adult whose children had all been identified with dyslexia and who realized that dyslexia was at the root of some of his own difficulties. When he courageously came forward to have his own dyslexia identified and supported within the workplace, his employer attempted to 'debunk' his dyslexic report and to claim that his difficulties were the result not of disability exclusion but of his own failings.

Despite abundant evidence from scientific and social research of dyslexic people's experience of exclusion, it is still seen by some employers and educators as more cost effective to exclude people with dyslexia than to support them. This is because this complex difficulty, which can include difficulty with seeing and coordination, which often includes other co-occurring conditions, and which affects a significant proportion of the population, appears to

Supporting Dyslexic Adults in Higher Education and the Workplace, First Edition. Edited by Nicola Brunswick.

be too time consuming and difficult to support. Conversely, because the dyslexic person is so able in many ways, those who do not understand the condition often do not believe that the individual has any real problems or need for support at all. In this chapter I hope to give some insights into the link between dyslexia and creativity and why supporting dyslexic people is not only socially responsible, but also richly rewarding and a worthwhile investment for the future.

Questioning and Challenging Conventions and Assumptions

There are many examples of famous people who have publicly acknowledged their dyslexia and whose creative abilities and resulting success is an inspiration for us all. The artist Tracey Emin is an excellent example of a dyslexic individual who challenges conventions and assumptions. Her work is powerful and controversial precisely because she challenges the assumptions and conventions that we have. Her work is frequently discussed in the media and she is internationally renowned and influential. Her installation piece *My Bed* for example, which was shortlisted for the Turner Prize in 1999, challenges our conventions on every level and is still discussed and critically evaluated despite not actually winning the prize.

Jamie Oliver, another famous dyslexic individual whose creativity has been focused in his work as a chef, has challenged conventions on school food, battery farming and education. His work has been powerful and influential and has led to major changes in deeply-held conventions that are notoriously hard to change, such as what we eat. Furthermore, in 2009 he was the chef for the world's leaders at the G20 dinner at 10 Downing Street in London.

In both of these cases the challenges have attracted controversy, debate, criticism and support. Jamie and Tracey have had the courage to hold true to beliefs formed from their creative understanding, despite being publicly mocked for these beliefs. One conjecture could be that they received public criticism for their ideas from an early age (at school, for example) so they have had to become exceptionally good at believing in themselves and not identifying with external factors. Another could be that, because they are dyslexic and creative, they are unable to express themselves in conventional ways because their ideas and their way of exploring and meeting the world, cause them to be on the leading edge of change.

The dyslexic actress Susan Hampshire said that her mother always believed in her and gave her a positive model for what she could do when she was confronted daily at school by what she could not do. Gosling (2007) suggests that all dyslexic students need to find teachers who recognize their skills, who believe in them, and who can help to bring their strengths out into the world. My guess is that both Tracey Emin and Jamie Oliver had such wonderful people in their lives; and that for every well-known dyslexic achiever and challenger there are hundreds who either fell by the wayside unseen or who were reviled by their teachers for the questions and challenges they raised, and who were thereby blocked from reaching their true potential.

Making Inventive Connections and Associating Things That are Not Usually Related

I have met many dyslexic students who are frustrated by the narrowness of an academic curriculum that segments subjects: a dyslexic management student who wanted also to study computer systems, or a dyslexic engineer who wanted also to study psychology. These were always exceptionally talented students who could make jumps and leaps in connections they had made in discussions with students from other courses, in library searches, or by linking something they had found in the media with something they were currently researching. The linear approach to study was uncomfortable and frustrating for them.

Children can often think laterally while their neural connections are still mobile and 'plastic'. Much of our early schooling is aimed at encouraging children into linear pathways that help us to develop our 'left brain' skills. Dyslexic children find taking that linear path much more difficult (Springer and Deutsch 1993). While this rigid approach causes difficulties for dyslexic children, in reading for example, it also gives them strengths in thinking 'outside the box', in making inventive connections and remarkable links (Meadows 2006).

Artists are often gifted lateral thinkers. We do not know if Leonardo da Vinci was dyslexic but we do know that he wrote backwards, used both hands to write and draw, and made extraordinary connections between things that are not usually related, all of which many dyslexic people do.

Envisaging What Might Be: Seeing Things in the Mind's Eye

Many dyslexic people are gifted at seeing things in the mind's eye. Thomas West details these abilities in his book, identifying dyslexic people such as Michael Faraday, who are evidently able to 'see' their ideas (West 1997). In some studies the right hemispheres of dyslexic people's brains are reported to be more developed than in non-dyslexic people, and we know that the right hemisphere is associated with non-verbal, visual strengths. As Miles (2007, p. 24) suggested:

> I think . . . there are physiological reasons for this to do with the two hemispheres and the symmetry of the two plana. This somehow seems and is still a bit speculative, to affect the balance of skills and one of the skills many of the Dyslexics seem to have is this holistic understanding, so they become Architects for example, [who] can envisage things in 3-D and all kinds of ways.

Many artists and designers describe how they see their work in their mind first, and the painting or sculpture is a manifestation of what they see. The furniture designer Terence Woodgate, for example, explained in an interview in *Icon Magazine Online* (Jackson 2004) that:

> Visualisation is one of my strengths as a designer. I think I'm particularly good with mechanisms. I can see the whole thing finished and working. I don't need paper. I like to design while driving or showering. I'm sure this is because part of my brain is distracted, leaving the creative side to dream. It's as though we dyslexics have a 3D graphics card integrated into our heads.

Dyslexic architects, such as Richard Rogers, also describe this skill. Similarly, Miles (2007, p. 24) wrote:

> I had a dyslexic orthopaedic surgeon [who] said he could somehow envisage the position of the bones, more than his colleagues could. There are many skills in that way and for those of us who are merely modal . . . I think I'm rather anti Dyslexic because they are horribly good at mending the car and mending the television sets and all those sorts of things, and folk like me are absolutely hopeless at such things, with great effort I did learn how to change a wheel when the car had a puncture, but you know it was very hard work, not the sort of thing I do naturally.

He then went on to describe a dyslexic priest who admitted:

> this is actually embarrassing when the car goes wrong, 'because I can spot it immediately but it's so embarrassing because I don't want to seem too clever so I've simply got to let

> the others have a go first', and he could spot this sort of thing instantly. (*Miles 2007, pp. 24–25*)

Visual–spatial thinkers can often manipulate and rotate an object or idea in their mind, and see it from all angles. The new computerized modelling software enables us all to see what this looks like, but many dyslexic artists and designers have always been able to put themselves into and around a three-dimensional space in their minds (see Brunswick, Martin and Marzano 2010). Often, a child who is struggling to read and spell, and whose work is messy and uncoordinated, will have an exercise book full of three-dimensional drawings of cars, houses or computer game designs.

Envisaging *what might be* can also be applied in imagining a different future or way of being. Many holistic, dyslexic thinkers have been involved in global issues and politics (e.g. Winston Churchill), philosophy and literature (e.g. Agatha Christie and Sally Gardner). Biggs (2007) and Saunders (2007) both suggest that it is imagination that is the key to creativity. We tend to assume that creativity is always the novel or the new, but creativity is actually more the organic process of the mind making lateral new connections in a profoundly imaginative way. Such skills are to be valued and encouraged in the workplace.

Trying Alternative and Fresh Approaches, Keeping Options Open

It is the ability to try alternatives that leads many dyslexic people into working in an arts environment. There will be alternative ways to express ideas and ways of communicating that depend on fresh approaches and trying alternatives, not seeking fixed solutions. Many occupations now require more of these skills. Rayner (2007), who is himself dyslexic, describes these approaches in his work in biological research where he communicates his ideas with painting and poetry as well as through his academic papers. Graves (2007, p. 50) similarly describes this in her work in the performaning arts, as she notes that:

> Creativity is certainly not confined to the dyslexic, but undoubtedly dyslexia can serve as a key to understanding something of the creative process which releases us from egocentricity.

Keeping options open is very important to a dyslexic person, who will rarely see one solution to anything. Multiple-choice questions are often very difficult for a dyslexic person who might see, for example, why two answers could be true. Closed paths are anathema when the fluidity of thought enables many different ways of looking at and seeing something.

Dyslexic people often find choosing which subjects to study in university, and which to pursue as an occupation, extremely difficult because they want to keep their options open. Which subjects to study will tend to be determined by which subjects are apparently easier for them to pass rather than by the subjects in which they could truly excel. Others leave education as early as possible and often try several different career paths before finding the one that best suits their interests and abilities.

Reflecting Critically on Ideas, Actions and Outcomes

Most dyslexic people are highly sensitized to criticism as they will have experienced this most of their lives. This leads them to reflect on the criticism in an attempt to find acceptance from an early age. Possibly as a result, their critical thinking and reflective skills are often finely honed.

Many dyslexic people also become perfectionists and suffer from the three Ps: perfectionism, procrastination and paralysis. As a result of these, the tutor or employer never sees the many brilliant ideas that the individual had, either in the mind's eye or sketched out on paper. By contrast, those who become artists are more likely to give themselves permission to reflect and to fail; they make test pieces, they have sketchbooks full of options and ideas, they make a mess and they make amends. As Biggs (2007, p. 100) notes:

> where dyslexics end up depends on whether they are helped . . . to find opportunities to develop as imaginative people.

Persisting in the Face of Resistance

Robert Sternberg, one of the major figures in contemporary creativity research and whose work has informed the curriculum developments in education, identifies in his article 'The nature of creativity' (2006, pp. 87–88) the way that creative individuals pursue:

> ideas that are unknown or out of favor but that have growth potential. Often, when these ideas are first presented, they encounter resistance. The creative individual persists in the face of this resistance.

Similarly, Thomas West (2008, p. 9) describes how William Dreyer, a strong visual thinker and dyslexic reader, developed:

> new ways of thinking about molecular biology. Sometimes he was almost entirely alone. He (with his colleague, J. Claude Bennett) advanced a new theory and new data about genetics and the immune system that was 12 years ahead of everyone else in the field. They all had to learn to think the way he did. Then, it was obvious. Because of this heresy, initially Dreyer could not get funding for his inventions from academic or foundation sources. His department head would get irate phone calls from other professors complaining about Dreyer's paper and talks. These professors could not see, until much later, that Dreyer had to be right.

For dyslexic people, persistence can become perseverance. The insight dyslexic individuals have that their idea has 'growth potential' causes them to insist upon it and to describe their thinking to others, sometimes to the point of perseveration. This does not mean that the ideas are wrong or not worth the investment of time and energy, but it does mean that others often find them uncomfortable. Maybe there is not a vocabulary to describe the ideas, or the ideas are challenging to the status quo, and the complexity and relevance of the idea is too difficult and time consuming for others to comprehend. Sternberg (2006) describes this persistence as investment theory, explaining that creative people choose and decide to invest (time, energy and thought) in ideas that are initially challenging and hard for society to accept. As he says:

> creativity requires a confluence of six distinct but interrelated resources: intellectual abilities, knowledge, styles of thinking, personality, motivation, and environment. (*Sternberg 2006, p. 88*)

These resources are explored further below.

Intellectual Abilities

There are three intellectual skills that Sternberg describes as being particularly important:

1 Synthetic skill – the ability to see problems in new ways and to escape the confines of conventional thinking.

2 Analytic skill – the ability to identify which of one's ideas may be worth pursuing and which may not.
3 Practical–contextual skill – the ability to know how to persuade others of the value of one's ideas.

Dyslexic people intrinsically know when they have intellectual skills but they often doubt themselves as they have usually had difficulty evidencing this through the normal educational route. In an interview with Shirley Cohen in 1999, William Dreyer described his difficulties with dyslexia in the following way:

> I knew I was different in the way that I thought, but I didn't realize why I was so dumb at spelling...and rote memory and arithmetic. . . . The first time I realized how different... brains could be...was when I bumped into Jim Olds (a professor). (*Cohen 1999, p. 2*)

He went on to describe this difference by saying:

> When I'm inventing an instrument or whatever, I see it in my head and I rotate it and try it out and move the gears. If it doesn't work, I rebuild it in my head. And he [Jim Olds] looked at me and said, 'I don't see a thing in my head with my eyes closed.' We spent the rest of the evening...trying to figure out how two professors – both obviously gifted people at Caltech in the Biology Division – could possibly think at all, because we were so different . . . and I realized that I had some amazing shortcomings as well as some amazing gifts. (*Cohen 1999, p. 2*)

This doubting of one's abilities can make it difficult for a dyslexic individual when it comes to the practical contextual skill of knowing how to persuade others of the value of one's ideas. In the workplace this can often mean that dyslexic individuals' ideas are discounted even if they have a much better, more creative idea with long-term benefits while non-dyslexic individuals with a simpler, less creative and beneficial, but more easily understood and articulated solution, receive acceptance.

Knowledge

Sternberg (2006) describes how knowledge can both hinder and help creativity, in that some knowledge of structures and information helps in responding to change and difference but too much knowledge can result in entrenched ways of thinking. Einstein is reported to have said that 'Imagination is more important than knowledge. Knowledge is limited. Imagination encircles the world.' Dyslexic people who are creative often have a 'knowability of the world' – a vast store of tacit knowledge accrued during years of trial and error, talking with others, heard and found information, and development of knowledge through experience and developing practical skills. Many dyslexic people have not gained their knowledge through reading and therefore it is often not explicit knowledge such as that gained through traditional hierarchical infrastructures that supports their creativity. Rather, it is this knowing that enables them to leap between different aspects of knowledge they have gained and to make unique connections as the creative thought process emerges.

Styles of Thinking

Charles Schwab, an internationally successful financier who is dyslexic, is quoted in *The New York Times* as saying that he:

> . . . had developed a different way of looking at things. 'Along the way, I've frustrated some of my associates because I could see the end zone of a particular thing quicker than they could, so I was moving ahead to conclusions…I go straight from step A to Z, and say: "This is the outcome. I can see it."' (*Turner 2003, p. 10*)

In the same piece, Sally Shaywitz, director of the Learning Disorders Unit at Yale University, describes this ability to see solutions as being typical of dyslexic adults, explaining that 'What distinguishes them is that they really think outside of the box' (p. 10). As with William Dreyer's descriptions above, there are many dyslexic people who ably describe this different way of thinking, and there are many non-dyslexic people who can describe their difficulty in understanding the way dyslexic people think.

Catering for different learning styles has become slightly more mainstream in education. What Sternberg (1997, pp. 30–31) calls the 'legislative thinking style' is, he says, particularly important for creativity in education and in the workplace, as he says:

> Legislative people enjoy doing things the way they decide to do them. They prefer problems that are not prestructured for them, but rather that they can structure for themselves . . . [they] also prefer creative and constructive planning-based activities, such as writing papers, designing projects, and creating new business or educational systems. Often, very successful entrepreneurs succeed precisely because they are legislative and want to create their own way of doing things.

Of course, not all dyslexic people are creative and not all creative people are dyslexic. However, there is abundant evidence that successful, creative dyslexic people do think in a different way, and they tend to be self-governing in their choice of activity and problem solving. The reason for dyslexic people having this ability is not clear but it is certainly the case that the type of thinking involved in creativity requires deep and long and lateral thinking. Interrupt this thinking partway through (perhaps for an assessment), and what emerges is a jumbled mass of partially resolved sentences as the creative embryo develops. What is clear is that when this creative thinking ability is nurtured, whether in education or in the workplace, dyslexic people succeed, but when it is not, dyslexic people fail. Sternberg (2006, p. 89), for example, reported that:

> legislative people tend to be better students than less legislative people, if the schools in which they study value creativity. If the schools do not value or devalue creativity, they tend to be worse students. Students also were found to receive higher grades from teachers whose own styles of thinking matched their own.

Personality

Sternberg (2006) also describes how numerous research studies have identified personality attributes for 'creative functioning'; these include a willingness to overcome obstacles, to take sensible risks, to tolerate ambiguity, and self-efficacy.[1] He reports how creative people are willing to stand up to conventions and that none of the aspects of creative thinking are fixed. In one study he and his colleague found that risk-taking tended to be associated with the

[1] A belief in one's ability to achieve a goal.

production of art work rather than with the writing of essays. On further investigation they found that some assessors:

> tended to mark down essays that took unpopular positions. [They] learned therefore that one of the risks people face when they are creative . . . is that the evaluators will not appreciate the risks if they go against their own beliefs. (*Sternberg 2006, p. 89*)

A clear example of this kind of unconventional, risk-taking behaviour is seen in the business dealings of Richard Branson, a man who has

> made a career out of playing David to the other guy's Goliath…He delights in taking on, and out-manoeuvring large corporations. (*Dearlove 2002, p. xiv*)

Branson's dyslexia is well publicized, and his ability to take sensible risks and excel in business is clear. Nevertheless, frustration of his risk-taking creative leaps, such as those experienced with his failed National Lottery bid,[2] still appear to cause him distress.

Many successful dyslexic entrepreneurs have been identified and their personal qualities, including resilience, adaptability and the ability to formulate original insight, are well known. It is therefore understandable that those who are challenged by this creative approach to conventions are unable to recognize their own part in excluding these creative abilities from education or the workforce.

Motivation

There is another aspect to the willingness to take risks and challenge conventions that supports the intrinsic motivation necessary for creativity. This is a sense of the value of the choices a creative individual is making. The value is not usually financial but is seen as a gain in another way. For example, an excluded dyslexic child might find some value in taking negative behaviour choices to 'get back' at the excluding environment. A dyslexic adult might choose, and many do, to contribute to the body of knowledge around dyslexia to make changes for the next generation of dyslexic people.

For creativity, the motivation must be intrinsic and self-initiated rather than extrinsic and rewards-based, and therefore it is often encouraged within creative dyslexic families and dyslexia-friendly businesses that can weather the ambiguity and sensible risk-taking involved, knowing that this leads in time to creative leaps. This is similar to weathering children's 'boredom' or uncertainty as they come into school holidays and out of external organized activities in order to allow them time to relax, play, find their intrinsic selves and make their own choices. It also enables creative individuals to develop the self-belief they will need in order to survive repeated rejection of their creative ideas and to continue, nevertheless, to be creative.

People rarely produce truly creative work unless they are passionate about what they are doing but the focus needs to be on the inherent value of the work rather than on the financial rewards that it might bring. The dyslexic artist Howard Hodgkin once said in an interview[3] that those art college lecturers who encouraged him helped him to recognize the inherent value of his work, and to believe that 'painting was a worthwhile thing to do'.

[2] In the year 2000, Richard Branson made an unsuccessful bid to run the UK National Lottery on a non-profit making basis.

[3] From a BBC interview with Alan Yentob in *Imagine: a portrait of the painter* in 2006.

Environment

A supportive environment that rewards creative ideas is essential for creative people to be able to bring their ideas to fruition. Through the many historical repressions of creativity across the globe, creative people have found pockets of resistance and an (often secluded) environment where they could continue to express and work with their creative thoughts. In art this is particularly evident in paintings such as Picasso's *Guernica* and Klee's *Revolution of the Viaduct*, which emerged during repression but found acknowledgement only years later.

There are abundant claims for (mainly educational) supportive environments for people with dyslexia. What these environments often offer, however, is support to help dyslexic people to adapt to linear methods of thinking, rather than support to enable dyslexic people to gain success for thinking the way that they think. As a result, many dyslexic people choose to go into creative environments where they can, often indirectly, find this support.

In successful dyslexic people in all walks of life we now have abundant evidence of this creative, dyslexic strength at work. When work and education environments let go of their narrow reliance on linear values and embrace creative diversity, the entire population benefits. We already see evidence of this in creative and thriving communities and some claim that this is the dawning of a new creative age. Creative dyslexic people will be part of this future and I hope that, as our understanding grows, we will be more able to recognize the real value that they bring to society, so that ignoring them is neither an economic nor an emotionally intelligent option.

Conclusion

There are immense creative rewards for those who teach, employ and support dyslexic people. We now understand a great deal more about how the brain works and we can see the visual–spatial skills in dyslexic brains being activated. Many dyslexic people are highly creative, and by using the UK Government definitions for creativity (SEED 2006), together with recent research into the nature of creativity, I hope this chapter has identified and clarified some implications for education and employment.

There is certainly more work to be done to explore how creativity may be fostered and developed in these environments, and how this is to be achieved in colleges, universities and workplaces will continue to engender an active and lively debate. However, it is satisfying to think that future generations of dyslexic individuals may have their skills recognized and applauded, and the litany of criticism their parents and grandparents experienced may become a thing of the past.

References

Biggs, I. (2007) Art, dyslexia and creativity, in *Cascade – Creativity Across Science, Art, Dyslexia, Education* (eds M. Kiziewicz and I. Biggs), University of Bath, Bath, pp. 98–103.

Brunswick, N., Martin, G.N., and Marzano, L. (2010) Visuospatial superiority in developmental dyslexia: myth or reality? *Learning and Individual Differences*, 20, 421–426.

Cohen, S. K. (1999) *Oral History Project Archives*, California Institute of Technology web site: http://resolver.caltech.edu/CaltechOH:OH_Dreyer_W, accessed December 12, 2010.

Dearlove, D. (2002) *Business the Richard Branson Way*, Capstone Publishing Limited, Oxford.

Gosling, W. (2007) Being dyslexic in higher education, in *Cascade – Creativity Across Science, Art, Dyslexia, Education* (eds M. Kiziewicz and I. Biggs), University of Bath, Bath, pp. 63–67.

Graves, J. (2007) Dance, desire, dyslexia – random thoughts on creativity, in *Cascade – Creativity Across Science, Art, Dyslexia, Education* (eds M. Kiziewicz and I. Biggs), University of Bath, Bath, pp. 42–51.

Jackson, L. (2004) Dyslexia. *Icon Magazine Online*. Available at: http://www.iconeye.com/read-previous-issues/icon-013-%7C-june-2004/dyslexia-%7C-icon-013-%7C-june-2004, accessed September 30, 2011.

Kiziewicz, M. and Biggs, I. (eds) (2007) *Cascade – Creativity Across Science, Art, Dyslexia, Education*, University of Bath, Bath.

Meadows, S. (2006) *The Child As Thinker: The development and acquisition of cognition in childhood*, Routledge, London.

Miles, T. (2007) Celebrating dyslexia, maths and music, in *Cascade – Creativity Across Science, Art, Dyslexia, Education* (eds M. Kiziewicz and I. Biggs), University of Bath, Bath, pp. 24–26.

Rayner, A. (2007) Inclusional perspectives – making space for creativity in science, in *Cascade – Creativity Across Science, Art, Dyslexia, Education* (eds M. Kiziewicz and I. Biggs), University of Bath, Bath, pp. 71–78.

Saunders, G. (2007) Imagination, in *Cascade – Creativity Across Science, Art, Dyslexia, Education* (eds M. Kiziewicz and I. Biggs), University of Bath, Bath, pp. 79–83.

SEED (2006) *Promoting Creativity in Education: Overview of key national policy developments across the UK*, SEED, Edinburgh, available at http://www.hmie.gov.uk/documents/publication/hmiepcie.html, accessed October 3, 2011.

Springer, S. and Deutsch, G. (1993) *Left Brain, Right Brain*, W.H. Freeman, San Francisco.

Sternberg, R.J. (1997) *Thinking Styles*, Cambridge University Press, Cambridge.

Sternberg, R.J. (2006) The nature of creativity. *Creativity Research Journal*, 18, 87–98.

Turner, R. (2003) Executive Life; in Learning Hurdles, Lessons for Success. *The New York Times*, November 23, p. 10, available at: http://query.nytimes.com/gst/fullpage.html?res=980CE5D8123BF930A15752C1A9659C8B63&scp=1&sq=Executive%20Life;%20In%20Learning%20Hurdles,%20Lessons%20for%20Success&st=cse, accessed September 29, 2011.

West, T. (1997) *In the Mind's Eye*, Prometheus Books, Amherst, NY.

West, T. (2008) It's time to get serious about the talents of dyslexics. *Perspectives on Language and Literacy*, 34(4), 9–11.

Index